RADICAL PROTESTANTISM
IN SPINOZA'S THOUGHT

Spinoza is praised as a father of atheism, a precursor of the Enlightenment, an 'anti-theologian' and a father of political liberalism. When the religious dimension of Spinoza's thought cannot be ignored, it is usually dismissed as some form of mysticism or pantheism.

This book explores the positive references to Christianity presented through out Spinoza's works, focusing particularly on the *Tractatus Theologico politicus*. Arguing that advocates of the anti-Christian or un-Christian Spinoza fail to look beyond Spinoza's *Ethics*, which has the least to say about Christianity, Graeme Hunter offers a fresh interpretation of Spinoza's most important works and his philosophical and religious thought. While there is no evidence that Spinoza became a Christian in any formal sense, Hunter argues that his aim was neither to be heretical nor atheistic, but rather to effect a radical reform of Christianity and a return to simple Biblical practices. This book presents a unique contribution to current debate for students and specialist scholars in philosophy of religion, the history of philosophy and early modern history.

To my mother

quid comparabile habebat
honor a me delatus illi
et servitus ab illa mihi?

Radical Protestantism
in Spinoza's Thought

GRAEME HUNTER
University of Ottawa, Canada

ASHGATE

Published by
Ashgate Publishing Limited
Gower House
Croft Road
Aldershot
Hampshire GU11 3HR
England

Ashgate Publishing Company
Suite 420
101 Cherry Street
Burlington, VT 05401-4405
USA

Ashgate website: http://www.ashgate.com

British Library Cataloguing in Publication Data
Hunter, Graeme
    Radical Protestantism in Spinoza's thought
    1. Spinoza, Benedictus de, 1632-1677
    I. Title
    199.4'92

Library of Congress Cataloging-in-Publication Data
Hunter, Graeme.
  Radical protestantism in Spinoza's thought / Graeme Hunter.
    p. cm.
  Includes bibliographical references and index.
  ISBN 0-7546-0375-X (alk. paper)
  1. Spinoza, Benedictus de, 1632-1677 – Religion. 2. Philosophy and religion. 3. Protestantism. 4. Spinoza, Benedictus de, 1632-1677. Tractatus theologico-politicus.
I. Title.

B3999.R4H86 2004
99'.492—dc21

2004007479

ISBN 0 7546 0375 X

Printed and bound by Antony Rowe Ltd, Chippenham, Wiltshire

#54929600

Contents

Acknowledgements

I gratefully acknowledge the University of Ottawa for the sabbatical that made writing this book possible and the friends and colleagues who made it better. A special debt is owed to Leslie Armour, Syliane Charles, Steven Nadler and David Novak. Thanks to Glenn Hunter for putting together the appendix and to my family for their patience and encouragement.

List of Abbreviations

The works of Spinoza are always cited by page number in Spinoza [1925], and according to the following scheme of abbreviations:

Ethics: **E**

Examples:

2Ea3: *Ethics* part 2, axiom 3.
3EAffd3: *Ethics* part 3, definition 3 of the emotions
4EAppCap3: *Ethics* part 4, appendix, chapter 3.
3Ed2: *Ethics* part 3, definition 2
1Ep12: *Ethics* part 1, proposition 12.
1Ep20c: *Ethics* part 1, proposition 20, corollary
1Ep33dem: Ethics part 1, proposition 33, demonstration.
2Ep49s: *Ethics* part 2, proposition 49, scholium.
4EPref: *Ethics* part 4, preface.

Correspondence: **EP**

Example: **EP43**: Letter 43

Tractatus de Intellectus Emendatione: **TIE**

Tractatus Politicus: **TP**

Example: **TP 8, §37**: *Tractatus Politicus*, chapter 8, section 37.

Tractatus-Theologico-Politicus: **TTP**

Example: **TTP 13**: *Tractatus Theologico-Politicus*, chapter 13.

Introduction

In the middle years of the seventeenth century religion and philosophy were still inextricably tangled: metaphysics had not yet emancipated itself from theology, ethics did not exclude religious precepts, political philosophers still had to reckon with the power of the Church. Virtually every major philosopher of that period was a Christian and even those who arguably were not had much to say about Christianity. Baruch Spinoza was born, flourished and died in that period.

Spinoza's early life in the Jewish Community of Amsterdam and his later expulsion from it made him an outsider to the European mainstream. Still, it would be strange if he reflected as little of the religious temper of his own time as is commonly supposed. There is a conception of Spinoza, widespread in the secondary literature, according to which he transcended the religious opinions of his age, while hiding the extreme consequences of his views under an artful veneer of religious conformity. He is said to have anticipated the critiques of Christianity normally associated with later centuries, but to have phrased them in such a way that only very skilful readers could understand them. To this select minority he revealed that anything in religion over and above nature is merely superstition.

Of course there is also a large and diverse body of scholarship devoted to Spinoza's religious thought, in which such broad claims are qualified and disputed. But specialized studies are slow to influence the cruder picture of a philosopher which creates the popular conception of him and establishes what scholars may say about him without a footnote and without fear of contradiction. Where Spinoza is concerned that picture is and has been for some time as represented in the previous paragraph.

Introductions to Spinoza's thought are the best place in which to encounter the picture of which I speak and that is as it should be. One function of introductory works is to instruct beginners about what can be taken for granted regarding their subject. So a student picking up Stuart Hamsphire's useful introduction of half a century ago would read:

> [Spinoza] has a direct interest in freeing others from the passive emotions and from the blind superstitions which lead to war and to the suppression of free thought. But in fact the enlightened and the free are always a minority, and men in general are guided by irrational hopes and fears, and not by pure reason. For these reasons Spinoza, anticipating Voltaire and the philosophical Deists of the next century, admits that popular religions are

useful, and that with their childish systems of rewards and penalties they are properly designed to make the ignorant peaceful and virtuous; to the uneducated and unreasoning, morality cannot be taught as a necessity of reason; it must be presented to them imaginatively as involving simple rewards and penalties. The free man therefore will criticize Christian doctrine or orthodox Judaism or any other religious dogma, first, when it is represented as philosophical truth, secondly, on purely pragmatic grounds, if it in fact leads its votaries to be troublesome in their actual behaviour; ...[1]

In the decades following the publication of Hampshire's work a great deal of research was done on Spinoza's actual relations to Jewish, Christian and radical communities in Holland and the results of that new scholarship were reflected in Alan Donagan's introduction to Spinoza's thought, published in 1988. Yet the idea of Spinoza as transcending the religious preoccupations of his own time and rejecting Christian views in favour of scientifically respectable ones survived undisturbed:

> While Descartes before him and Leibniz after were trying to synthesize traditional theology with the new science, [Spinoza] was trying to naturalize it; and if we read him as we read Descartes and Leibniz, we shall misunderstand him as most of his contemporaries did ... by restoring to [his Ethics'] theological terms the pre-naturalized senses of which he strove to rid them.[2]

Hampshire and Donagan are alike at least in this: they instruct their readers that they may safely treat Spinoza as both anticipating the thinking of later times and reductive in his religious outlook. They imply that any hints of Christian thought found in Spinoza's writings are only vestigial. Spinoza's dissatisfaction with the orthodox mainstream of Holland is taken as a dismissal of Christianity in all its forms. These introductions to Spinoza's thought convey the common picture of it accurately enough. But that picture routinely underestimates Spinoza's real debt to parts of Christian thought, as I shall try to show.

To wrestle against a commonplace presents special challenges. For one thing the basic picture is subject to numerous protean extensions. Spinoza may be represented as anticipating atheism, or deism, or secularism or liberalism or naturalism or combinations of them. And his independence of Christianity may often be more effectively suggested by never acknowledging any religious dimension of his thought than by arguing against any particular one. And, of course, commonplaces gather authority simply by going unchallenged.

The conventional picture of Spinoza's religious outlook is easiest to maintain if one's focus is firmly on the *Ethics*. The present book owes its origin to my first systematic study of the *Tractatus theologico-politicus* (TTP), in which I seemed to encounter a very different Spinoza, one that prompted me to look for the evidence for the non-Christian picture of him I had so long taken for granted. I thought it would be easy to find. Instead I discovered the evidence to be sparse and ambiguous and there seemed to be a great deal that pointed in the other direction.

It soon became clear to me that I would be wasting my time if I tried to rectify the many ways in which Spinoza's debt to Christian theology is undervalued. It would require making too many small points, few, if any, of which would be significant in themselves. I would do better, I saw, to present the Christian dimension of his thought positively and directly. Because I was working against a commonplace widely received and of long standing I resolved to proceed cautiously, revisiting first Spinoza's life and then his writings and keeping an open mind about his attitude toward Christianity. An open mind, assisted by some pointed questions: Was Spinoza really emancipated from the Christian preoccupations of his time and place? To what extent does he aim at a naturalistic reduction of Christianity? Are his religious views heretical or merely unorthodox or neither? If my answers to these questions are correct, they will challenge the picture of the religiously "progressive" Spinoza sketched above. They will also put in question many of the findings of the literature that specializes in Spinoza's religious thought. The authentic Spinoza, if he was as I take him to have been, was religiously radical, but still very much under the umbrella of Christian thought.

The account of Spinoza I am proposing does not depend on any newly discovered writing, but on the recovered meaning of familiar ones. It depends especially on a contextualized reading of several chapters of his TTP and a subsequent rethinking of what he must mean elsewhere, if he is not to contradict what he says there. Spinoza is normally read differently: as the philosopher of the *Ethics* with whom the theologian of the TTP must somehow be reconciled. I have found it convenient to move in the opposite direction, beginning with the TTP and then investigating to what extent its doctrines are consistent with those of the *Ethics*.

I do not pretend to be the first to think that Spinoza has better Christian credentials than is commonly supposed. The first to make that point was Spinoza's friend, Jarig Jelles, who said it in the preface to the first edition of Spinoza's works in 1677. And the thought has been echoed on several occasions since, though to my knowledge always more diffidently than in the present study. The interested reader will find references to and discussions of these affirmations in the pages that follow. But even in its most timid manifestations, the thesis defended here has been forcefully and sometimes even bitterly denied. For that reason I am not merely adding my signature to a minority report, but defending a strong version of it against those who have endorsed it too weakly as well as those who have rejected it too harshly.

Though many of Spinoza's writings reflect his attitude to Christianity, I have two reasons for focusing on the TTP. First, it contains not just isolated observations but a complete theory about the nature of Christianity and its proper place in society. In the second place, it is also a mature work, published in Spinoza's lifetime and therefore likely to convey his considered opinion.

It has also been necessary to devote a good deal of attention to the *Ethics*, however, even though it was not published in Spinoza's lifetime and is less overtly concerned with Christianity. It could not be ignored because most scholars consider it to be more representative of Spinoza's real philosophical outlook than is the TTP, and many think that, on religious matters, the two texts point in different directions. If it were necessary to choose between them, then, the presumption in favour of the *Ethics* would diminish the authority of the TTP. For that reason it was necessary to show that, where Christian theology is concerned, there was no necessity to choose. The religious teachings of the TTP are fully compatible with what is taught in the *Ethics*.

You know you are battling against a commonplace when the reactions to your project are less expressions of interest than of incredulity or dismay. Such has been my frequent experience, when explaining what I have been writing about over the last couple of years. From acknowledged experts to those possessing only the most superficial acquaintance with Spinoza, a daunting number of those to whom I have communicated the idea of this study have seemed to know in their hearts that Spinoza was opposed to every form of Christianity and that what I propose could not possibly be true.

I would sometimes respond that Spinoza's TTP could qualify as Christian simply on the strength of the contribution it made to the development of Bible criticism and so to liberal Christian theology. That might silence the beginner, but more experienced readers would counter that Spinoza's attention to Christianity, like his use of specifically Christian ideas and vocabulary, was insincere. If I presented evidence of his sincerity, it would be construed as only feigned sincerity, due either to Spinoza's devious nature or to an inclination to ambiguity inherited in some fashion from his Marrano ancestors.

Those who assume Spinoza's treatment of Christianity was merely window-dressing of course see no need to investigate its internal structure. But to enter into its detail, as is done in Chapters 4, 5 and 6 of this book, is to find internal coherence and order far beyond anything that would be employed merely as a disguise. So, at least, would run my final line of defence to anyone patient enough to listen. The clincher for the other side was always the appeal to the *Ethics*. What about the appendix to the first part, with its attack on Christian providence and superstition? What about Spinoza's commitment in part five to salvation through knowledge of the third kind? I have devoted the longest chapter in this book (Chapter 7) to answering these objections. There I have tried to demonstrate not only the consistency of the TTP with the Ethics, but even how its doctrines illuminate the very parts of the *Ethics* with which they at first appear to conflict.

I do not hold that Spinoza's radical approach to Christianity is the key to all his thinking or even that it is the most important element of his thought: only that he shared the benevolent concern for the future of the Christian faith common among intellectuals of his day. Just as one can write about Spinoza's moral philosophy or his natural philosophy without exaggerating their importance, so one can write of the degree to which his philosophy is shaped by radical Protestant Christianity without denying that other forces were also at work. Nothing said here rules out other influences on Spinoza's philosophical development, such as those of Jewish philosophy, or of Cartesianism or even of anti-religious radicals like Franciscus Van den Enden. For example, the argument developed by David Novak that Spinoza envisioned a restructured Judaism "continuing what he saw as the political strengths of Judaism with the spiritual strengths of Christianity"[3] is certainly complementary to what is put forward here. This book is only directed against interpretations that impute to Spinoza a rejection of Christianity in all its forms.[4]

Some may deny that there can be any meaning in terms like "Christian philosophy" or "Christian thought" for Spinoza, since he distinguishes so carefully between theology and philosophy. But that is a non-sequitur. If philosophy is carefully distinguished from theology, then it cannot be theology. But nothing stops it from being Christian. That term extends to more than just theology. The notions of piety, salvation, beatitude, love, and miracles, to name just a few, are all important to Spinoza's philosophy and all are shaped by his radically Protestant reading of the New Testament.

In defending the importance of radical Christianity in Spinoza's thought I have leaned upon two general positions, one historiographical, the other hermeneutical. They are best acknowledged from the outset.

Spinoza has a history of being adopted by his radical successors, who have found in his writings inspiration for their own religious (or, more frequently, irreligious) positions. Some have used him to justify unequivocal rejection of Scripture,[5] others in aid of atheism,[6] or materialism,[7] to name just three important appropriations of his name and legacy. That Spinoza's work lent itself to such extensions is beyond dispute, but it is of historiographical importance to remember that they are extensions. The fact that later religious radicals exploited Spinoza's ideas hardly entails that Spinoza had been trying, but failing, to articulate doctrines just like theirs. The progressivist fallacy is to see in philosophers of one period stammering attempts to express the views of a later one, instead of what they obviously are: competent expressions of their own opinions. The quotation from Stuart Hampshire cited above provides an illustration with the assertion that Spinoza "anticipates" Voltaire and eighteenth century deism. I argue instead that such anticipations, if they occurred at all, were fortuitous, and that Spinoza's religious thinking is rooted in a form of radical Protestantism indigenous to his own time.

The hermeneutical point undergirding my main argument is so innocuous that it is surprising it would ever need to be acknowledged, much less defended. I claim that Spinoza, except when employing conventional literary devices like humour, quotation, exaggeration or irony, ought to be supposed to mean what he writes. This normally uncontested assumption needs to be acknowledged in Spinoza's case because he has been thought by many philosophers, including some very good ones, to have adopted an esoteric form of writing in which he can say one thing to an ordinary reader and mean the opposite to a sophisticated one. I am far from the first to notice the inevitable pitfalls of such an interpretation, but I have here supplied my own reasons for opposing it both as a general principle and as a means of understanding Spinoza in particular.

I have avoided calling Spinoza a Christian, though I may seem to imply it by saying that his writings take a radical Protestant point of view and that he is sincere in taking it. However, as will become clear in Chapter 2, the question of whether or not he ever formally joined or ritually participated in any Christian community is probably unanswerable, and not just from lack of data. The radical Protestantism to which he is attracted is characterized in part by its disdain for ritual tokens of community.

My argument is a simple one and I have tried to keep the writing simple also. Except for Chapter 7 there is little that undergraduates with a course in Spinoza under their belt will have difficulty following. On the other hand, I have also hoped my claims would be taken seriously by Spinoza scholars, and to that end have tried to disclose my sources as fully as possible and in their original language (usually Latin). As much as possible these scholarly matters have been kept to the endnotes and the endnotes to them. My policy has been that what is essential to the argument should normally be part of the body of the book.

Spinoza's writings are cited according to the Gebhardt[8] pagination, a practice I have adhered to despite the critical and annotated Akkerman edition of the TTP[9] that is now available and surpasses in accuracy Gebhardt's version of that text. My reason for continuing with Gebhardt-references is twofold. In the first place, the Akkerman edition is keyed to Gebhardt, so that anyone using it will be able to follow my references with ease, though the converse would not be true. In the second place, because most of the relevant secondary literature is keyed to Gebhardt, it is easier to compare my claims to those I dispute if the textual basis of the dispute is clear.

I have also tried to make the Gebhardt-references accessible even to those who do not read Latin. For the *Ethics*, this has been done by including generic references to the many natural subdivisions of that text. In most cases they suffice to break down the text into short easily located portions. (For more details consult the List of Abbreviations.) In the *Tractatus theologico-politicus*, however, generic references only go down to the level of chapters. For that reason I have appended for that one text a concordance relating each Gebhardt page to the corresponding pages in two standard English translations.

Finally, a note on religious vocabulary. Words like "scripture", "church" and "god" are sometimes used generically and sometimes as proper names. Uses of the latter kind are capitalized not in the interest of piety but of clarity.

Notes

1   Stuart Hampshire [1951] *Spinoza* London: Penguin, 202.
2   Alan Donagan [1988] *Spinoza* Chicago: University of Chicago Press, 34.
3   David Novak [1995] *The Election of Israel* Cambridge: Cambridge University Press, p. 47.
4   Thomas Cook, Robert Misrahi and Yirmiyahu Yovel are among those with whom I have fundamental disagreements.
5   See Miguel Benitez [1990], "Du bon usage du Tractatus théologicopoliticus: La religion du chrétien" in O. Bloch [1990], 75.
6   See Jacques Moutaux [1990], "D'Holbach et Spinoza" in O. Bloch [1990], 153ff.
7   See Marita Gilli [1983] "L'influence de Spinoza dans la formation du matérialisme allemand" in *Archives de philosophie* 46 (1983), 590-610.
8   See Spinoza [1925] in Bibliography for details.
9   Spinoza [1999] *Oeuvres* vol. 3. *Tractatus theologico-politicus/Traité théologico-politique* Ed. Fokke Akkerman Paris: Presses universitaires de France.

PART I
CONTEXT

Chapter One

A Jew In Amsterdam

Tradition and Trade

The thriving Jewish community into which Baruch Spinoza was born in 1632 existed only by historical accident, having taken precarious root there a scant three decades earlier. And yet its story is also very old – in a way even timeless – for it is part of the long tale of the persecution of European Judaism and its irrepressible, triumphant rebirths.[1]

The Jews who began arriving in the Netherlands in the late sixteenth century were the descendants of the *Sephardim* (Spanish Jews) whom Spain had forced either to convert to Christianity or flee for their lives a century before. Though anti-Jewish sentiment had already been running high in Spanish territories since the 1390s, it was not until 1492 that Ferdinand II of Aragon and Isabella of Castile finally took the decisive step of ordering their immediate conversion or expulsion. Jews who chose to remain in Spain were called *conversos*, or, if their conversion was suspect *crypto-judios*. The vulgar name for the latter group was *marranos* (pigs).[2] Despite its derogatory meaning, "marrano" has remained a standard term for designating this population in the scholarly literature.

About 120,000 Jews fled to Portugal where, for a few years, they were allowed to continue practising their faith. Even when Portugal followed Spain's lead and demanded their conversion to Christianity, the *Cristãos Novos* (or New Christians) as the Portuguese called them, were still free at least of the dreaded Inquisition and could be secret Judaizers if they chose. Further heavy blows were soon to fall upon them, however. The second crisis for the *conversos* was not reached until the middle of the sixteenth century when Portugal established its own Inquisition. A third followed in 1580, when Portugal was united with Spain under Philip II. At that low point in their fortunes began a new diaspora of Spanish/Portuguese Jews in which they emigrated to various destinations in Europe, the Americas and the Middle East. A certain portion of these, including Spinoza's ancestors, came to the Netherlands.

Although the Jews were not always warmly received in the Netherlands, life there must have seemed good in comparison to what they had left behind. Jews were granted freedom to practise their religion in 1619 and could become citizens after 1657. Ironically in the 1620s it was more politically dangerous in the Netherlands to be a Christian of any other than Calvinist persuasion than to be a practising Jew.[3]

Materially and socially Jewish prospects were also good. By the latter part of the seventeenth century the fledgling Sephardic community was on average a little richer than its Dutch counterpart and Amsterdam had become known as "the Dutch Jerusalem". The spiritual diversity and dynamism of the Sephardim which had expressed itself in the century's early years by their having three different and partly competing religious communities reached a new level of maturity when the three joined to become the "Talmud Torah Community" in 1639.

Unity can of course be a mixed blessing just as dissension is sometimes a mitigated evil. Although the union of the three congregations at least officially put old matters of contention behind them, it also made dissent from the views of the one remaining community more dangerous. To fall out with *Talmud Torah* would mean exclusion from the entire Sephardic society of Amsterdam. The new authorities lost no time in making their new powers plain to the community. Soon after the establishment of Talmud Torah they declared: "The *ma'amad* [lay board of governors] has an absolute and incontestable authority; no one may avoid its resolutions, under punishment of *cherem* [excommunication]".[4] Not many years later, Spinoza would feel the full weight of that new and indisputable authority in his own life.

This period of doctrinal concord and economic prosperity came to pass during Spinoza's childhood. It was two decades earlier that business interests had brought Spinoza's grandfather Isaac d'Espinosa and his great uncle Abraham to the Netherlands. Isaac had settled in Rotterdam, Abraham in Amsterdam. Later, around 1623, Isaac's son Michael married into his uncle Abraham's family and fortune, the latter taking the form of an import-export business. Michael, who would later be Baruch Spinoza's father, thus settled in Amsterdam primarily for business reasons. And for those reasons he remained even after his childless marriage to his cousin Rachel ended prematurely with Rachel's death in 1627. As was not uncommon in those days, Michael remarried within a year. His second wife was one Hannah Senior, who would later be the mother of Baruch.

By the 1630s Michael d'Espinosa had become a successful entrepreneur in the Jewish community,[5] occupying leading roles both in civic and in religious capacities. In addition to serving on the *ma'amad*, or lay board of governors of Talmud Torah, Michael belonged to the board charged with overseeing the school – a point to consider, when it comes to understanding Michael's attitude and contribution to the education of his talented son, Baruch.

The earliest biographers seem at first glance to disagree strongly about both the quality of Spinoza's early education and his father's attitude toward it. One portrays Michael as a man who hated the speculative bent he detected in his son from its earliest manifestations. On this view Spinoza's humanistic and theological impulses would all have been pursued against his father's wishes. Another biographer says that Baruch's father permitted him to study Hebrew and the like, but only *faute de mieux*, because he could not afford the business education that, in the father's judgement, would have been better. A third reports that Baruch had a "better than average" education, involving expenses which only more prosperous families could normally afford.[6]

It is no longer possible to go behind these reports to form an independent opinion, but it is easy to see how such different pictures might agree more nearly than at first seems the case. Successful businessmen are often less than enthusiastic about the unremunerative interests and talents of their children. To Michael's practical mind Baruch's speculative temperament may have seemed to be a handicap, particularly since the elder Spinoza would have been conscious of the always precarious position of Jewish communities in Europe. He may well have thought the time unpropitious for indulging a merely speculative cast of mind. It always is.

On the other hand, this same pragmatic outlook would have required the father to recognize and encourage the real strengths of his son. Michael's experience with education committees suggests that he must have had some respect for and understanding of educational matters. It is possible, then, that some *quid pro quo* was reached in which Michael provided the education that suited his son's disposition on the understanding that Baruch would go into the family business. If the great parental challenge is to make one's children both cultivated and employable, without confusing the two, Michael d'Espinoza seems to have risen to it more effectively than many parents do.[7]

To the Sephardic community Spanish was the great language of culture and it was therefore also the language of instruction at the Talmud Torah school. In the early years the curriculum would have focused on reading, memorizing, reciting, chanting and interpreting the Bible, especially the Pentateuch.[8] Ferrara's Spanish Bible translation of 1533 would not merely have been studied but in large part also memorized by the students. Yet the Hebrew Scriptures were also studied in their original language. A visitor to the Portuguese Jewish schools at about the time Spinoza was starting there praised them for their academic excellence, particularly in Hebrew and grammar.[9]

The scholarly *Compendium of Hebrew Grammar* Spinoza would compile late in his life gives eloquent testimony to the rigour of the programme of Talmud Torah.[10] In addition to formal study of the Bible Spinoza would also have been expected to participate in the serious worship life of the community. Throughout most, if not all, of his school years, the curriculum would involve daily corporate worship, including evening prayers and the singing of psalms.

Beyond elementary school, which finished with the fourth grade, when students would be approximately 14 years old, there were higher stages leading ultimately to Rabbinical training, but it is doubtful whether Spinoza went much beyond the elementary level.[11] On the other hand it is likely that he attended the Keter Torah *yeshiva* (school) during the 1650s[12], where he is thought to have studied with the rabbis Mortera and Menasseh ben Israel.

Spinoza left no record of what he thought of his own early schooling, nor is education a subject of frequent comment in his writings. However his *obiter dicta* on the topic make one think that, notwithstanding Talmud Torah's many merits, he would have thought its approach to education less than optimal.

Spinoza came to view early education as fundamentally a *moral* transaction between the generations, one that must take place in full conformity with nature. For example, Spinoza believes that women cannot be educated to the same level as men because they are naturally weaker both in mind and character.[13] Nevertheless when due allowance is made for such differences, human beings of both sexes are found to be susceptible of moral improvement through what today would be called behaviouristic means. All children can be taught to feel pain at the thought of some actions and pleasure at others. Parents can encourage proper development "by denouncing one type of action and often scolding their children on its account, while on the other hand prompting and praising another type". Parental intervention of this kind will "bring it about that sadness is associated with the one and joy with the other".[14] By such means the nature of children can be moulded by their education until, in the most successful instances, they learn to live wholly according to the dictates of their own reason.[15]

Since education's great goal is the formation of adults who reason autonomously and well, the sectarian dogmatic curricula in which confessional schools of the type Spinoza attended take such pride would have to be regarded as pedagogically questionable. But the idea of state-funded schools had even less appeal. They would be incapable of fostering the right kind of attitudes, for they are also more interested in coercing minds than in cultivating them.[16] What Spinoza really favoured was a *laissez-faire* free-market approach to education so radical that no modern state has yet dared to adopt it. "In a free republic", he asserts, "the arts and sciences would reach their highest perfection, if everyone who desired a licence to teach were granted one, but at his own expense and at the peril of his own reputation".[17]

The extreme democratization of the classroom Spinoza proposes is made more intelligible in the light of his other observations on teaching cited above. Since education's highest purpose is, as far as one's nature permits, to learn to live by the dictates of right reason alone, neither academic degrees nor political or religious agendas necessarily qualify teachers to impart it. To be effective teachers must themselves live according to reason and know how to cultivate that skill in others.[18]

Education, for Spinoza, turns out then to have little to do with the curriculum of religious schools such as the one he attended or their Christian counterparts. No doubt he was glad to have acquired the knowledge and skills his schoolmasters had given him and there is no evidence of his having resented the particular forms of worship with which their transmission was linked. But the mature Spinoza saw genuine education as involving the cultivation of a mind's resources more than the acquisition of a dogmatic outlook of even the most meritorious kind.

•   •   •

The scanty information that remains concerning Spinoza's early life suggests that he completed his primary education in 1649 and then entered into his father's import-export business.[19] The seven years he subsequently spent in business coincided with what has been called the "fifth phase" of business expansion for the Sephardic merchants of the Netherlands, a boom that lasted from the end of the Thirty Years War and the signing of the Spanish-Dutch peace at Münster in 1648 to the significant fall of sugar prices in 1655-7.[20]

Baruch's step-mother, his father's third wife,[21] died in 1653, followed by his father within a year. But Baruch and his brother Gabriel had economic burdens to bear that made those emotionally dark days even darker. It fell to them to take over the management of the family business at a time when trade generally was entering a slump. Furthermore Michael d'Espinoza had made some poor business decisions of his own prior to his death that would leave his heirs "plagued by creditors" for years to come.[22] The spectre of business failure continued to haunt Baruch throughout the short time in which he was a director of the family enterprise. However, if it contributed nothing else to his development, at least it made him shrewd. According to Dutch law one was officially a minor until the age of 25. That fact permitted Baruch to declare himself a legal orphan in 1656, and so to be freed of some of his father's debts.[23]

Devotion and Dissent

Economic life, with all its uncertainties, could not have been more perplexing to the young Spinoza than the religious turmoil amid which he grew up, whether he confined his gaze strictly to the immediate community of Portuguese Jews, or extended it more broadly across the enveloping Dutch Christian society or the sectarian confusion in Christian Europe as a whole. What a colourful picture of religious diversity Europe could have displayed to a detached observer! But where was detachment to be found? To most thinking people inter-religious contacts were a minefield of dogma and prejudice whose nearest contemporary equivalent may be the ideologically poisoned atmosphere of the so-called culture wars. Moreover, piety and dissent, orthodoxy and heresy, could appear in such deceptively similar forms that only the most discerning religious intelligence could say which was which. Spinoza would later formulate his own rule of discernment in a memorable way.

> The piety or impiety of opinions cannot be determined by considering them in themselves, apart from works. The only reason for saying that a man's belief is pious or impious is the degree to which he is either moved by it to obedience or licenced by it to sin and rebellion. This is so much the case that if believing a truth causes someone to be obstinate, then his faith is impious, and it is pious if it makes him obedient, even though it be based on a false belief.[24]

Spinoza's emphasis on obedience over dogma, his equation of obstinacy with impiety, could seem to entail that pious people should live in conformity with the system of beliefs into which they are born. Yet by the time those words were written, their author had moved far away, both geographically and spiritually, from the Talmud Torah community. Therefore if we are not to charge him with hypocrisy, the obedience of which he wrote must have involved principles deeper than conventional dogma.

To get an unclouded understanding of Spinoza's own sense of piety is one of the challenges of this book. The word itself, along with many other terms in its semantic field, belongs to a vocabulary which few people regularly use today. Beyond the role such words play in the jargon of ecclesiastical specialists, many religious terms have been reduced almost to lexical fossils, appearing only in stock phrases, conveying little of their former significance. An effective way of conveying what piety meant to Spinoza and his contemporaries however may be to look at some of their lives, especially at the ones made notable either because they had so much of it or so little. Both Spinoza's Sephardic community and the Dutch Christian society that enveloped it can furnish examples of great piety and impiety, including men whose spiritual thought and conduct helped shape the young Spinoza's religious imagination. Acquaintance with their lives can at least furnish a context for Spinoza's early struggle with Judaism.

The noted Jewish apologist and controversialist of the Amsterdam community, Isaac Orobio de Castro, was interested in both the theory and practice of piety. He was troubled not just by the universal problem that in many people's lives precept and practice do not always correspond, but by the systematic way in which among the Sephardim pious orthodoxy actually tended to diminish as education increased (Révah [1958], p. 179). We ought not to read any Enlightenment irony or satisfaction into Orobio's observation. It would also be wrong to attribute crypto-atheism to the many doubters in the Dutch Sephardic context simply on the basis of their doubts. Though some of them may have anticipated Enlightenment attitudes, the unique situation of the Jews in the Netherlands makes its religious unorthodoxy unique also. It was easy for *conversos* to be sceptical without being irreligious. Having in many cases been educated in the Roman Catholic universities of Spain during the period of their coerced Christianity, they were deeply aware of both the ideals and the shortcomings of an *alternative* orthodoxy. Is it then so surprising if many found it difficult to draw the line between purity and impurity of belief with the same assurance as could those who had known only a single faith? Spinoza's definition of piety, cited earlier, is a good illustration of how scepticism about dogma can be combined with a respectful attitude toward piety as such.

It is true that "rejectionism", as it has been called, was unusually prevalent among the Sephardim and attempts to explain it have long been a subject of scholarly controversy.[25] Still the number of dissenters must be seen in proportion. In a community of about 2500, whose rules were unusually demanding and comprehensive, severe disciplinary action (excommunication) was taken against members no more than about once a year.[26] And many of those excommunications were for terms as short as a single day.

In thinking about unbelief one must not lose sight of the truism that religious communities are made up of believers, rather than sceptics. Nor can any religious enclave survive long, if living faith is confined to the ignorant. Thus one could safely have guessed the existence of articulate and orthodox Jewish believers in Amsterdam, even had there not been the abundant empirical evidence of it that we possess in fact. There as elsewhere, informed belief was more prevalent than the radical doubt with which it coexisted.[27]

The prolific rabbis Mortera and Menasseh ben Israel, with whom Spinoza studied, are good examples of learned orthodoxy. Another is Rabbi Moses Raphael D'Aguilar, whom Spinoza must also have known. Orobio mentions Aguilar as one of the influential figures in his own intellectual development. His particular gift seems to have been in the realm of apologetics, justifying the fundamental beliefs of Judaism.

When Aguilar returned to Amsterdam in 1654 after more than a decade's absence he quickly became an influential member of the brotherhood of the *Keter Torah* under Rabbi Saul Levi Mortera. In 1659 he was appointed to succeed Rabbi Menasseh ben Israel as teacher in the Yeshiva Ets Chaim. Orobio considered him "a sage in whom Jewish and secular scholarship were synthesized". Orobio's recent biographer, Yosef Kaplan, describes Aguilar as possessing "authority both in Jewish sources and in the culture and philosophy of classical antiquity".[28]

Orobio de Castro himself, although he did not come to Amsterdam until 1662, two years after Spinoza's departure, can serve as another example. He was a thoughtful, orthodox believer and an eloquent apologist living in the Portuguese Jewish community. His reaction to one of the disputed questions of the age – whether or not God will deny salvation to all who are not of the true Faith – sheds light on how a reflective orthodox thinker approached a contentious theological question. Since it is also a debate on which Spinoza expressed a view, it puts their differences of outlook into bold relief. More importantly it helps explain why one major Jewish thinker of the period was able to find an intellectual home within his own tradition, while another could not.

The question at issue really concerns God's judgement of outsiders to the true faith, and it was debated far beyond the Jewish community of Amsterdam. Its Christian counterpart lay in the ancient dictum *nulla salus extra ecclesiam* (no salvation outside the Church). Whether to accept it at all and, if so, within what conception of "the Church", were questions vexing every denomination in post-Reformation Europe. The Sephardic community in Amsterdam faced it in a differently accented form. Their question was whether or not non-Jews could be saved (or, in their words, "whether Gentiles have a portion in the world to come")? The moderate view was that Gentiles could be saved, provided they obeyed the seven so-called "Noahite laws". These laws were the ones given by God to Adam and Noah prior to the delivering of the Ten Commandments to Moses. Now it was taken for granted by all parties in the debate that these Noahite laws were also discoverable by unaided reason. Precisely that assumption gave the Jewish version of the question its decisive form: could Gentiles fulfil the Noahite laws by obeying them *merely* as commands of reason?

Neither an affirmative nor a negative answer to this question seemed altogether satisfactory. If Gentiles only had to be obedient to reason, then it would not only be possible to be saved outside the Jewish faith but even without acknowledging the Jewish God. Moreover the privilege of being chosen by God, as the Jewish people were, would begin to seem more like an unfortunate burden.

On the other hand, if Gentiles had not only to obey the Noahite laws but also to recognize them as particular revelations from God, that seemed to presuppose a degree of familiarity with Jewish Scriptures and history which was simply unavailable to most people in most periods. To imagine eternal punishment being inflicted on people whose offence lay in lacking knowledge they were precluded from having seemed unconscionable to most reflective persons.[29]

Spinoza would later be very critical of "the Jews" on just this point. Quoting Maimonides as the source of their doctrine, which he (Spinoza) categorically rejects, he says that the Jews take the position that the Gentiles must not merely observe the Noahite laws, but observe them *as revealed* in order to be saved.[30]

Orobio agreed that this was what Maimonides said and was no less troubled by it than was Spinoza. Unlike Spinoza, however, Orobio did not dismiss that proposition as "a mere figment". Ironically neither party guessed that the text of Maimonides then in use was corrupt at precisely this point, and that he in fact shared the outlook of both his modern critics.[31] However the different ways in which Orobio and Spinoza express their disagreement remain no less instructive lessons in religious interpretation than if their understanding of Maimonides had been correct.

Like Spinoza, Orobio considered Maimonides' supposed doctrine an offence to reason.[32] However since pious regard for his tradition forbade him to do what reason seemed to command, that is, to reject it, he decided that the proper course in such a matter was to suspend judgement. This he justified by reminding himself that judging Jews and Gentiles was in any case the sole responsibility of God. As Kaplan puts it:

> Even if one can detect in [Orobio] an inclination to maintain an equilibrium between accepting the authority of Halakhah (Jewish Law) and the critical evaluation of issues in the light of reason (as evidenced by his inability to accept without demur all the answers propounded by recognized authority), nevertheless in the last resort, he bowed to Halakhah and rabbinic tradition.[33]

Why does the high regard for tradition in thinkers like Orobio not impress Spinoza? Part of the answer is that there is simply nothing more fundamental to Spinoza's thought than his firm commitment to reason as arbiter. Yet Spinoza has not put religion behind him as philosophers would begin to do a century later. Even his regard for reason is coloured by the religious character of his mind, as his major writings attest.

Orobio's and Spinoza's attitudes toward devotion and dissent can be observed once more in their differing reactions to one of the Amsterdam community's most notorious dissenters, Juan de Prado, a *converso* who, as it happens, had been friendly with both men at different periods of his life. Just as Orobio and Spinoza took strikingly different, but comparably principled, positions on Jewish doctrine, so they did on Prado's unorthodox views.

Shortly after Orobio's arrival in Amsterdam in 1662, he received a letter postmarked from Antwerp from his old friend, Prado, whom he had not seen in almost twenty years. They had been friends in childhood and classmates at the Spanish university of Alcalá in the year of 1635-6. Orobio had met him at least once since, in 1643, and had been aware even then that Prado had begun to affect some of the heterodox ideas of the deists. But many years had passed since then and under normal circumstances Orobio would presumably have rejoiced to see his friend again and gone to meet him with an open mind. However circumstances were not normal. Since 1657 Prado had been under a solemn ban, forbidding members of the Jewish community to enter into contact of any kind with him.

The main factors leading to Prado's excommunication were as follows.[34] In 1655, already in his early forties, Prado had arrived in Amsterdam as a *converso* refugee, about to begin a new life as a Jew. He joined the Keter Torah Yeshiva and presumably drew upon the medical training he had received in Spain to support himself as a physician. But it was not his medical remedies that would make him famous. His radical religious views soon gathered a following among young students, one of whom was Spinoza, while at the same time stirring up the animosity of the leaders of the community.

The indefatigable scholarly delving of I.S. Révah, has given us a picture of Prado's views sufficiently complete to judge that they were a variety of deism.[35] The aspects of Prado's thought that Révah believes to have made the deepest impression on the youthful Spinoza were his rejection of revelation as usually understood, his assertion of the autonomy of reason in all matters of speculation and morality, his belief that the laws of nature had been fixed immutably by God at creation and that a core of them were of moral force and knowable by all men.[36]

The officials of Amsterdam's Jewish community began to move against Prado in 1655. When faced with the threat of excommunication, however, he backed down and recanted all his views. If Spinoza could thus far be described as Prado's follower, he now outdid his master, refusing to recant even when Prado did. The result was Spinoza's own excommunication in 1656, a stage in his life to be discussed more fully in the following chapter.

The insincerity of Prado's retraction made it a shabby, humiliating occasion. But it is not difficult to sympathize with his predicament. He was a recent, impecunious arrival in Amsterdam, already well into middle age. His knowledge of Dutch was minimal, thus making him completely reliant on the Sephardic community for his livelihood. More than reliant! He more than once received financial aid from the Synagogue's charitable fund.[37] The prospect of excommunication must have terrified him. What but destitution could await him after such a sentence?

Even retraction, however, did no more than delay his day of reckoning. Because his new profession of faith was insincere, Prado soon reverted to his old habits of thought and speech, with the result that he was denounced and finally excommunicated after all early in 1657.

Neither his ideas nor his life improved subsequently. Sometime in the early 1660s he moved to Antwerp, where he continued to eke out an existence as a physician. In 1667 things had become so bad that he sought permission from the Spanish Inquisition to return as a Roman Catholic to Spain. When that was denied he seems to have fallen apart, losing all regard for religion. After the death of his wife, he lurched into a life of unbridled sensuality to the limit that his pinched purse could afford.

A dramatist would find it difficult to dispose of such a character in a believable way, but life is less fastidious. One day, as he crossed a bridge on horseback his mount threw him. He plunged into the water below and was gone.

Some took Prado's end as a judgement of providence.[38] To Spinoza, of course, it would not have seemed so. But assuming the news of his sometime mentor's end reached his ears, it must have encouraged Spinoza to think that he had been right and Prado wrong in facing the threat of excommunication. To waver compounds the danger of dissent.

Though the Jewish community officially washed its hands of Prado in 1657, neither Orobio nor Spinoza can be said to have done so at the personal level. Spinoza's friendly relations with Prado are known to have continued after the latter's excommunication up until Spinoza's departure from Amsterdam three years later.[39] Orobio's gesture came later. But though what he offered Prado then was bitterer than friendship, he at least seems to have offered it as a friend.

When Orobio received the unexpected letter from Prado under the circumstances already mentioned, he approached the Jewish authorities for permission to reply. Notwithstanding their ban, the *ma'amad* granted its permission because of Orobio's declared intention to put his apologetic skills to work in an effort to win the outcast back. The main fruits of this unsuccessful attempt at reclaiming Prado's soul were three epistolary treatises composed by Orobio and, though not actually published, widely circulated in the Jewish community.

In summary of Orobio's thought his biographer Yosef Kaplan writes:

> [F]or him, there is no contradiction between Scripture and natural reason, there is no more lofty religious teaching than that of Judaism, nor any way of life more ethically sublime; every single precept is binding, every custom justified: the Oral Law, the whole complex of Halakhic ordinance, the protective screen of supernumerary prohibitions, the rulings reached by the rabbis on specific issues - all these constitute a single, coherent system, the parts of which were not patient of being dismantled.[40]

Since that was the outlook at which this gifted, well-educated Jewish intellectual had arrived, his effort to win back his old classmate bears the stamp of friendship no less than did Spinoza's ongoing relations with him.

Granted Orobio's belief that people have souls and that souls can be in peril, his motivation in regard to Prado was not merely comparable to Spinoza's ongoing friendship, but, from a religious point of view, superior to it. In continuing his friendly relations with Prado Spinoza simply flouted the ban of the Jewish community. Orobio persuaded the community to a higher understanding of itself and its ban in an effort to reach a member whom he believed had gone astray. But the comparison of these two intellectuals,

Orobio and Spinoza, also calls to mind Spinoza's definition of piety, with its stress on action over doctrine. It is perhaps not surprising that seen in that light Spinoza's fidelity to Prado as a friend appears more meritorious than Orobio's abstract preoccupation with doctrinal correctness. The points of coincidence and contrast with Orobio suggest, however, that had Spinoza been looking for intellectually respectable ways of remaining a Jew he could have found them. While one can defend the wariness of dogma that made Spinoza a radical dissenter, it may also have blinded him to possibilities of traditional piety that were not intellectually disgraceful.

•　　　　•　　　　•

The surrounding Dutch society was also marked by devotion and dissent. The Spinoza scholar Wim Klever makes the case for Spinoza's having been influenced more deeply by the defrocked Jesuit Latinist, Franciscus Van den Enden, than by Juan Prado or other Marrano dissenters.[41] Van den Enden had a colourful history. Expelled from the Jesuits in 1633, he later appears as a *paterfamilias* in Amsterdam, supporting his family by running a bookshop and dealing in art. That business failed in 1652, however, and he fell back on the grammatical training he had received as a Jesuit, opening a school of Latin. To it in due course went the children of many of the leading families of Holland. It was there that Spinoza received his introduction to Latin, and, once so equipped, to the writings of Descartes.

On the basis of fascinating archival material he has discovered, Professor Klever claims to demonstrate a substantial philosophical debt of Spinoza's to Van den Enden. On his reading, Van den Enden would be the source of Spinozistic naturalism, his scientific outlook and even of the atheism widely attributed to him in the seventeenth century. Klever sees Spinoza not merely as Van den Enden's student, but as his follower in a school of radical political and metaphysical thought.

To agree that Klever has established the likelihood of an influence and opened up an important body of literature for investigation, is not to pronounce on whether the influence was as profound as Klever believes. Certainly the society of Van den Enden did nothing to soften Spinoza's suspicion of Roman Catholicism, which was common ground, perhaps even a bond, between Amsterdam's Marrano population and the surrounding Calvinistic culture. Even at the end of his life Spinoza exhibits overt hostility to the Church of Rome.[42] But there is massive evidence, a good deal of which will be discussed in this monograph, that Spinoza did not reject Christianity as a whole as Van den Enden did.

Van den Enden's apostasy late in life was of course no more typical of the religious mentality of Amsterdam than was his youthful Catholicism. If, as I have argued, religious orthodoxy predominated even among *conversos*, with their peculiar inducements to doubt, how much more would this be true among the single-minded, self-confident Dutch. The religious disputes which marked the Christian community during Spinoza's formative years were vehemently concerned with what orthodoxy entailed, but none of the disputants would have dreamed of putting the need for it in question. For example the views even of radical dissenters such as the Remonstrants, among whom Spinoza would ultimately find his closest friends, can be traced to the persecution of Arminians by the Reformed Church following the Synod of Dort in 1619.[43] Yet what made that Synod so acrimonious was that both sides held orthodox belief and pious living to be at risk. The disputants on both sides, beginning with Arminius and Gomarus themselves, were theologians of notable piety and exemplary lives.

•   •   •

The idea here is not to provide an inventory, but only a sample, of the patterns of devotion and dissent that can reasonably be supposed to have influenced Spinoza's religious development. Even the briefest account, however, would be incomplete if it omitted that paradigmatic example of Marrano dissidence, the life of Uriel Da Costa. Although he ended his luckless days in 1640, when Spinoza was only 8, his spiritual career rocked the Amsterdam community and is sure to have made a deep impression on Spinoza. No one acquainted with Da Costa's story can fail to read it as a cautionary tale, but it takes greater skill to know what moral to derive from it. There are those who see Da Costa in romantic terms, as a heroic, "freethinking" deist who blazed the trail Spinoza would follow, one that led on past him to Enlightenment atheism.

That picture is highly questionable. It leaves out of account the deep religious concerns that Da Costa expresses to the end of his life. Moreover, even if the romantic picture were true, it gives us only a retrospective understanding of Spinoza. Neither he nor Da Costa *intended* to anticipate the Enlightenment any more than people writing and thinking today intend to match their beliefs to those of future centuries. Though religious and philosophical thinkers often respond to the past and invariably to the present, only prophets address themselves to the future. To Spinoza Da Costa must have been known simply as a notorious non-conformist. There is little direct evidence for his thought having influenced Spinoza, but neither is the long tradition that it did an incredible one.

Da Costa was born in the mid-1580s in the city of Porto, Portugal. His family was of Jewish descent, but they appear to have become sincere Catholics. Da Costa himself testifies to the sincerity of his father's Catholicism. Moreover his family, which belonged both to the minor nobility and to the well-to-do, could under no circumstances have enjoyed such a high status in the Portugal of those days, had they been in any way religiously suspect. In his autobiography, which was also his last testament, Da Costa does not conceal the pride he felt in his high birth and he shows a keen awareness of its obligations as well as its privileges.[44]

Da Costa was raised as a Roman Catholic and educated in the arts and pastimes that suited his high station. At university he studied law. Every indicator in the young man's situation foretold for him a life of prosperity and influence. But appearances were deceptive. His great expectations were unrealized and he passed with the inexorability of tragic drama through disappointment to ignominious death. The word "tragedy", often loosely applied to lives which are merely sad, is appropriate here. Da Costa's life offers all the elements of tragedy and has in fact been dramatized as such.[45]

To use a dramatic term, Da Costa's fatal flaw was in itself a common characteristic of his age: he was deeply anxious about his personal salvation. This concern led him to seek assurance about the efficacy of Roman Catholic rites for absolution of sins. Though Protestants would have applauded such investigations, the doubts they betrayed would not have escaped censure in seventeenth century Catholic Portugal. Da Costa's method of resolving doubts would have been even more suspect. He began an independent reading of the Gospels in an attempt to discover the scriptural warrant for the Roman rites regarding absolution of sin. I.S. Révah has shown that a focus on Scripture was common in Marrano circles, but the influence of Protestant practice is also likely.[46]

Whatever its origin, Da Costa's study of the Bible led him to the belief that the Roman rites were without biblical warrant. This unsettling conclusion prompted him to wonder whether as a consequence he must reconcile himself to the fearful damnation which Catholic doctrine promised those who died in their sins. But this, he clearly recognized, would follow only if the Roman Catholic teaching about the afterlife were itself defensible. Reason prompted him to think it was not.

By this time Da Costa's intellectual progress had taken him into an area of political as well as spiritual danger. He continued to think of life in religious terms, though for him Roman Catholicism was religiously and rationally discredited. So where could he go? In a leap which puzzles readers today, he seems to take it for granted that a move toward Judaism would follow. But as Révah points out, not everyone who leaves Catholicism becomes a Jew. Révah's conjecture that Da Costa's Marrano connection explains the leap is certainly plausible. Interestingly, however, Da Costa himself offers a different, if less satisfactory, explanation. He ascribes his turning to the study of Judaism not to any atavistic quest, but simply to his knowledge that on the precise matter that disturbed him – the question of salvation – Jews believed differently from the now discredited Christians. It was in the hope that Judaism might bring him closer to an answer that he began to read what he calls "Moses and the Prophets", i.e., what his Catholic teachers would have called the Old Testament. His reading persuaded him that obedience to the Mosaic Law was all God actually requires of mankind. As that discovery became a conviction with him his thoughts turned toward conversion to Judaism.

It is unclear in the autobiography and probably in the mind of its author whether from the very outset he saw "the Law" narrowly, as involving mainly the ten commandments, or whether it originally included the wider range of dietary laws and other customs which Moses also enjoined upon the people of Israel. Nor does he make it clear at what point he came to view the rewards and punishments set out by the Law as confined to the present life. In any case, probably sooner rather than later, he began to take a narrow view of both the Law's scope and its sanctions. The same independent study that had led him to this judgement of the Law gave him a correspondingly limited view of what becoming a Jew would entail. That was the error which would bring about his undoing.

Da Costa's opinions were already unorthodox, but the cost of conversion was so high for him that it dispels any doubt about his sincerity. Merely to mention his conclusions to his mother and brothers was to put his privileged situation at risk. But he did more. He was so persistent that he ultimately persuaded them of his views and developed a plan for their joint conversion. Knowing that Jews were free to practise their religion in Amsterdam, but that emigration from Portugal was illegal, the family devised a plan of escape. However it entailed the complete sacrifice of their material goods and the risk of their very lives. Uriel in particular left behind him a comfortable life, a fashionable house and an enviable social position.

Upon arrival in Amsterdam he submitted to the ritual circumcision required by the Jewish law. Perhaps this was the first thing to rouse him from his utopian dream of finding in Amsterdam the hoped-for community of believers practising Judaism as he understood it. When he learned how Judaism was actually practised Da Costa began to harbour doubts about it similar to those which had earlier pushed him out of Roman Catholicism. He blamed the Jews for having gone too far beyond the "customs and ordinances" given to Moses. He accused them of Pharisaism, quoting from the Vulgate version of Jesus' famous indictment of the Pharisees in Matthew 23.

It is not surprising that the Jewish community did not appreciate this sort of insurrection from within, especially from an insignificant refugee. Not only would it be disturbing to the faith of others, but the community felt pressured by the surrounding Christian society not to become known as a haven for heretics. Therefore they threatened Da Costa with excommunication. He responded by writing a book in his own defence, to demonstrate "the nullity of Pharisaic traditions and observances". The war escalated on both sides: more vindications came on his side; excommunication was their ultimate reply.

For the next fifteen years Da Costa lived as an outsider to the community and became theologically a stranger to it. With the passage of those years he had ceased to regard even the part of the Mosaic Law he accepted as inspired by God. But at the same time he was weary of the difficulty of being a stranger and alone. Even if it meant, as he disparagingly put it, playing the monkey among the monkeys, he decided that he must be reconciled with the community.

That reconciliation, when it came, was short-lived. After only a few days he was denounced to the authorities by his nephew for not observing the dietary laws. Systematic ostracism began to be practised against him. What he found most difficult to accept was that his most assiduous detractors were members of his own family. But when word got out that Da Costa had advised two Christians who were thinking of converting to Judaism to think again, the whole community joined in the call for his excommunication. This time he endured isolation for seven years, once again made all the more bitter by implacable hostility and malice from his own family. Those who did not go out of their way to harm him, he complains, nevertheless rejoiced at his misfortunes. Attempts at legal redress within the community met with only the usual insolence of office and the law's delay.

Da Costa's will ultimately was broken. He decided he must at any price come to terms with the community, though it was a grievous blow to his *amour propre* as a man well-born. If he could no longer endure life as a pariah, however, there was no choice but to settle on their terms.

Not surprisingly second reconciliations, being rare, had to be bought more dearly. To begin he would be asked to repudiate publicly all he had in good faith believed and done and to make a solemn promise never to think or act in that way again. This done, he would be stripped to the waist, lashed with thirty-nine strokes and then, stretched across the threshold of the

Synagogue, he would allow all the men women and children of the community to kick him or step on him as they left.

Da Costa endured it all. Afterwards he went home and, with remarkable *sang-froid*, wrote the moving autobiographical sketch which would also be his final testament. He called it *A Specimen of Human Life.* Next he found his pistol and attempted to shoot the family member who had been his principal adversary. Like so much in Da Costa's life, the shot went astray. His second found its mark, however, ending the sufferer's unhappy life.

The Sartrean dictum "Hell is other people" might be a fitting epitaph for Uriel Da Costa. But the poignant last words of his memoir give the best indication of what organized religion meant to him in the end:

> Remember this: my name in Christian Portugal was Gabriel. Among the Jews – whom I wish I had never approached – I was called Uriel. The change was of small importance.

All this drama occurred when Spinoza was eight years old. But as his own convictions developed Da Costa must surely have figured prominently in his mind, at least as an illustration of what not to do. Perhaps it was with Da Costa in mind that Spinoza held firm under pressure that caused Juan de Prado to recant.

·   ·   ·

Readers of the twenty-first century have difficulty just grasping the issues involved in the religious struggles of the seventeenth. Few feel any emotional connection with them. That is where the advice of the historian Pieter Geyl is useful. He reminds us not to make unfavourable comparisons between the wealth and fruitfulness of the Netherlands' art and poetry in the seventeenth century and what seems to be the dusty irrelevance of their religious disputes. The latter do not betoken some "extraordinary lapse" in moral development but are themselves an expression of the same wealth and fruitfulness. "[T]he age lives in them and even in its apparently most accessible manifestations is not to be understood without them".[47]

All the more is this observation true for Spinoza himself, whose religious views were refined in that furnace within a furnace, the Sephardic community within the larger Christian society of the Netherlands. The reactions of the devout and the dissident among Spinoza's contemporaries reveal the patterns of religious submission and challenge in the light of which Spinoza would make his own way towards excommunication and beyond.

Notes

1   The best short account of this community and Spinoza's life in it is found in the opening chapters of Nadler [1999], to which I am much indebted.
2   See I.S. Révah [1995c], 30/14.
3   See Méchoulan [1991], p. 25f.
4   Nadler [1999], 56.
5   The earliest biographies are collected in one volume in Gebhardt [1914]. They are divided over the question of whether the family was well-to-do or not. Perhaps this is not surprising. Like most families whose income depends on business, the Spinozas' fortunes were up and down at different times. However Nadler thinks it is fair to say that at least in the 1630s they were well-to-do.
6   Gebhardt [1914], 11f, 39, 53f. In order the biographers are Maximilien Lucas, Christian Kortholt and Johannes Colerus.
7   Cf. Révah [1958], 175f.
8   The Pentateuch is the first five books of the Old Testament, Genesis, Exodus, Leviticus, Numbers and Deuteronomy. The first of these books tells the story of the beginning of the world, the choosing of Abraham as a patriarch whose descendants, the Jews, would become God's chosen people. Exodus recounts how the Jews were led out of Egypt by Moses and given the Law, called in Hebrew "Torah", according to which God expected them to live. The last three books of the Pentateuch elaborate and interpret the Law.
9   Nadler [1999], 61.
10   See the preface to the Grammar (Spinoza [1925] 1, 286) and the editorial comments by C. Gebhardt in the same volume, 626.
11   Nadler [1999], 65.
12   Ibid, 90.
13   Spinoza [1925], 3, 360 = TP 11/4.
14   Spinoza [1925], 2, 197 =3Ed27(after P59).
15   Spinoza [1925], 2, 269 = 4eApp9.
16   Spinoza [1925], 3, 346 = TP 8/49.
17   *loc. cit.*
18   Spinoza [1925], 2, 269 = 4eApp9.
19   Nadler [1999], 81, finds little evidence to support the older view that Spinoza actually pursued Rabbinic studies.
20   See Israel [1984], 41-44, 50.
21   Spinoza's mother died in 1651.
22   Nadler [1999], 86.
23   *op. cit.*, 119.
24   Spinoza [1925], 3, 172 = TTP 13.
25   A succinct review of the three main scholarly explanations of rejectionism can be found in Kaplan [1989], 160ff.
26   Méchoulan [1991], 56.
27   For a brief account see Méchoulan [1991], 97-102.

28   Kaplan [1989], 112f.

29   Kaplan [1989], 117f.

30   Spinoza [1925], 3, 79f.= TTP 5.

31   Kaplan [1989], 119f.

32   Kaplan [1989], 357f.

33   Kaplan [1989], 122.

34   The discussions on which I have principally drawn for this sketch of De Prado's life and teachings are Kaplan [1989], 122-178 and Révah [1958].

35   For comprehensive discussions of what is known see Kaplan, 138-145; Révah [1995a], 237/375 - 242/380.

36   Révah [1959], 51.

37   Révah [1995a], 232/370.

38   Kaplan [1989], 159.

39   Révah [1958], 198f.

40   Kaplan [1989], 166.

41   Klever [1991], 616.

42   Spinoza [1925], 4, 322f = Ep 76 (to Burgh).

43   Kolakowski [1969], 168.

44   The original Latin of the autobiography, entitled *Exemplar humanae vitae*, is printed together with a German translation in *Die Schriften des Uriel Da Costa* ed. C.I. Gebhardt. Amsterdam: Curis Societatis Spinozanae, 1922. There is no easily available English translation. My summary here is based on this edition.

45   *Uriel Acosta*, by Karl-Ferdinand Gutzkow (1847).

46   I.S. Révah is certainly right in dismissing those who interpret Da Costa's case as pure, romantic individualism. Révah's discovery that Da Costa's independent reading of Scripture fits a fairly typical seventeenth century Marrano profile also offers the best explanation of his later immediate reversion to Judaism without any Protestant interlude (see Révah [1995b]). However it offers no explanation of the beginning of Da Costa's journey. His having initially been prodded into undertaking his religious investigations by uncertainty about his personal salvation declares a classic Protestant theme. Next, his manner of pursuing this question, beginning as it does with an independent examination of the *Gospels*, strongly suggests the influence of Protestant biblicism.

47   Geyl [1966], 38.

Chapter Two

Conflicts and Communities

Abominable Heresies; Monstrous Deeds

The business career of Spinoza came to an abrupt end in the summer of 1656, when the Talmud Torah community pronounced against him the harshest *cherem* (order of excommunication) in their history. Because of the "abominable heresies" and "monstrous deeds" which had come to light as the result of testimony from "trustworthy witnesses", the *ma'amad* determined that Spinoza must be "expelled from the people of Israel".[1]

Ze'ev Levy documents the astonishing legacy of mistrust of Spinoza created by this excommunication. Among some Jewish religious thinkers and philosophers it has lasted down to the present day.[2] But at the same time the excommunication marks one of the transitional moments in Spinoza's life and remains an indispensable key to understanding his development. It was at least the herald, if not the progenitor, of his later philosophical development.

Exactly what the monstrous deeds and heresies were for which Spinoza was exposed to such severe treatment by his community remains a subject of discussion. The writ of excommunication indicts the guilty party and exhorts the community accordingly, but makes little attempt to justify its harshness. It consists of a formulaic denunciation followed by an injunction to all believers to forego Spinoza's company. The first section reads (in part) as follows:

> By decree of the angels and by the command of the holy men, we excommunicate, expel, curse and damn Baruch de Espinoza, with the consent of God, Blessed be He, and with the consent of the entire holy congregation ... and with all the castigations that are written in the Book of the Law. Cursed be he by day and cursed be he by night; cursed be he when he lies down and cursed be he when he rises up. Cursed be he when he goes out and cursed be he when he comes in. The Lord will not spare him, but the anger of the Lord and his jealousy shall smoke against that man, and all the curses that are written in this book shall lie upon him, and the Lord shall blot out his name from under heaven. And the Lord shall separate him unto evil out of all the tribes of Israel, according to the curses of the covenant that are written in this book of the law.[3]

The leaders of the community supplemented this set piece by an order of their own pertaining to the sequestration of Spinoza:

> We order that no one shall communicate with him either orally or in writing, that no one shall show him any favour, no one shall live under one roof with him, or tarry within four yards of him. No one shall read anything he writes.[4]

Because such solemn warnings from the *ma'amad* were scrupulously observed by the community, it is obvious that Spinoza's business contacts would be severed for the term of the ban. And since Spinoza would under no condition have risked becoming a second Uriel da Costa by seeking reconciliation, his excommunication effectively brought mercantile life to an end for him the day it was pronounced: 27 July 1656.

A great deal has been written about the motivation behind the ban, both of those who issued it and of the one against whom it was pronounced. Concerning Spinoza's alleged "heresies", Nadler provides a list of nearly 20 reasons for excommunication accepted as valid at the time. Of these he thinks it likely that Spinoza had already begun to hold at least two views which would have earned him condemnation. First, he denied the immortality of the soul, at least in the form that it was then understood. In the second place he disputed the divine origin of the Torah. To hold just one such proposition would have been sufficient to have brought down upon him the full wrath of the community.[5]

Maximilien Lucas, one of the early biographers, reports that two of Spinoza's "most intimate friends" initially wormed some of his controversial views out of him and then, when Spinoza tried to avoid further incriminating contact with them, denounced him to the religious authorities.[6] Neither he nor subsequent biographers, however, have found any of the "monstrous deeds" also mentioned in the *cherem*. Were there any? No doubt we must treat the word "monstrous" as a technical term from the polemical religious vocabulary of his time and place. But even in this restricted sense it is not obvious how the young philosopher offended.

If clues as to what prompted the community's severe measures against him are available, it would be reasonable to look for them in Spinoza's actions just prior to the excommunication or in his reactions in the immediate aftermath. Though the information we have concerning this period of the philosopher's life remains sketchy, a sufficient amount has been rediscovered and illuminated by recent scholarship that at least a partial account of the ban's motivation can now be given.

A Utrecht theologian by the name of Salomon Van Til, writing in 1684, reported that Spinoza had written a kind of *Apolgia pro vita sua*, under the title "A Justification for Leaving Judaism". Van Til adds, however, that on his friends' advice Spinoza withheld it from publication, incorporating its main points into his mature work, the *Tractatus Theologico-Politicus* (henceforward TTP).[7] Since no copy of the "Justification" has so far been discovered, we must judge its character from what we see in the TTP.

The "Justification" has contributed to Spinoza's reputation for anti-Semitism in some circles.[8] But that charge should neither be lightly made nor uncritically allowed to stand. To judge from what remains of the "Justification" in the TTP, it was certainly not anti-Semitic in the sense of being an attack on "Jewry,"[9] i.e., on Jews as an ethnic group. Anything of that kind would obviously have involved an element of self-hatred for which I can see no evidence in Spinoza's writings.[10] And while it is incontestably true that he rejected Judaism as a religion, that cannot be called anti-Semitic in any *morally* objectionable sense.

There is, however, one act of Spinoza's that might be construed as anti-Semitism of a very limited kind. In the immediate aftermath of the excommunication, his biographer Colerus reports, Spinoza deliberately chose the Christian name of Benedict.[11] Taken in conjunction with Uriel da Costa's poignant remark, mentioned in the previous chapter, about the practical futility of such gestures, Spinoza's act could be read as a vindictive, even if pointless, attempt to thumb his nose at the community that had expelled him. But such a reading is far from compelling. What seems more likely is that Uriel da Costa was wrong about what is in a name, or that, knowing that he was about to take his own life, he was evaluating such changes *sub specie aeternitatis*. Spinoza may have had pragmatic reasons for changing his name, hoping thereby to escape any disadvantages attendant on having a Jewish name in the Christian community in which, henceforward, he would have to live.

Spinoza's reactions to the excommunication, however construed, may turn out to be less indicative of its motivation than were his activities in the years and months leading up to it. That will be so, at least, if Richard Popkin's remarkable story of Spinoza's first publications proves able to withstand scholarly scrutiny.[12]

By an improbable coincidence it seems that the year of Spinoza's excommunication coincided with the year fixed in the chronologies of certain Millenarian Christians for the conversion of the Jews. These predictions in turn chanced to coincide with the Messianic expectations of certain Jewish leaders, among them Menasseh ben Israel. Stimulated by such auspicious signs English Quakers had sent a mission led by a certain William Ames[13] to the populous Jewish communities of the Netherlands. To reach their audience most effectively they wanted to have translated into Hebrew two pamphlets written by the famous Quaker, Margaret Fell[14]. The first pamphlet is actually a letter addressed to none other than Spinoza's sometime teacher, Menasseh ben Israel. It is entitled, *For Manasseth-Ben-Israel; The Call of the Jews out of Babylon.*

William Ames reported to Fell on 17 April 1656 that a Hebrew translator for the pamphlet had been found. He was an excommunicated Jew whom Ames believed to be a Christian:

> There is a Jew at Amsterdam that by the Jews is cast out (as he himself and others sayeth) because he owneth no other teacher but the light and he sent for me and I spoke toe him and he was pretty tender and doth owne all that is spoken; and he sayde tow read of moses and the prophets without was nothing tow him except he Came to know it within; and soe the name of Christ it is like he doth owne.

Popkin believes the translator Ames found was Spinoza. If so, it is of great significance that Ames' meeting with and commissioning of Spinoza took place *more than three months before* the excommunication. If Manasseh ben Israel, the addressee of the pamphlet, was aware of its existence, then one of Spinoza's "monstrous deeds" – from a religious point of view one of the most monstrous imaginable! – is accounted for. If it was known that a member of the Amsterdam Synagogue had conspired with a Christian mission to convert the entire Jewish community of Amsterdam, that would surely be viewed as conduct monstrous enough to deserve the severest condemnation. It would also explain why Spinoza never thought reconciliation an option.

Spinoza's Personal Motivations

Whatever the exact nature of Spinoza's heresies and monstrous deeds may have been, no scholar has suggested that he entered upon them rashly or in reaction to some merely contingent event. Neither Spinoza nor his early biographers portray the excommunication as something that *befell* him. Yet conjectures about which personal convictions may have set him on collision course with his community have varied widely.

In the view of Spinoza's first biographers, the turmoil of 1656 had its earliest antecedent not in any event or circumstance outside Spinoza's control, but in the opinions the young thinker came to form, and in his determination to follow them at any cost. The composite picture that emerges from their different brief accounts is something like the following. After studying the Bible and the Talmud in the *yeshiva*, Spinoza began privately to learn Latin in Van den Enden's school. In the hands of so gifted a student, knowledge of Latin was sufficient to open up for him all the writings of the learned, and especially those of the natural philosophers (natural philosophy being what we today call natural science).

The new and exciting paradigm of natural philosophy in the Netherlands of the early seventeenth century was the physics of René Descartes. The biographers say that Spinoza's imagination was captured by Cartesian physics and that reading it created in him an expectation of more rigorous standards of argument and proof than he had found among his rabbinical teachers. Inevitably he was led to apply that new standard to their teachings and as a result to put them in question.[15] Intellectual dissatisfaction of this kind may have prompted, or itself been prompted by, a more widespread impatience with rabbinical authority, which some scholars have seen as the root cause of his ultimate separation from the Jewish community.[16] Others have argued that Spinoza was led away from Judaism by deistic opinions he absorbed from heterodox friends and teachers, most of whom were also Cartesians.[17]

Spinoza's own rare pronouncements on this period of his life coincide at least with the one point in which all his biographers and commentators agree, namely, that the *cherem* was not thrust upon him but, in some mysterious way, chosen. He is quoted as having said that it forced him into nothing he would not have done anyway, had he not wished to avoid scandal.[18] However unpleasant the process of excommunication may have been in itself, the ban seems to have put Spinoza exactly where he wanted to be. But where was that? Certainly it involved freeing himself from the moral authority of the Jewish community. But some his own writing strongly suggests that his desire to leave was motivated less by the anti-Semitism with which he has sometimes been tarred than by a dislike of the position that he had come to occupy as a Jew – that of a businessman. If business life was what he most disliked, then it explains why the severing of his business connections was unable to break Spinoza's will, as it had been able to do in the cases of both Uriel da Costa and Juan de Prado. It would have less force against a man who saw his previous business life as a threat to his very salvation and had prepared well in advance to enter into another. One of his early writings suggests that Spinoza may have been such a man.

The *Tractatus on the Emendation of the Intellect* (henceforward TIE) opens with a first-person account of a spiritual crisis. Commentators warn against taking the picture it presents as "strictly biographical",[19] but on the other hand it is difficult to think that such an impassioned meditation on finding the right path in life could have been unaffected by the crisis Spinoza had recently passed through.[20] In his commentary on the TIE Bernard Rousset judiciously distinguishes between its Cartesian form, its Stoic content, and its source in its author's "experience".[21]

The narrator of the TIE ascribes his changed outlook to a moral or perhaps religious crisis brought on by *fear*. He had grown afraid that his life was morally or religiously unacceptable. In language which is unoriginal, though charged with authentic emotion, he describes a transformation that many of history's religiously and morally sensitive consciences have undergone, beginning with the suspicion that their lives have strayed off course.

> I thus perceived that I was in a state of great peril, and I compelled myself to seek a remedy with all my strength, however uncertain it might be. I was like an invalid labouring with a deadly illness who, when he sees he will surely die, unless some remedy can be employed, seeks it with all his might. He does not care how uncertain it may be, since it represents all his hope. All the trash (*illa omnia*) pursued by ordinary folk not only provides no remedy for the preservation of our being, but even stands in its way. Riches not infrequently cause the death of those who possess them; they are inevitably fatal to those possessed by them.[22]

The conviction had grown upon the narrator that he was on the slippery path of an unexamined life, pursuing uncritically the spiritually fatal goals of riches, honour and pleasure. Was there a time when Spinoza was pursuing these things? To the extent that he was in business, it must be granted that he was in pursuit of riches. There is no biographical evidence independent of the TIE of his having been inordinately interested in the other two. This does not exclude the possibility of his having detected or suspected these tendencies in himself, however, as spiritually sensitive people are known to do.

All three pursuits in any case have one moral defect in common: their objects are perishable things and therefore not finally productive of happiness. For that reason, the narrator tells us, we should cultivate towards them an attitude of indifference, saving our love for "a thing that is eternal and infinite and feeds the soul with pure joy".[23]

To learn self-control and so redirect his love is the first condition the narrator stipulates for escaping his predicament. But if that had been sufficient in Spinoza's own case, he could surely have achieved it within the Jewish community. Thus, if the TIE is drawing upon Spinoza's personal experience one would expect the narrator to prescribe some further necessary condition for a good life. And there is one. The narrator speaks of the necessity of achieving self-control *in community with others*. The seeker must also find a "society (*societas*) of the requisite kind in which as many as possible could achieve the same end with the greatest ease and security".[24] The Jewish community with its rigid religious hierarchy did not seem suitable to Spinoza for that purpose.

It is not difficult to see in this double goal of self-control and community the foreshadowing of what some have thought to be the dominant concern and tension of Spinoza's philosophy, namely to work out the conditions under which the attainment of individual salvation would be consistent with an open society that erects no dogmatic barriers against others who are following their own paths toward purity of life.[25] It is certain that, as André Malet has stressed, the opening paragraphs of TIE are no mere edifying discourse somehow to be separated from Spinoza's deepest philosophical commitments.[26]

Collegiants

One of Spinoza's closest friends after the excommunication (and perhaps before) was Jarig Jelles, a Dutch businessman who passed through a religious crisis of his own in the mid-1650s, after which he also abandoned his business career. His description employs terms strikingly similar to those used by Spinoza:

> Whoever loves this world, which is to say, whoever loves idle fame, pleasure and riches, will pay the highest penalty: he will not be able to inherit the Kingdom of God. The kingdom of Mercy, however, which leads to the kingdom of Glory involves achieving dominion over the emotions. And we enter into this kingdom when we are led by the Spirit, by the light of the understanding, by truth.[27]

Jelles' religious crisis preceded Spinoza's, though Spinoza was the first to write about it. Thus it may be that Spinoza owes something to Jelles in taking his decision to break with business life, just as it seems likely that Jelles is

Spinoza's debtor for his formulation of his reasons. The important point for present purposes in any case is the similarity of the two cases.

It is of interest because Jelles belonged to a group of radical Protestants of Holland's so-called "second reformation", whose ambition was to cultivate both a kind of individualism and a kind of community resembling what Spinoza was seeking. The religious communities they established were called "Colleges" and so the frequenters of them became known as "Collegiants". Defining themselves less by dogma and rite than by personal piety and community, the Collegiants were able to welcome the exiled Spinoza into their midst. A letter to Spinoza from Simon de Vries in 1663 is indicative of the importance at least some Collegiants recognized his philosophy to have. He tells Spinoza that his *Collegium* regularly meets to read, discuss and defend Spinoza's views.[28]

The importance of this religious community in Spinoza's development has been recognized since K.O. Meinsma's book *Spinoza en zijn Kring* (*Spinoza and his Circle*), published in 1896, and appearing in German and then in French translations in the course of the twentieth century. Meinsma's findings have of course not gone completely unchallenged,[29] but the arguments produced against his thesis have not been thought compelling by many scholars.[30]

To follow Meinsma, on the other hand, helps make sense of some of the puzzles surrounding the excommunication. It would tell us why Spinoza, unlike either Da Costa or De Prado, seemed to welcome it. He did so because it posed no threat to him. He knew in advance of an alternative community in which he would be warmly received and whose outlook would be more congenial to his own.

If Spinoza formed an attachment of some kind to this new religious community it would also explain why he discussed his early crisis in positive, quasi-religious terms in the TIE, rather than in terms of the anti-Jewish hostility he is assumed to have had by some Jewish commentators, or in the secular-scientific terms that one would expect from the accounts given by his early biographers. His attachment to a Christian community would also offer an explanation of Spinoza's "almost visceral" intimacy with the New Testament, which, as André Malet points out, could hardly have been acquired outside a believing community.[31]

Finally, as already mentioned in connection with the Quaker translations, the Collegiant connection would help explain the "monstrous deeds" for which he was excommunicated. Among the offences which made excommunication mandatory were "engaging in common prayer with persons who had never been members of the synagogue" or "engaging Gentiles in theological discussions".[32] If it is true, as some have suggested, that Spinoza began attending Collegiant gatherings as early as 1654, then he could not have avoided being guilty on both of those charges.

It is also significant that frequenting the Collegiants could easily have aroused among his enemies within the Jewish community the suspicion that Spinoza had converted to Christianity, or at least that he was contemplating it. One of his early biographers claims that he did in fact become a Christian,[33] though most subsequent commentators have not agreed.

Spinoza may first have entered into relations with the Collegiant community of Amsterdam as early as 1654,[34] and may have done so through a variety of doors. Perhaps he met them by merely turning up at their meetings, or he may have made his Collegiant acquaintances through his business connection with the Amsterdam Exchange.[35] It is even possible that he met them at his own synagogue, since several of the Collegiants, possessing both scholarly knowledge of Hebrew and philo-Semitic tendencies, were regular attenders there.[36] And of course none of these possibilities excludes any of the others. Spinoza's first Collegiant friends included Pieter Balling, Pieter Serrarius, Simon de Vries, the publisher Jan Rieuwertsz and others.

Origin of Collegiantism

The rise of this small, but highly influential, religious movement could be called an accident of Dutch history. Paradoxically, its decidedly anti-Calvinistic voice arose just as Calvinism appeared to have swept away its foes at the Synod of Dort in 1619. At that Synod the Gomarists, who favoured the exclusive authority of the Reformed (Calvinist) Church utterly routed their Arminian opponents, who had lost their political influence the year before, with the fall of the Oldenbarnevelt regime. The Synod moved swiftly to revoke the Arminian ministers' licences to preach, with chilling results for the Dutch religious climate. The range of permissible religious expression in Holland noticeably narrowed and her nascent religious toleration appeared to be imperilled: "The Church was tied much more straitly to her creeds; ... the Calvinists set the tone for several generations to come", says the historian Peter Geyl.[37]

Since the interdict against non-Calvinist preachers included even small assemblies in private homes, conventional thinking had it that those of Arminian persuasion must either recant or be driven underground.[38] Their enemies thought the same and congratulated themselves on having dispatched the Arminian threat.

Some more imaginative Arminians, however, thought of a third option. Why not meet without a minister? In this way the strictures of Dordt could be respected and the community of Arminian believers preserved intact. But for this to happen, it would be necessary to reorganize themselves on radically democratic principles, so that the ministerial function could be taken over by the ordinary believer, with or without theological training. In keeping with these reforms they began to call their meeting places not Churches, but Colleges, and the Collegiant movement was born.

What began as a necessity soon became a virtue in Collegiant eyes and more than one Arminian minister who offered his clandestine services was shocked to learn that the Collegiants had grown to prefer the form of worship that had so recently been forced upon them.[39] The numbers of those who liked it grew by surprising leaps and bounds. Between 1620 and 1650 it spread throughout the whole of the Dutch Republic.[40] Democratic participation in the ministry appealed to many people in other denominations as well, especially other socially marginal sects, such as Mennonites and Quakers, who found an unconditional welcome in the broad-minded Collegiant assemblies. In fact, so many Mennonites were attracted to Collegiant gatherings, and they were won so entirely to the new form of worship, that the Dutch Mennonites were left depleted, demoralized and divided by the second half of the seventeenth century.[41]

The attempt of the Reformed Church to extinguish Arminian thinking by repression thus backfired in a way no one could have anticipated. By their very success in the Synod of Dordt, the Gomarists called forth the Collegiant version of Arminian Christianity, a rival no less challenging in its theology, but more durable in its organization. In the midst of repression was born a movement that has been called the most radical and perfect expression of Dutch religious tolerance.[42]

What Collegiants Believed

Detailed accounts of the origin of the Collegiants and of their teachings are readily available in the writings of Meinsma, Fix and others cited in the bibliography of this book. For present purposes a brief outline of their beliefs will suffice.

The location of Collegiant headquarters in the quiet town of Rijnsburg belied the noisy activism that came with being part of the

Netherlands' "second Reformation". Despite having arisen more or less by chance out of the religious strife surrounding the Synod of Dordt, and despite their notable lack of dogma, the Collegiants nevertheless soon began to find a theological justification for their religious convictions going back into the earliest roots of Reformation theology.[43]

When it came to opposing Rome, the Collegiants were of one mind with their Reforming predecessors. Rome was the Babylon referred to in the Revelation of St. John, and the Pope was the Antichrist.[44] They were critical of the Reformation not so much for failing to achieve its goal of purging Babylon as for believing it attainable in the first place. The fundamental error of the great reformers had been their failure to understand the real source of the religious apostasy they were trying to undo. As a consequence of that first error, they had also not seen how to be faithful witnesses to Christ in the world as it is.

The corruption that made reform necessary went back further than Luther and Calvin had believed. It began in the age of Constantine, when the Roman Empire had officially become Christian. The early Church, the Church of the apostles, could never have entered into such a cozy alliance with the State.

In those days the Church still enjoyed two gifts of the Holy Spirit, one of which had ceased in the age of Constantine. The lost gift was that which they called *Heerlijkmaking*,[45] which in the theological jargon of the day referred to a glorious (*heerlijk*) union with the Lord (*de Heer*). As long as the Church had possessed such glory it had need of neither dogma nor State support; but once it was lost, neither dogma nor state support could restore it.

The loss of this gift left the visible Church, organized as it was by dogma, tradition, hierarchy and possessions, and vexed by inter-denominational hatred, in a position so vulnerable that mere reform was insufficient. Nothing short of the second coming of Jesus Christ would be able to restore her to glory. In the interim Christ's true followers, who were scattered among all the denominations of the visible Church (except, of course, the Roman one), must carry on with the only remaining gift, that of *Heiligmaking*, or holiness.

The first great error of the Reformation, then, had been to think that the Church could be reformed by human hands. The second, which resulted from the first, was to try to further the cause of Christ by the futile means of seeking in high places support for new creeds.

The Collegiant alternative was to lead a life built entirely upon the single gift of holiness that remained. In practice this meant living a pious life, surrounded where possible with others who were pursuing the same goal.

Where there was no *heerlijkmaking*, there could be no "church", if by that term was meant what the Reformed Church called "a holy congregation".[46] Much of what the Calvinists said in their *Belgic Confession* concerning the Church would have been perfectly acceptable to the Collegiants, but they would not admit the Reformed church (or any other) to be a "holy congregation". That is why they declared their own assemblies to be merely gatherings of ordinary people whose purpose was to pursue holiness together. "The religious community proclaims itself a secular institution, called to strengthen collectively its religious values, but deprived of any charismatic glory of a religious group in its ideas, activities and rituals".[47]

Out of their denial of even the possibility of corporate holiness arose the Collegiants' casual attitude toward the inherited creeds and articles of faith, which other Christian organizations took so seriously. But how could the Collegiants dispense with them? In the absence of a creed, or some comparable standard of measurement, how could anyone be certain of being acceptable to God? Here the Collegiants depended almost exclusively on the discerning power of what they liked to call the *innerlijke licht* (inner light).

Andrew Fix sees the Collegiant theology of 'light' as part of the development from inner-light spiritualism to natural-light rationalism. He sees it, in other words, as a significant transitional moment between the still Christian outlook of the seventeenth century and the secular attitude of the Enlightenment.[48] It is to Fix's credit, however, that he is able to preserve the essential tension of the transitional moment, without collapsing the Collegiant's self-understanding into the position into which it would later evolve. Not all historians are so careful. It is easy to suppose that if a later age takes up the thoughts of an earlier one and uses them for a different purpose, that later purpose must have been what the earlier age was trying to articulate all along. This is a particular temptation when the later age is our own or in sympathy with our own. All history then becomes a stammering attempt to say what "now we know". I shall argue that this is a danger not just in looking at the Collegiants but, of special concern here, in relation to Spinoza.

For present purposes it is important to stress the danger of this elementary historical fallacy and to resist it by understanding the Collegiant doctrine of the inner light in its historical integrity, without reference to any appropriation of it by later times. The best Collegiant guide to the significance of the "light" is probably that of Spinoza's good friend, Pieter Balling, who published his *Het Licht op den Kandelaar* (*The Light upon the Candlestick*) in 1662.[49]

Balling begins by lamenting the way in which the religious disputes of his day made all salvation seem to depend on the most recondite points of doctrine and jargon. (Pascal's satirical *Provincial Letters* can be read as confirmation and commentary on this point.) Like Pascal, Balling recognizes that such disputes, even granting that some of them may have theological merit, will never help common people, but only drive them to despair. But he also believes he knows a remedy for that despair, one that will permit them to turn away from idle words and endless disputes towards a source of spiritual discernment that they have within themselves. This he describes as "the true light, which enlighteneth every man that cometh into the world".[50]

The words quoted are of course taken from one of the most famous passages of the Bible, the procemium of the Gospel of John, which no one of that biblically literate age would fail to recognize. They would also know that the Gospel writer intended those words to describe and introduce the figure of Jesus Christ. Balling later makes the same explicit connection:

> This light then, Christ the truth, etc. is that which makes manifest and reproves sin in man, showeth him how he is strayed from God, accuseth him of the evil which he doeth, and hath commited, yea this is it which judgeth and condemneth him.[51]

The light of Christ is not only judgemental, however. It is also an uplifting guide. Balling continues on the same page:

> This is it which leads man in truth, into the way to God, which excuseth him in well-doing, giving him peace in his conscience, yea, brings him to union with God, wherein all happiness and salvation consist.

It is true that Balling prefers to use the term light rather than to talk of Christ,[52] but this is because he recognizes the Biblical warrant for identifying them, not because he wants to reduce one to the other. If it is more difficult for ordinary people to understand the recorded teachings of Christ, then let them simply pay attention to the demands of *the Light*, for Scripture is not the unique witness, but only a "co-witness" to what is also taught by the light.[53] "The light is also the first principle of religion", he goes on to say:

> For, seeing there can be no true religion without the knowledge of God, and no knowledge of God without this light, religion must necessarily have this light for its principle. ... Without this light, there is no power or ability at all in man to do any good.[54]

By the identity of terms already noted, to say that there is "no knowledge of God without this light" is to say that every way to God leads through Christ. And this is a point that needs to be emphasized in discussing the religious sensibilities of the Collegiants. For all their resistance to dogma, Christocentrism seems to be a characteristic of Collegiant thought.[55] They find in Christ not only the "power to do good", which human beings otherwise lack, but also the key to eternal life: "The light, Christ, ... is a living word, and translateth man from death to life".[56]

The universality of this doctrine of light was a needed counterweight to the Collegiant doctrine that religious assemblies had merely secular value. If there is no institutional source of salvation, people must despair of it altogether, unless it is available to each individually. But everyone has direct access to the light, which was also called Christ, the Spirit, the Word, "seeing these all denote but one and the same thing".[57]

When the low value the Collegiants placed on religious assemblies is put together with the universality they attribute to the light, their reputation for "anti-clericalism" is easily explained. What could justify conferring special privileges of ministry and interpretation on one person, as do those who believe in the supernatural effect of the sacraments or the supernatural calling of ministers of the Word? In justifying their anti-clericalism, Collegiants would recur "innumerable times" to the fourteenth chapter of Saint Paul's first Corinthian letter.[58] There the apostle commends a democratic order of service of just the type the Collegiants favoured, in which each man in the assembly is invited to preach (προφητεύειν (verse 31)).

The belief that sacraments such as Communion or Baptism had a merely symbolic value was certainly of a piece with the other Collegiant positions. Kolakowski summarizes the whole drift of Collegiant thought very well in saying: "Salvation, obtainable only individually, also requires guarantees that can be individually obtained – that is, it becomes dependent on individual moral efforts as an essential condition".[59]

Looking back at the Collegiants from the twenty-first century, with the example of contemporary liberal Protestant denominations in mind, might lead one to expect that Collegiant tolerance and lack of dogma would also have been accompanied by a lack of zeal. But this would be a mistake. Pieter Balling might stress that it was no part of Collegiant doctrine to "draw thee off from one society of men, to carry thee over to another".[60] But this was only because of the inefficacy of all "societies of men". He was very serious about winning his readers for the *light*. So was his fellow Collegiant, Daniel Zwicker, writing in 1658. He describes his personal mission as follows:

I am neither a Lutheran, nor a Calvinist, nor a Remonstrant, neither Orthodox nor Papist nor Socinian nor Mennonite nor member of any other of today's sects. On the other hand I hope to reform each one separately and all of them together according to the one divine truth whose student I am.[61]

Rijnsburg

Sometime near the beginning of 1660 Spinoza left Amsterdam and went to live at the centre of Collegiant spiritual life, in the town of Rijnsburg. While it is true, as Nadler points out,[62] that he no longer had family ties to keep him in Amsterdam, since those who were still alive were forbidden by the ban to have contact with him, it nevertheless remains a puzzling move. Why would he want to leave the place where most of his friends and contacts lived?

Biographers old and new, however, assure us that friends were part of the problem. So overwhelming were their visits and attentions that it left Spinoza insufficient time to accomplish the ambitious scholarly projects he desired to complete. But if a search for peace and quiet explains his leaving Amsterdam, it makes his destination of Rijnsburg puzzling. Why would Spinoza have gone to the citadel of Collegiant worship and reflection, where he would soon be encumbered with as many distractions as before, which indeed came to pass? Freudenthal is surely right to conjecture that Rijnsburg was not merely the accidental destination that followed on Spinoza's leaving Amsterdam, but that he sought it out for its own sake, presumably *because* of its central position in Collegiant life.[63]

Readers familiar with Spinoza's religious thought will see that there are obvious parallels between it and Collegiant teachings. Like the Collegiants Spinoza has little regard for dogma and ritual, but much, as has already been seen, for simple piety. There is certainly an interesting parallel to be drawn between the goals of personal purity and community which Spinoza espouses in the opening pages of the TIE, and the similar aspirations of Collegiant life. It is also worth noting how closely the life Spinoza led following his excommunication approximated to the Collegiant ideal of a man who made strong personal demands of himself, while showing tolerance to others.

Overlaps in technical vocabulary should not be neglected either. The Collegiant use of such terms as "*verstand*" and "rede" and "algemene kerk" may correspond to Spinoza's "intellectus", "ratio", and "ecclesia universalis".

But Spinoza could hardly have affiliated himself with any organization less informative about what affiliation means. Collegiants are the paradigmatic examples of Leszek Kolakowski's "unchurched Christians". There was no official act of membership, nor did being a Collegiant exclude continuing membership in other faith communities. Pieter Balling, for example, remained a Mennonite.

Did they even welcome members who did not confess Christ as their saviour? Fix doesn't think so, but Kolakowski says they did.[64] In either case they would surely have been satisfied if Spinoza were prepared to admit, as he does in the TTP, that Christ is the way of salvation,[65] however unorthodox his view of Christ and salvation may be.

One function of the College at Rijnsburg was to provide services of Communion and Baptism for the entire Dutch Collegiant community. As many as possible were expected to send their representatives to the services held for Communion twice annually.[66]

The degree to which Spinoza participated in the religious activities of the Rijnsburg community or personally identified with its Christianity cannot be inferred from what is presently known of his life and writings. But neither is it crucial to find out in order to recognize a link with Collegiant thinking. If he had been baptized or received Communion, it would certainly make him more recognizably Christian by the standards of the mainline denominations, but it arguably would not have made him any more Collegiant. It is sufficient for present purposes to recognize that there was a Christian community among whom the excommunicated Spinoza found his closest friends, with whom he was in ongoing dialogue, and whose radical Protestantism Spinoza found congenial to his own thinking. Among them he felt free to practise the piety and seek the community which were integral to his conception of the good life. When Spinoza tells Ostens years later that "Turks and other Gentiles, if they worship God by the exercise of justice and charity towards their neighbour ... have the spirit of Christ and are saved"[67] he is clearly speaking *like* a Collegiant. There are no doctrinal or institutional tests to apply to discover whether or not he was also speaking *as* one.

In the TTP Spinoza will defend a minimalistic religion with noticeable affinities to the teachings of the Collegiants. Without presupposing any explicit Collegiant affiliation on Spinoza's part I shall argue on the basis of the text alone that the religion in question is Christianity.

Notes

1   Nadler [1999], 120.
2   See Levy [1987], 2; also Brykman [1972], 62ff; Lévinas [1984], 155).
3   For the full text, see Nadler [1999], 120.
4   Freudenthal [1899], 116.
5   Nadler [1999], 137.
6   Gebhardt [1914], 13-15.
7   Salomon Van Til: *Het Voor-Hoof der Heydenen*. Cited in Révah, [1958], 205.
8   See Levy [1987], 2; also Brykman [1972], 62ff; Lévinas [1984], 155.
9   To distinguish among the terms Jewry, Judaism and Jewishness, so necessary to speaking clearly about Spinoza's reaction to the *cherem*, I have learned from Levy [1989], p. 12f.
10   Pace Brykman [1972], 62, 67.
11   Gebhardt [1914], 52.
12   See Popkin [1984] and [1985], from which the following account is derived.
13   Not to be confused with the better known Puritan divine of that name who died in Rotterdam in 1633.
14   Later Margaret Fox, wife of George Fox, the founder of the Society of Friends (Quakers).
15   Four different explanations of Spinoza's departure from Judaism are given by the early biographies contained in Gebhardt [1914]: Jelles, 3f; Lucas, 12ff; Bayle, 45; Colerus, 56.
16   See Levy [1989], 35.
17   See for example in Révah [1958]; Klever [1991].
18   Gebhardt [1914], p. 18.
19   De Dijn [1996], 11.
20   That is, assuming, with Mignini [1987], that the TIE was written close to the time of the excommunication. De Dijn [1996], 5, takes a different view.
21   Spinoza [1992] *Traité de la réforme de l'entendement*, ed. and trans. by Bernard Rousset Paris: Vrin, 148.
22   Spinoza [1925] 2, 6f = TIE, §7.
23   Spinoza [1925] 2, 7 = TIE, §10.
24   Spinoza [1925] 2, 9 = TIE, §14.
25   Alexandre Mathéron devotes his book *Individu et communauté chez Spinoza* (Paris: Les Éditions de Minuit, 1969) to demonstrating that the combination of complete individual liberation with unrestricted community was one of Spinoza's deepest motivations.
26   Malet [1966], 78.
27   Jarig Jelles: *Belydenisse des Algemeenen en Christelyken Geloofs*. Translating from Gebhardt's paraphrase in Gebhardt [1932], 351.
28   Spinoza [1925] 4, 38ff = EP 8.
29   His most significant critic was Madeleine Francès [1937].
30   See for example Malet [1966], 123^2, 232; Kolakowski, [1969], 207; [1990b], 392ff.
31   Malet [1966], 286f.
32   Nadler [1999], 125f.
33   Johannes Colerus, Chapter 3, in Gebhardt [1914], 56.
34   Meinsma [1983], 152.
35   See Kolakowski [1990b], 403.
36   See Popkin [1988], 39.

37   Geyl [1966], 78.
38   For more detailed accounts of the fascinating political and religious struggles surrounding the Synod of Dordt, see Israel [1995], 399-464; Geyl [1966], 70-83; Fix [1990], 160f.
39   Kolakowski [1969], 169.
40   Fix [1990], 162.
41   See Fix [1990], esp. 176.
42   Cf. Kolakowski [1990a], 266.
43   See for example Kolakowski [1969], Chapter 3.
44   Kolakowski [1969], 203.
45   Fix [1991], 102.
46   Belgic Confession, Article 27.
47   Kolakowski [1990a], 271.
48   Fix [1991], 212, 252.
49   The seventeenth century English translation is reproduced in Bedjaï [1983] from which all the following citations are taken.
50   Bedjaï [1983], 72.
51   Bedjaï [1983], 73.
52   Bedjaï [1983], 72: "We give it rather the appellation of light, than anything else, otherwise it is all one to us whether ye call it, Christ, the Spirit, the Word, etc. seeing these all do note but one and the same thing".
53   Bedjaï [1983], 78.
54   Bedjaï [1983], 74.
55   Compare Fix [1991], p. 117.
56   Bedjaï [1983], 76f.
57   op. cit., 72.
58   Kolakowski [1990a], 263.
59   Kolakowski [1990a], 264.
60   Bejaï [1983], 71.
61   Daniel Zwicker: *Irenicum Irenicorum* [1658]. Cited in Kolakowski [1969], 226.
62   Nadler [1999], 181.
63   Freudenthal [1927], 126. Nadler [1999], 181 states that the Rijnsburg College was no longer very active by the time Spinoza arrived there, because it "met only twice a year". What did meet biannually was a kind of synod attended by representatives of all the Dutch Colleges in which services of communion and baptism were celebrated. But these were in addition to the other activities of the Rijnsburg College. (See Fix [1990], 162.)
64   Kolakowski [1990a], 270; Fix [1990], 162.
65   Spinoza [1925] 3, 21 = TTP 1.
66   Fix [1990], 162.
67   Spinoza [1925]4, 226 = EP 43.

PART II
CHRISTIAN PHILOSOPHY?

Chapter Three

A Bible Gallery

Spinoza's Inspiration

Not many studies of Spinoza's philosophy have inquired closely into its Christian dimension. The few that have are remarkable for the caution they exercise in attributing any significant Christian commitment to Spinoza.[1] That is why it is surprising that the noted Spinoza-commentator Robert Misrahi thought their very existence so scandalous as to merit the polemical response entitled, "Spinoza and Christian Thought: a Challenge".[2] If Misrahi knew of bold and unwarranted claims that have been made about Spinoza's Christianity, he did not disclose the source of them to his reader. In fact he cites no one in his article. He says nevertheless that his purpose is to "unmask [...] Christian interpretations of Spinoza's philosophy" and "to restore the genuine features of Spinozism – that is indeed of a practical atheism and of an ethical and political doctrine which was at that time subversive".[3]

Misrahi seems to use the word "subversive" in a postmodern, laudatory sense. Normally to call a doctrine subversive is to register one's personal disapproval of it, but no such force attaches to Misrahi's use of the term. On the contrary he implies that Spinoza's alleged subversion of Christian society was an entirely satisfactory outcome, which the unnamed Christian interpreters of Spinoza are wickedly conspiring to undo. They stand accused of making "a vain attempt to distort the meaning of Spinoza's philosophy ... to make it instrumental to Christian spiritualist idealism".[4]

Misrahi's article seems to have stopped the encroachments of the Christian spiritualist idealist reading of Spinoza, for I find it represented nowhere in recent Spinoza literature. But his attribution of cunning subversiveness to Spinoza appears to me to be a simple mistake. It is of course conceivable that Spinoza secretly believed Christianity to be a hoax or an imposition of priests upon gullible believers, as has more than once been alleged. Even were that granted, however, textual evidence would compel a candid reader to admit at the very least that Spinoza thought the hoax to be a useful one or the imposition a necessary evil.

Religion in Spinoza's eyes is closely connected to politics, as the title of his "*Tractatus Theologico-Politicus,*" implies. And Misrahi would surely concede that while Spinoza was a critic of Dutch society and longed to reform it, he had no desire to blow it up. But then he could have harboured no purely destructive thoughts about religion either, if for no other reason than that he saw the future of Dutch society as linked to its religious outlook. What was chiefly required, he thought, were rulers who would exert the authority that flows from absolute power to instruct the public in piety, and in conformity with public welfare.[5] I shall argue that Spinoza was no more concerned with subverting Christianity than he was with overthrowing Dutch society. His aim was indeed to alter the public conception of both, but for the sake of improving, not subverting them.

Misrahi's polemic is nevertheless useful in a couple of ways. First, it signals a resistance among some Spinoza scholars to the very idea of there being a Christian dimension to Spinoza's thought, a resistance that is undoubtedly shared by others who have not articulated it as fully, or whose chosen method of articulation is to ignore it.

In the second place some of his individual challenges to a Christian reading of Spinoza can serve as points of departure for discussing different topics of interest to the present study. One such challenge is of immediate importance and can be used as an introduction to the subject of this chapter.

Misrahi asserts that the Hebrew king Solomon stood much higher in Spinoza's esteem than did Jesus Christ and that this is significant for understanding Spinoza's philosophy. "Solomon", he says:

> is more than a legislator who rules – he is a philosopher who endeavours to understand, and it is as such that he may be said to be, from the doctrinal standpoint, the true source of Spinoza's inspiration, he Solomon the sage, and not Christ the righteous.[6]

I would like to look carefully at the textual justification for this claim, but also to widen the question Misrahi raises into the more general one that really ought to have preceded it: from what biblical figures, if any, did Spinoza draw inspiration?

Solomon is certainly one of the protagonists of the Old Testament to whom Spinoza accords both respect and attention. But he is not the only one. Another is the prophet and leader of the Jewish people, Moses. Spinoza also gives careful consideration to New Testament apostles, especially Saint Paul, and, of course, to Christ. A complete account of Spinoza's treatment of biblical figures would involve others, but at a minimum each of the four mentioned deserves consideration. In order to respond directly to Misrahi's claim, I shall begin with Solomon.

Solomon

What is it for one thinker to be "the true source of inspiration" to another? One can think of different senses ranging from the weak one of merely being admired to the strong sense of being the originator of doctrines which the other thinker knowingly adopts as his own. Misrahi does not specify where on that continuum he places the influence of Solomon on Spinoza, though the phrase "*the* true source" suggests something at the high end of the scale. Spinoza surely admired Solomon, but to call Solomon *the* source of doctrinal inspiration would be highly interpretive. Spinoza does not himself attribute that sort of influence to Solomon. If he finds Solomon interesting it is because of the wisdom for which the prophet-king was famous and because of a small number of doctrines he shares with Solomon as a result of that focus. Spinoza does not claim to have learned these doctrines from Solomon, however. When he considers Solomon's proverbs he explicitly says he is simply looking for "those which most clearly confirm our view".[7] When he has located these he points out that they therefore can be drawn "from Solomon's mind *as well*",[8] i.e., as well as his own.

Spinoza draws attention to six ways in which the thought of Solomon is in conformity with his own. All have to do with the prophet's emphasis on the intellect. Spinoza credits Solomon with having recognized that the source of true life lies in the human intellect and that true punishment consists in being deprived of that life. Spinoza also approves of Solomon's view that we find in the intellect the source of human happiness, tranquillity and beatitude and learn from it to have a wise fear of God. Finally, Spinoza commends Solomon for teaching that wisdom and science flow from the mouth of God and that true ethics and true politics are part of what that science contains.[9]

Spinoza considers these insights important, but apart from them he attributes no excellence to Solomon or his thought that he does not qualify with some corresponding criticism. Solomon may excel other prophets in wisdom, but not in other respects.[10] And even his wisdom is not uniformly great. In mathematics, for instance, Solomon did not rise above the understanding of common workers.[11] He also misused the very reason that set him apart, as when he placed himself above the law and thus fell prey to lusts that are beneath the dignity of a philosopher,[12] or when he disgraced himself as a philosopher by doubting providence or by marrying an Egyptian.[13]

Moses

Solomon's celebrated wisdom did not even suffice to make him in Spinoza's eyes the greatest of the prophets. That status belongs instead to Moses,[14] who exceeds Solomon (and all the other prophets) in virtue.[15] Moses had within him a "divine virtue" that enabled him to capture the minds of the fractious people of Israel, where mere charisma could never have succeeded.[16] He was also distinguished by being the first to recognize the "absolute essence of God", the first to whom God chose to reveal himself under the name of Jehovah.[17] His unique calling as a prophet was also reflected in the fact that God chose to speak to him through an actual voice rather than through dreams or visions, as he did with the other prophets.[18] Lastly, from a political point of view, Moses is by far more significant than Solomon, and it is not surprising that Spinoza devotes many more pages to discussing him.

Moses is the Old Testament character who interested Spinoza most. But even in Moses' case there is no evidence of anything one could call philosophical influence in the strong sense, as Spinoza's critical remarks about him make abundantly clear. Spinoza tells us that Moses was limited both by his own understanding of what God revealed to him and by that of the people to whom the revelation was given. Both prophet and people lacked Solomon's philosophical discernment. As a result Moses failed to see the real significance of the positive law communicated to him by God, and so he fell short of declaring what God actually intended. Through Moses the Law became a burden that the people of Israel had to bear in order to repay God for their deliverance from Egypt and in order to merit his ongoing favour. Moses could not rise to the "philosophical" understanding of the Law, which Spinoza finds nowhere in the Old Testament but only in the New. Instead of a burdensome Law, God intended to give the people "true liberty", which Spinoza understands as "the grace and gift of God",[19] vocabulary derived not from the Old Testament but directly from Saint Paul,[20] the apostle who is often called the founder of the religion of Christianity.

Saint Paul

Spinoza draws on Saint Paul not just as the pre-eminent critic of Judaism, but also with a sort of deference to his opinions that is without parallel in his treatment of Old Testament figures. On one occasion, for example, as Spinoza is passing in review central biblical texts which might be thought to confer a special "chosenness" on the Jewish people, a text attributed to Moses is passed over summarily. Then Spinoza comes to one from Saint Paul which he introduces with these words: "there is another text that impresses me more deeply" (*alium textum reperio, qui me magis movet*).[21] The text that impresses or, literally, *moves* him more is from Saint Paul's letter to the Romans (3:1f), and says that the people set apart by circumcision (i.e., the Jews) have an advantage over others because they have received the oracles (τὰ λόγια) of God.

Spinoza has no trouble interpreting this text in conformity with his own view. But why does it "move him" more? No reason is given at that place. We must infer it from other things Spinoza says about Paul.

In the first place Paul was an apostle, which Spinoza regards as a more significant calling than that of the prophets. Apostles' gifts include prophecy, but go beyond it. In addition to prophesying they can also teach with authority in their own right, as mere prophets cannot.[22] And Paul is the greatest of the apostles[23], rightfully called "the apostle".[24] Spinoza cites Paul to give authority to doctrines of the Old Testament prophets,[25] but not conversely. More striking still is the fact that Spinoza more than once cites Paul as lending authority even to doctrines Spinoza acknowledges as his own.[26]

I shall not argue on the basis of the texts cited that Paul was a bona fide "source" of Spinoza's thought in the strict sense of the term described above, though others have not hesitated to draw such a conclusion. André Malet went so far as to call Saint Paul "the father of Spinozism" on the basis of the ancestral link he believed he saw between Paul's hard determinism and that which he found in Spinoza.[27] But in my opinion such agreements are better seen as elective affinities rather than influences in the strong sense, unless they can be shown to be the latter by Spinoza's own words. None of the biblical characters considered thus far can be documented as having influenced Spinoza in the sense of being the identifiable and unique source of any of his doctrines.

To deny such strong influence is however in no way to diminish the significance of these religious figures in Spinoza's thought. I shall argue later in this chapter that Spinoza considers Paul to occupy an important transitional moment in the development of religious thought which Spinoza sees as involving and even culminating in his own philosophy. Before leaving this survey of potential biblical inspirations of Spinoza, however, we must consider Spinoza's treatment of the figure of Jesus Christ, whose apostle Saint Paul was.

Jesus Christ

Paul's authority, though real, was borrowed. It arose, as Spinoza recognizes, from Paul's having been made Jesus Christ's apostle to the Gentiles. Jesus could confer such authority because, according to Spinoza, he was Christ, in whom God manifested himself most fully.[28] Spinoza's treatment of Jesus Christ is of an altogether different quality from his treatment of any other biblical figure, including Paul. Probably there is no doctrine which Spinoza adopted simply because Christ proclaimed it. Nevertheless his affirmations of Christ and Christian teachings are strikingly appreciative. To speak of Christ as having exerted some form of influence is almost unavoidable when one takes into account – as even fierce opponents of a Christian reading of Spinoza must do – the care with which the philosopher at different points accommodates his own thought to a Christian outlook.[29]

Consider, for example, the description of Jesus Christ in the opening chapter of the TTP. Spinoza declares that Christ (and Christ alone) is able to perceive things contained neither in the primary foundations of our knowledge nor deducible from them,[30] thus effectively ascribing to Christ a knowledge that falls outside even the "infinite things in infinite ways", that are said in the *Ethics* to define the limits of the world. Christ alone is capable of receiving revelations immediately from God without the intermediary of either words or visions;[31] because "superhuman wisdom" (*sapientiam supra humanam*) took on human form in him.[32]

Admittedly, even such uncharacteristically dogmatic (and, to many scholars, puzzling) remarks about Jesus Christ do not prove that Christian doctrine was the source of any characteristically Spinozistic teachings, but they draw attention to the unique place Jesus occupied in Spinoza's thinking and contrast with the less significant one occupied by the other biblical figures we have discussed. The least of these, not the greatest, was Solomon.

Progressive Revelation

Comparing the influence of biblical figures on Spinoza by counting the number of doctrines they contributed to his teaching is, in any case, an exercise of limited value. Whether they exercised any direct influence or not, their real significance lay in shaping Spinoza's thought in a way that is more subtle, interesting and plausible. Spinoza holds to the orthodox Christian view that because God's infinite and eternal revelation outstrips the human capacity to grasp it, he therefore had to disclose it repeatedly and with different emphases to mankind.[33] Spinoza envisions a gradual human appreciation of doctrine moving from the earliest biblical manifestations of God (in Genesis) and culminating in Spinozism itself. It is this developmental understanding of revelation together with Spinoza's view of his own philosophy as the final expression of that development that is the key to understanding the real relationship between him and the central figures of the Bible.

The pivotal point in the development of revelation lies between the Old and New Testament. To recognize it we must understand why Spinoza thought the Jewish Bible to be incomplete. It was not because he believed the message of God to have changed or to have been deficient in its original state. The Old Testament suffered from a kind of "Cambridge" incompleteness, arising from the incapacity of the Old Testament's authors and readers to grasp the full significance of the revelation they received. Just as a proof that is perfect in itself may require restatement to an immature student, so what Christians came to call the Old Testament needed the reformulation it received in what they called the New Testament.[34] Of fundamental importance to understanding the purpose and structure of the TTP is the recognition of its assertion of this developmental view of revelation and the four distinct steps in which it consists. The first stage is that of the Old Testament prophets.

The Prophets

Spinoza defines prophecy as certain knowledge of any matter communicated by God through revelation.[35] But he defines prophets as interpreters of the divine revelation to those who do *not* have certain knowledge, and who therefore can only believe the revelation by faith. When prophecy is so defined it leaves two large gaps in the process of communicating the revelations of God. One is the gulf between God's infinite mind and the finite minds of his prophets; the second is the smaller but still significant gap between the prophets and their audience. In the case of Moses, Spinoza illustrates the second of these hindrances to communication by contrasting the prophet's "divine virtue" with the state of "wretched slavery and ignorance" into which the Jewish people had sunk.[36] The problems of translation between God and prophet and then between prophet and people thus constitute two a priori limitations upon any revelation of the Word of God.

Some prophets had great philosophical gifts – Solomon being the best example [37] – but they are not for that reason outstanding as prophets.[38] This is because prophecy is a gift of the imagination, rather than the intellect. Prophecy occurs when God disposes the imagination of a prophet in such a way that he comes to understand something not commonly known, though also not in principle beyond rational comprehension.[39] Usually this happens in a vision, and in that case its cognitive quality depends in part upon the imaginative faculties of the prophet himself.

Moses, the greatest prophet, was exceptional in this respect. He alone heard a divine voice that was wholly independent of his own imaginative powers. And although this distinction elevates him above his fellow prophets, he remains like them, in that his sayings are "merely modes of expression calculated to instil with efficacy and present vividly to the imagination the commands of God".[40] Moses' achievement was to communicate to the Jewish people a politically significant revelation from God. His mistake was a lack of discrimination, since he was unable to distinguish the universal moral significance of the decalogue (ten commandments) from the local and temporary significance of the ceremonial law.[41] On "the basis of what was revealed to [Moses], he perceived the method by which the nation of Israel could best be united in a particular territory, could form a body politic or state, and ... could best be constrained to obedience".[42] However he overlooked the universal moral significance of at least the decalogue. The opposite misunderstanding was also exemplified in the Pharisees. They treated the ceremonial law as if , like the decalogue, it were part of the moral key to human happiness.[43]

Moses' error in connection with the law led to another one concerning the interpretation of the sense in which the Jews are a "chosen" people. The belief that Jews are in some preferential and continuing sense "chosen" by God, and to that extent set apart from other peoples, is central to Judaism. Spinoza holds that this chosenness is reflected only in what from a secular point of view would be called the the Jewish people's exceptional good fortune (*fortuna*).[44] Spinoza allows, in fact he stresses, that their good fortune also has a theological dimension, in which it can be understood as God's providential leading of the people. But this leading is only manifest through external causes[45] and therefore always remains subject to naturalistic explanation.

On the other hand, all the moral goods that can be acquired by moral inquiry or by formation of the character, are accessible to all nations alike. Moses looked for nothing beyond the gifts of fortune, Spinoza says.[46] And therein lay his limitation.

In the partial truth of Moses' prophetic leadership of Israel the limitation of the prophets and of the entire Old Testament is disclosed. Moses' failure to see the full implications of the revelation he received is what makes the New Testament necessary. "[T]he prophets who preached religion before Christ preached it as a national law in virtue of the covenant entered into under Moses; while the apostles who came after Christ, preached it to all men as a universal religion".[47] As this passage suggests, the hinge between the stage of prophecy and that of the apostles is the life of Jesus Christ.

Jesus Christ

What sets Jesus Christ above the prophets is the quality of his mind. The prophets had many astonishing insights, but they of course knew nothing beyond what natural powers fit men to know. Christ did. Spinoza holds not only that Christ shared the perfect knowledge of God, but also that the way of life he prescribed, rather than a strict observance of the whole Mosaic Law, was "the way of salvation".[48] This is indeed nothing other than Jesus' own teaching about himself, namely that he was in himself the fulfilment (πλήρωσις) of the law and prophets.[49]

The ultimate source for the life, death and continuing influence of Christ is of course the collection of documents called the New Testament. It consists of four short biographies of Jesus, called Gospels, a history of the early Church, called "The Acts of the Apostles", a book of prophecy called "Revelation" and twenty-one letters to fledgling churches by the early disciples of Christ, who were called "apostles" (literally ambassadors or messengers, men who are sent on a mission of importance). According to Spinoza there needed to be such a book as the New Testament for the very reason that the message of the Old Testament, while true, was insufficiently understood. The world needed to learn that the blessing of divine election fell not on the Jews alone and not even on all the Jews. It fell on Jew and Gentile alike, provided they were prepared to acknowledge the necessity of obeying God's Law. The New Testament was needed because the Old Testament had not succeeded in conveying that message. The limitations of the prophets and their audience had been such that Old Testament had seemed to them to be the proclamation of the Law to a single nation. Moreover, that limited audience had also failed to distinguish the moral essence of the law from its contingent cultural setting. The New Testament brought a universal religion to all mankind, regardless of cultural setting.[50]

Spinoza does not think that God changed his mind, but only that he revealed his mind progressively to human beings. To explain this notion Spinoza selects a passage from the fourth Gospel in which the apostle John identifies the man, Jesus, with the eternal Word of God. "The Word of God", in Spinoza's paraphrase, "was *in* the world, but was not known *by* the world". Hence for Spinoza the eternal Word which was always in the world was necessarily subject to a gradual revelation in order that it should be known by the world. Taken in its fullness, however, this Word is acknowledged by Spinoza as the "true" and "catholic" religion.[51]

Spinoza is heterodox in rejecting the doctrine that Christ rose from the dead,[52] but he holds nevertheless that the "true" and "catholic" religion was fully revealed in Jesus' life and death. In this way the revelation in Christ was greater than it could possibly have been in the limited minds of a Moses or even of a Solomon.[53] However, even full revelation within a super-human mind does not escape the second of the limitations encountered by ordinary prophets: it is still subject to the finite receptivity of its human audience. Jesus' message was furthermore limited by time and place, by the fleeting duration and remote locale of his life and ministry. For those reasons the full meaning of the message he brought was not immediately propagated to the world, and therefore Jesus appointed the men who were called his apostles, whose commission was to go into the whole world proclaiming the Gospel.

The Apostles

The apostles were prophets[54] who rarely prophesied. That is, they seldom depended on revelation, except in some of their preaching and other oral communications. And when they did depend on revelation, they confirmed what they said by signs.[55] Spinoza does not deny that the apostles received the gift of prophecy; he emphatically asserts it. But it was the apostles' supplementary power which set them apart from mere prophets and made them more important for Spinoza's purposes. To the apostles was given (*concessa est*) not only the power of prophetic preaching (*virtus praedicandi*) but also, and more importantly, the authority to teach (*authoritas docendi*).[56] The revelation received by the apostles therefore supercedes that given to the Prophets.[57]

It was this *teaching authority* which they revealed in the letters they authored, all of which were dictated solely by the light of reason (*a solo lumine naturali dictatas*).[58] And, since the light of reason illuminates all mankind, their message, unlike that of the prophets, had the potential of being received by all. This is what made the apostles suitable ambassadors of the *universal* revelation of Christ.

One might think that the religion taught by the apostles was not drawn from reason alone, since much of it is mere narration of the life of Christ.

However Spinoza responds that because the essence of Christ's teachings (and in note 27 of the TTP Spinoza says he means chiefly the so-called "Sermon on the Mount") is for the most part moral, the apostles' authoritative writing can be apprehended by the natural faculties of all people (*potest unusquisque lumine naturali facile assequi*).[59] It might seem, therefore, that the writings of the apostles can be nothing other than the final revelation of God.

Superior though they are to prophecy, however, even the apostolic writings do not escape the limitations intrinsic to all communication. Since the apostles write according to reason, their writings and authority are in the first place limited by the quality of their own reasoning abilities. This is the apostolic counterpart of the limitation imposed by the imagination of the prophets. And of course the apostles also have in common with the prophets the necessity of dealing with the limited understanding of their readers. Spinoza stresses the way in which both these apostolic limitations have left indelible scars on Western history.

The apostles' different ways of reasoning account for the inevitable disagreements that arose among them, some of which are documented in the New Testament itself. The best example is probably the famous dispute between Paul and James concerning the relative place of faith and works.[60] Saint Paul insisted that since all our works are tainted by original sin, they count for nothing in the sight of God. If we are to be saved from eternal damnation, therefore, it must be by grace alone in recognition not of our righteousness, but of our faith.[61] By contrast the apostle James says that faith without works is dead and ineffective for salvation.[62] Historically the Church has of course attempted to harmonize these positions in different ways, but no single way of reconciling them has been found satisfactory by all Christian denominations.

The effect of the audience in shaping what is received is particularly obvious in the apostolate of Saint Paul. His calling was to be the apostle to the Gentiles, which meant speaking intelligibly to the non-Jewish population of the Roman Empire, most of whom were cultural and intellectual debtors to Greece. Therefore Paul was obliged to make more overt use of reasoning than did any of his fellow apostles.[63] It was his calling to the Gentiles that brought him directly into conflict with the apostle Peter.[64]

That the limitations of apostles and their hearers should have an impact on what the apostles wrote is hardly surprising. Indeed some of their disagreements often appear inevitable even with the hindsight of history. For example, passing time has not resolved the uncertainties of Christians regarding the proper balance to be struck between faith and works. A trace of the same controversy can also be observed in the secular context, in ethical debates about whether the intentions with which we enter into an action have more ethical importance than the action's consequences.

On the other hand Christians have also been bitterly divided over other questions that seem insignificant with the passage of time. For example, it is difficult to see that a great deal turns on the question of whether penance should be called a sacrament, or only a ceremony. And it is hard to enter imaginatively into the minds of pious Christians who once found it a matter of fundamental importance to decide whether, during the rite of Communion, the Host should be elevated or not. It is understandable that philosophers of Spinoza's ability were disgusted that such issues divided believers in the seventeenth century. Moreover, as those living in the aftermath of the Reformation were acutely aware, neither the inevitability of some disagreements nor the often quibbling character of others prevented them from being the cause of schism in the Church and bloodshed in the streets. Ever since ancient times, the unavoidable or accidental differences of religious style and insight have given rise to the bitter (and all too often bloody) divisions of the Church. And some of these were introduced by the apostles themselves.[65]

Not all Christians have been willing to admit the divisive impact that their faith has had. In the middle of the twentieth century the theologian Ernst Käsemann was still able to shock his students by saying that "the New Testament canon does not constitute the foundation of unity of the Church. On the contrary, it provides the basis for the multiplicity of the confessions".[66] It is interesting to reflect that Spinoza said much the same thing in 1670 and not so amazing that his contemporaries found it shocking.

The apostles contributed to universality and peace insofar as they propounded Christ's simple truth, but they engendered discord and schism, whenever they added to it, Spinoza held. And, being human, how could they avoid occasionally trespassing beyond the narrow lines of truth? Those doctrines propounded by the apostles which do stray outside simple truth, Spinoza calls *philosophical speculations*. That is why he insists that controversy will only cease to divide the Church when "religion is at last separated from philosophical speculations".[67]

Now, since the doctrines of the Church will always be propounded by human teachers, speculation might appear to be inevitable and therefore it might seem that nothing can prevent perpetual schism and decay. The growing Protestant sectarianism of Spinoza's time would only be one lamentable manifestation of the instability at the core of the Church. Furthermore it would be seen to derive from a fatal flaw in the human condition that must therefore lead to a tragic outcome.

No human being can carry in his simple head more than a finite portion of the whole truth. Being infinite, the whole truth transcends our grasp. And even if, *per impossibile*, what we understood were perfectly true, our ability to communicate it would be severely restricted by the capacity of other people to understand it. A less careful thinker than Spinoza (or a more modest one) would have concluded, therefore, that we must resign ourselves to a religious war of all against all.

Spinoza Himself

So it must have appeared in 1670; so it appears to many people today, as they try to account for religiously motivated terror and violence. But Spinoza's ambition in writing the TTP was not merely to depict the tragic dimension of religious belief but to rescue the Church from it. Spinoza felt capable not only of providing his unsparing analysis of the predicament of his age, but also of pointing to a way beyond it.

His main insight depended on a fact that everyone knew, but the significance of which no one else had recognized: he was the first to comprehend the full meaning of the fact that the apostles were the authors of the New Testament. It implied that they themselves did not possess the New Testament, and therefore that the post-apostolic age had an advantage that even the apostles themselves had not enjoyed. We who live later inherit from them not only the instrument of their creation, the whole Scripture, but also a task which they themselves could not complete,[68] yet which may be possible for us.

The availability of the New Testament in addition to the Old may allow us, if we adopt the careful exegetical rules Spinoza sets out in the seventh chapter of the TTP, to "edit down religion to the fewest and most simple dogmas which Christ taught to his followers" (*ad paucisssima et simplicissima dogmata, quae Christus suos docuit*).[69] "Philosophical speculations" will thus be eliminated and a final revelation, a *vera religio*, will have come to be at last. Moreover the small number, simplicity and self-evidence of the doctrines thus discovered will be accessible to even the meanest intelligence and so the natural limitations of those who receive the revelation will be overcome.

The idea of reducing the Gospel message to its essentials was not new, even in Holland. As early as 1611 Hugo Grotius had attempted to minimize Christian dogma for irenic purposes[70]. Neither was it new to think that the proliferation of Protestant sects was a scourge and one which God in time would remedy. The philosopher Dirck Volkertsz Coornhert writing in the declining years of the sixteenth century had "urged true believers patiently to await the coming of new, divinely inspired apostles who would be sent by God into the world to reform the decayed visible churches and to reunite all of the many Christian sects into one universal church of Christ".[71]

There was a powerful reason why Spinoza envisioned a new stage in development of Christianity coming about through his own philosophy. It was because the favourable political circumstances in which he found himself had allowed him the freedom to work out a fully justified epitome of Christian teaching that other circumstances simply would not have permitted.[72] The significance of this freedom will be discussed more fully in the next chapter. But because Spinoza exercised it prudently, always submitting his personal judgement to the strict exegetical rules already mentioned, he could claim to have discovered for the first time the true dogmatic basis of the Christian religion. The dogma he would put forward would all be free of philosophical speculation, and therefore would escape even the limitations of Spinoza's own mind. But since, on the other hand, it would also be of the utmost simplicity and self-evidence, it would not be affected by the narrow intellects of the public to whom they are proclaimed. To have an intellect at all would be to find such a dogma acceptable.[73]

It is true that there may still be as many interpretations of these fundamentals of the faith (*fundamenta fidei*) as there are believers, but that will not necessarily lead to discord. Spinoza says that people must be judged not by the interpretation to which they give verbal assent, but by the evidence of piety or impiety in their actions.[74]

Spinoza will conclude his chapter on the apostles (TTP 11) with unusual exuberance, and with an advertiser's sense of timing. He proclaims the singular desirability of what three chapters later he will take credit for having achieved. "Happy would be the age," he assures us, "in which that simplification of Christian dogma could be accomplished"!

Simplifying Christian dogma is the task to which Spinoza devotes the fourteenth chapter of the TTP, which he himself says contains "the main topics to be set forth in this treatise" (*praecipua ... quae in hoc Tractatu intendo*).[75] And what he there presents he describes repeatedly in the most religiously ambitious terms. It is "evangelical doctrine", "the whole law", "the definition of the faith", "the dogmas pertaining to the universal or catholic faith" and "the fundamental principles of the whole of Scripture".[76] In a nutshell, if Spinoza is right, he has found the pure teachings of Scripture for which the whole Church had been searching since the Reformation. He has found what the first Reformation aimed at, but failed to achieve – a true basis for unity. It has fallen to Spinoza to take a step in theology that was impossible even for the apostles. It is not so much, as Alexandre Mathéron asks us to consider, that Christ was a Spinozist.[77] He was no more so than were Solomon or the apostles. It is only that for historical reasons Spinoza was able to express Christ's message in its definitive form.

There follow in Chapter 14 of the TTP an enumeration of seven general "dogmas" which it is unnecessary to set down here, for they will be discussed in detail in the sixth and seventh chapters of this book. They have aspects in common with different creeds of his day, and even with Maimonides' explanation of the fundamental principles of the Law in the *Guide for the Perplexed* (Pt. III, Chapter 27f). They also resemble the Ten Commandments in one respect at least, namely, in dealing first with God and then with the duties and privileges of being his human creatures. But they are not equivalent to any of these analogous texts. They represent, in the eyes of their author at least, an advance over all of them.

Spinoza's seven dogmas involve only general facts about God and our relationship to him. They are all logical consequences, he says, of the one fundamental revealed truth, namely that we owe God obedience. These truths, according to Spinoza, are all we know and all we need to know about religion. They are meant to be literally, as well as metaphorically, the last word about Christianity.

Was it then Spinoza's intention to provide a creed around which the religious factions of Christendom would unite. If so, as Alan Donagan has remarked, his religious project was "still born".[78] The dogmas launched no new religious movement even in Holland. But just to acknowledge that failure would mark a step forward in understanding Spinoza, because it would involve at least a recognition of the Christian dimension of what he hoped to accomplish, a rarity in the secondary literature on Spinoza. And though his programme had failed in practice, it would remain no less admirable in theory. It could still be said that Spinoza had a clearer insight into the predicament of Christendom than did most of his contemporaries and offered a more compelling solution to it.

If this interpretation were correct, Spinoza, like his Collegiant friends, would have been seeking to establish a version of Christian faith that would bring Christians together, rather than divide them, while attracting open-minded adherents of other faiths into the same big tent. By means of a radical second reformation, Spinoza would have sought to end the divisions the first reformation had brought about. To paraphrase one of his own early formulations of the good he sought, Spinoza was trying to lay the foundation for a Christian society in which as many as possible could achieve the good life in community with one another.

In Chapter 6 I shall argue that this interpretation is however only partly right. Spinoza indeed had the outlook of a radical protestant with an agenda of unity, but he had in mind a subtler way of achieving it than merely through the founding of a new sect, however inclusive it might be.

To understand the extent to which his thought was Christian it is necessary to see it in the context of his mature political theory, from which Spinoza refused to divorce it, as the title *Tratctatus theologico-politicus* reminds us. It will therefore be necessary first to study the interplay of those two dimensions of the TTP before returning to a consideration of the exact nature of Spinoza's radical Protestantism.

Notes

1   For example, Léon Brunschwicg [1951] 110, says that "the TTP presents the principles of a rational Christianity". Jean Lacroix [1970] 106, detects "a certain Christianism in Spinoza". Sylvain Zac [1985] 490, after a careful and useful examination of texts, concludes: "The most plausible hypothesis is that Spinoza does not identify himself with Christianity, although the idea of Christ plays an important part in the economy of his own philosophy".
2   Misrahi [1977], 387-417.
3   Misrahi [1977], 387.
4   Misrahi [1977], 387.
5   Spinoza [1925] 3, 236 = TTP 19.
6   Misrahi [1977], 416.
7   Spinoza [1925] 3, 67 = TTP 4.
8   Spinoza [1925] 3, 68 = TTP 4: " ex mente Salomonis etiam".
9   Spinoza [1925] 3, 66f = TTP 4.
10 Spinoza [1925] 3, 29 = TTP 2.
11 Spinoza [1925] 3, 36f = TTP, 2.
12 Spinoza [1925] 3, 41 = TTP 2.
13 Spinoza [1925] 3, 87f; 318 = TTP 4; TP 7, §24.
14 Spinoza [1925] 3, 153 = TTP 11.
15 Spinoza [1925] 3, 75 = TTP 5.
16 Spinoza [1925] 3, 239 = TTP 20.
17 Spinoza [1925] 3, 169 = TTP 13. Cf. Exodus 6: 1-8.
18 Spinoza [1925] 3, 17f; 39 = TTP 1; 2.
19 Spinoza [1925] 3, 41 = TTP 2.
20 See e.g., Ephesians 2:8; also Romans 5: 15-17.
21 Spinoza [1925] 3, 54 = TTP 3.
22 Spinoza [1925] 3, 155 = TTP 11.
23 Spinoza [1925] 3, 158 = TTP 11.
24 Spinoza [1925] 3, 169 = TTP 13.

25 See also e.g., Spinoza [1925] 3, 68 = TTP 4.
26 See Spinoza [1925] 3, 198 = TTP 16: "... et Pauli authoritate confirmavimus." See also Spinoza [1925] 4, 307 = EP 73.
27 Malet [1966], 101.
28 Spinoza [1925] 4, 350 = EP 75 "... dixi, Deus sese maxime in Christo manifestavit, quod Johannes ut efficacius exprimeret, dixit verbum factum esse carnem".
29 For example Madeleine Francès (Spinoza [1954], 8) attributes the disconcertingly Christian appearance of Spinoza's *Short Treatise* to Spinoza's desire to wean people gradually from Christianity's anthropomorphic outlook.
30 Spinoza [1925] 3, 20f = TTP 1.
31 Spinoza [1925] 3, 21 = TTP 1.
32 Spinoza [1925] 3, 21 = TTP 1.
33 Though Cardinal Newman is sometimes credited with being the originator of this view, it in fact goes back to the New Testament, as Newman himself recognized. Saint Paul, for example, refers to the Jewish Law as "a schoolmaster to lead us to Christ" (Galatians 3: 24). Spinoza's early critics recognized that he was adapting "the ancient notion of divine accommodation" but regarded it as "a treacherous ploy". See van Bunge [2001], 115.
34 Spinoza [1925] 3, 163 = TTP 12.
35 Spinoza [1925] 3, 15 = TTP 1.
36 Spinoza [1925] 3, 74 = TTP 5.
37 Spinoza [1925] 3, 62ff = TTP 4.
38 Spinoza [1925] 3, 29 = TTP 2.
39 Spinoza [1925] 3, 15 = TTP 1.
40 Spinoza [1925] 3, 153 = TTP 11.
41 Spinoza [1925] 3, 70 = TTP 5.
42 Spinoza [1925] 3, 63f = TTP 4.
43 Spinoza [1925] 3, 71 = TTP 5.
44 Spinoza [1925] 3, 47 = TTP 3.
45 Spinoza [1925] 3, 46 = TTP 3.
46 Spinoza [1925] 3, 54 = TTP 3.
47 Spinoza [1925] 3, 163 = TTP 12.
48 Spinoza [1925] 3, 21 = TTP 1. This is of course not because Christ abolishes the Law, but because he fulfils it. See Matthew 5: 17.
49 Cf. Matthew 5: 17.
50 Spinoza [1925] 3, 163 = TTP 12.
51 Spinoza [1925] 3, 163 = TTP 12.
52 Spinoza [1925] 4, 314 = EP 75 and 328 = EP 78.
53 Spinoza [1925] 3, 45 = TTP 3.
54 Spinoza [1925] 3, 151 = TTP 11.
55 Spinoza [1925] 3, 155 = TTP 11.
56 Spinoza [1925] 3, 156 = TTP 11.
57 Spinoza [1925] 3, 221 = TTP 18.
58 Spinoza [1925] 3, 155 = TTP 11.
59 Spinoza [1925] 3, 156 = TTP 11. Spinoza's focus on the "beatitudes" is much closer to orthodox Christianity than it is to the deism of which he is often suspected. Pope John Paul II in his address to World Youth Day in Toronto, on 26 July 2002 made a very Spinozistic point: "The joy promised by the beatitudes is the very joy of Jesus himself: a joy sought and found in obdience to the Father and in the gift of self to others".
60 Spinoza [1925] 3, 157 = TTP 11.

61   See Romans 4; Ephesians 2: 8f.
62   James 2:17-26.
63   Spinoza [1925] 3, 158 = TTP 11.
64   Galatians 2: 11-21.
65   Spinoza [1925] 3, 157 = TTP 11.
66   Harrisville and Sundberg [1995], 11.
67   Spinoza [1925] 3, 157f = TTP 11.
68   Spinoza [1925] 3, 158 = TTP 11: "quod Apostolis impossibile fuit".
69   Spinoza [1925] 3, 158 = TTP 11.
70   See van Bunge [2001], 22f.
71   Fix [1991], 89.
72   Spinoza [1925] 3, 7 = TTP pref.
73   Spinoza [1925] 3, 10 = TTP pref.
74   Spinoza [1925] 3, 11 = TTP pref.
75   Spinoza [1925] 3, 180 = TTP 14.
76   Spinoza [1925] 3, 174ff = TTP 14.
77   Matheron [1971], 121ff.
78   Alan Donagan [1996], 373.

Chapter Four

Religion and Politics in the TTP

Why did Spinoza Write the TTP?

Spinoza seems to have interrupted the writing of his great work, the *Ethics*, in order to write another book – also destined to be great – the *Tractatus Theologico-Politicus* (TTP). Why would a writer put aside a project calling for all his energies – a systematic presentation of his philosophy – to begin another? That question is part of a wider one: why did Spinoza write the TTP at all? What is it really about? It is strange that such a question should be controversial even among those who have studied Spinoza most carefully. Yet even the general aim of the book is among the topics still under discussion: If the TTP is a "theological-political" treatise, which of its two main subjects has priority?

The general aim is sometimes taken to be political. Geneviève Brykman, for example, warns against selective readings, especially those which get little further than the first half of the book, fearing that lazy readers will miss the book's essentially political intent.[1] The error into which they might slip would be to think the TTP to be mainly a religious work or, worse still, a Christian one.

In their zeal to warn readers away from misinterpretations, some scholars advance bold, though debatable, hermeneutical hypotheses. Madeleine Francès, while admitting that there is a disconcerting quantity of Christian language in Spinoza's writings, explains that it is placed there by Spinoza as a device by which Christian readers can be drawn into Spinoza's way of thinking before they realize that it really undermines the religion they take it to support.[2]

Jonathan Israel takes a broader view of the subject. He depicts the primary thrust of the TTP as an appeal for intellectual liberty. He also explains why Spinoza permitted it to interrupt the writing of the *Ethics*. According to Israel the attitudes of Dutch readers needed to be softened up in several areas, including their religious and political views and especially their acceptance of censorship. The TTP was written to change people's minds, to make them more receptive to the argument of the *Ethics*. In Israel's own words the "express purpose" of the TTP was :

to advance "liberty to philosophize" by demonstrating the necessity and also the innocuousness of intellectual freedom – and one of the main aims ... was to lessen popular reverence for the authority of the public Church, and its spokesmen, by changing the public's attitude towards Scripture ... Spinoza himself believed that the forces of censorship in the Dutch Republic at that time represented a formidable obstacle to his philosophical activity and plans to publish. He saw, correctly I would argue, that he needed to clear a path for his *Ethics* by first delivering a heavy blow to the power of censorship and intolerance in the United Provinces of his time.[3]

It is not clear that Spinoza was well enough placed socially to deliver a very "heavy blow" to the opinions and practices of the United Provinces, but Israel is no doubt right that Spinoza would have liked to do so. However Israel omits something of even greater importance. Securing the liberty to philosophize was an "express purpose" of the TTP, but not its chief one. Intellectual freedom is not an end in itself. It is only the indispensable foundation of practical and religious life, which are the ultimate ends for which Spinoza wrote the TTP.

I am not alone in thinking the TTP to be fundamentally about religious questions. The Spinoza scholar Filippo Mignini takes its main focus to be religious, though he is fully aware of how critical Spinoza is of religion as he found it. Mignini believes the aim of the TTP to have been the reduction of revealed historical religion to what is merely rational. Spinoza wished to "recover the nucleus of truth" at the core of revealed religion and to show its compatibility with whatever is taught by the natural light.[4]

The confusion surrounding the fundamental intention of the TTP is warrant for reconsidering what Spinoza himself says about it, both within and outside the work itself. There is only one explanation outside it.

In a letter to his friend Henry Oldenburg, composed sometime in 1665, Spinoza admitted to being busy with a treatise on the meaning of Scripture. That makes it sound as if his original intention was to write a book of a religious character, an impression that is reinforced by the three circumstances that he lists as motivations for writing it.[5] The first is what he called "the prejudices of theologians". He hopes the TTP will uproot these prejudices at least from the minds of more discerning (*prudentiorum*) readers.

Spinoza's second motivation for writing the TTP is that ordinary people (*vulgi*) are constantly charging him with atheism. He hopes to disabuse them of (*averruncare*) this unwarranted suspicion.

Finally, Spinoza wishes to defend freedom of thought and speech (*philosophandi dicendique*) in every way he can against the exaggerated authority and petulance of "rabble-rousers".[6]

To judge by these reasons, it appears that Spinoza is hoping to cure two different readerships of three different errors. The error to which discerning readers are particularly prone is theological prejudice. The letter does not go into the nature of the prejudice Spinoza has in mind. But readers of the TTP discover that Spinoza accuses both Jewish and Christian theology of elevating into dogma many unnecessary doctrines and rituals. It is not that Spinoza wishes to see believers universally discard all these inherited beliefs and practices. But he will argue that they should learn to see them as the inessentials they really are so that, henceforward, each believer will be free to form and maintain his private opinion about them.

The fact that the TTP is addressed to discerning readers is worthy of emphasis. It is not, therefore, a popular work, aimed at preparing non-philosophers for the more complex arguments of the *Ethics*. Any such conjecture regarding the purpose of the TTP would be refuted by the preface to the finished work in which Spinoza explicitly discourages ordinary people (*vulgi*) from reading it.[7]

Nevertheless, without underestimating the philosophical rigour of the TTP, it is worth noting that Spinoza may at one time have entertained the idea of writing it for a wider audience. And though the finished book may no longer address the wider public directly, it still is concerned with repudiating the charge of atheism popularly brought against him. Here Spinoza resembles Socrates trying to unravel the web of suspicion spun about him in the popular mind by Aristophanes. Both philosophers recognize that a preconceived opinion among readers often makes it difficult for them to understand a writer's real intentions.

To recognize this fact is not to change it, however. In the TTP Spinoza demonstrates again and again that he is not an atheist, though many of Spinoza's contemporaries and even some of ours have refused to learn the lesson.[8]

The third error Spinoza hopes to address, a weakness for demagoguery, is common to both the learned and the unlearned. The TTP aims to reduce the dangerously inflated authority of rabble-rousers (*concionatores*).

Spinoza's attacks on theological prejudice and demagoguery, the first and third aims of the TTP, may be connected if, as Ernestine van der Wall has argued, the "theologians" Spinoza has in mind were the Voetian Calvinists, who favoured the use of state authority to suppress all novelty in theological matters.[9] If they are meant, then the theologians and the "rabble rousers" are the same people and the three original aims of the TTP are exclusively theological. But whether or not his targets can be identified this way, the project of the TTP as Spinoza understood it in 1665 was decidedly more theological than political. It must now be investigated whether or not that was the case with the published work.

One immediately striking fact about the TTP as we have it can be observed simply from the table of contents. Fifteen of the twenty chapters into which the work is divided are theological in content; only five are political. The identical proportion of three to one is also observed in the pages of the preface. If theme were determined by length of discussion, then the TTP would be primarily a religious writing.

The epigraph, a quotation from the first letter of St. John, also encourages a religious view of the work: "This is how we know that we remain in God and he in us: because he has given us something of his spirit".[10] It is true that Spinoza will later offer an interpretation of this verse in which the spirit of God is equated with love,[11] but that is not an implausible construction of John's meaning and no more implies anything heterodox in Spinoza than does his choice of a biblical epigraph in the first place. Indeed I shall indicate below the length to which Spinoza goes, *pace* certain commentators,[12] to integrate John's doctrine of love with the views of other apostles.

Using this verse from 1 John also resonates with the outlook of Collegiants. As pointed out in Chapter 2, they based much of their undogmatic theology on their interpretation of what it meant to have the "spirit" of Christ.

The subtitle of the TTP is also significant. Its logic, though not simple, captures the argument of the whole work. The subtitle declares:

> that liberty of thought (*philosophandi*) can not only be permitted without injury to piety and to the peace of the republic, but that it is impossible to suppress it without likewise suppressing the peace of the republic and piety itself.

Reduced to its bare logical bones the subtitle says this: freedom is not only compatible with piety and peace, but necessary to them. But what sense of "necessary" does Spinoza have in mind? As the preface will make clear, Spinoza means not so much the logician's "necessary condition" as the practical philosopher's "necessary presupposition". He will argue that liberty of thought and speech must already be *in place* for the practice of piety and peace to be possible.

Next comes the preface. Though it quickly leads Spinoza into the minefield of religious controversy, it takes him there by the safest possible route. He begins with the neutral topic of pagan religions. They are based on a fear of nature, Spinoza says, arising from the pagans' imperfect grasp of natural things. Out of fear grows superstition, which manifests itself in the worship of false gods. When false gods fail, as they must, there will be a demand for new gods and the resulting conflict of dogmas will lead to religious wars.[13] In war, deception and fanaticism are enlisted by religious leaders of all sides to keep their followers loyal to their cause. No situation could be less favourable to the development of freedom of thought and expression than that of religious war.

Readers of Spinoza's day, living in the aftershock of the Thirty Years War, could hardly fail to see the connection to Christianity's internecine conflicts. Taking nothing for granted, however, Spinoza makes the parallel explicit.[14] Far from exemplifying Christian piety, many self-proclaimed Christians are little different from the pagans described earlier, exalting only credulity and prejudice and prepared to make war on everyone who judges differently from themselves. Thus where religious leaders are permitted to seize control of the powers of state, there can be no possibility of free reflection about religion.

That is why Spinoza declares it to be so serendipitous a thing that he is living in Holland, a state in which the religious authorities do not exercise despotic power and where it is possible to come to a true understanding of the meaning of Scripture. It is this happy chance which allows Spinoza to accomplish the "welcome and useful task" of showing that piety and peace in fact depend on and presuppose liberty of the very kind the Netherlands happen to permit.[15] And this, Spinoza goes on to say, is the main thing he wants to show in the TTP.

The gist of his argument is this: the unprecedented liberty which had evolved in the Netherlands for historical and political reasons is still a precarious achievement at the time Spinoza is writing the TTP. But there is a sufficient amount of it to permit him to lay before the public a project as important as it is challenging, one that involves a radical reformation of the teachings of Christianity.

As it turned out Spinoza was either too optimistic about the degree of latitude he had in the Dutch Republic or else he was just being diplomatic. Jonathan Israel argues contrary to a long, but apparently mistaken, scholarly tradition that Spinoza's works did not circulate freely in the early years but that condemnation and repression of them was almost instantaneous.[16]

At the time of writing, however, Spinoza is envisioning not sordid reality but an ideal. If a reformation of the kind he puts forward can become the new orthodoxy (leaving aside for the moment the precise political measures that would be necessary to bring about such a change[17]) it will in turn perpetuate the very liberty the Netherlands now enjoy, while anchoring securely the practice of true justice and charity. In other words, Spinoza's philosophical opportunism in writing the TTP can be the occasion for establishing the best political order, one that will permit the practice of true religion.

The Christian sects Spinoza wanted to humble probably included most of those around him, except for the most forward-looking Collegiants. The rest exhibited two main faults. First, they sought to use political power to force their unnecessary beliefs and practices on the public, as discussed above. Their other shortcoming was doctrinal. What they described as "the deepest mysteries" (*profundissima mysteria*) were merely philosophical speculations drawn from Plato and Aristotle. These they would try to twist into orthodoxy by tortuously deriving them from the Bible.[18]

To put Spinoza's objections in succinct and technical language, he opposed both dogmatic and scholastic exegesis of Scripture. The first was the commonplace of pulpit sermonizing, the second, in its Protestant no less than its Catholic form, was the norm in the universities.[19]

It was for the sake of finding an alternative exegetical method that Spinoza "resolved", as he says, to examine the Scriptures anew in a spirit of commitment and freedom, and to affirm nothing about them, to admit no doctrine to be found in them, that they did not disclose to him with the utmost clarity.[20] Once having shown that the freedom he exploited in examining Scripture is in fact sanctioned by Scripture itself, he then proposes to exhibit its connection with civil peace.[21]

That is how political freedom comes to be the subject of the last five chapters of the TTP. But its coming last should not deceive us into thinking that political liberty must therefore be the ultimate good, subordinating even freedom of religion to itself. As already explained, the importance of political freedom resides in its being the material condition on which a religiously good life depends. Spinoza, in agreement with the mainstream of western philosophy, sees religion as an inescapable and central part of human communities. And it is only when religious freedom is guaranteed, he says, that everyone can be freely and fully committed to obeying God and to upholding charity and justice.[22]

If the preface is understood in the way just sketched, it complements and illuminates the three goals which Spinoza mentioned to Oldenburg in 1655. Seizing the freedom that was contingently available in his time and place, Spinoza argues against dogmatism, atheism and despotism, in favour of a liberty of thought which he urges the state self-consciously to expand and enshrine in law. Such liberty is not only conducive to the security of the state, it is, more importantly, the key to pious and charitable living.

This interpretation of the aims of the TTP is also confirmed by what Spinoza writes at the end of Chapter 14, the chapter in which he presents what he takes to be the basic dogmas of the "catholic faith". The faith in question, I shall argue, is intended to be a liberal form of Christianity as understood by radical Protestants.[23] When properly understood, it promises to allow everyone "the greatest possible freedom of thought", to damn as heretics and schismatics only those who teach doctrines that cause division and strife, and to count as faithful all those who do their best to lead lives of justice and charity. In the concluding paragraph of Chapter 14 Spinoza tells the reader that these were the main things he hoped to prove in this treatise (*in hoc Tractatu*).[24]

Religion in the TTP

Spinoza often does not refer to Christianity, preferring the more neutral term "religion". How good is the evidence that the religion discussed in the TTP, whose creed is ultimately formulated in Chapter 14, really is some form of Christianity? No one has made any systematic effort to assemble all the passages that bear on that question. Nor is it my goal to attempt such a task. But it will be useful to outline some of the salient aspects of Spinoza's "religion" that are clearly drawn from the outlook of the radical Protestants. A final look at the evidence can be taken when I study in detail the argument of Chapter 14, in the sixth chapter of this book.

The religion put forward in the TTP unmistakeably involves a critique of Judaism as Spinoza found it. His critique is based, moreover, on an obviously Christian reading of the Jewish Scriptures. Spinoza calls the Jewish Scriptures by the Christian term "The Old Testament", presupposing as his point of reference those additional books which Christians add to the Jewish Bible and call "The New Testament". As André Malet succinctly put it, Spinoza purifies the Old Testament by using the New.[25] It is difficult to see how this way of reading the Jewish Scriptures could be construed as excluding Christianity, though it might also include a very liberal Judaism of the kind Spinoza is sometimes thought to have had in mind.

Spinoza's reading of the Bible is not just generically Christian, however. It has a recognizably Protestant character. He aspires to reclaim from Scripture not what Christian tradition has read into it, but a pre-dogmatic message that antedates that tradition. In this aspiration he is a child of the Reformation, though he is certainly no orthodox disciple of any of its leaders. Spinoza sidesteps all confessionally coloured lines of interpretation for the same reason that the original Reformers rejected the traditional Catholic reading of Scripture – not because they wished to abandon Christianity, but in order to recover its original shape.

Spinoza's fundamental hermeneutical principles are Reformation commonplaces: Scripture is self-interpreting (*Scriptura sui interpres*) and ought to be the sole basis for religious teachings (*sola Scriptura*).[26] But what is Scripture? Spinoza's conception of it resembles that of Martin Luther who understood the Bible more as the message of a "living voice" than as a fixed canon of writings.[27] Spinoza explicitly says that the Scripture is not to be identified with a certain set of books. In fact, that is why its simple message can be said to be uncorrupted, and indeed incorruptible.[28]

So understood, Scripture is the Word of God and can be known to be such, Spinoza says. It teaches true religion (*veram religionem*).[29] Like the Protestant reformers before him, Spinoza goes out of his way to stress that this "true" or "catholic religion" he is writing about is not new, except to people who never understood it properly.[30] Paraphrasing John 1:10, Spinoza says: "The Word of God has always been in the world, but not known by the world".[31] Spinoza stands here in the tradition of John Calvin, who likewise defended his teaching by identifying it with the original and authentic Word of God: "By calling [my teaching] 'new', [my detractors] do great wrong to God, whose Sacred Word does not deserve to be accused of novelty", Calvin wrote.[32]

If Spinoza was as much a Protestant as I have suggested, why did he seem so dangerous to Protestant Holland? The answer is simple: because Protestant traditions were among the ones he was putting on trial. The established Protestant churches were no longer radical. Like other radicals they had turned conservative as soon as they saw their reforms satisfactorily established. They had all acquired some form of the traditional and ritualistic trappings that Martin Luther once vividly described as "the Babylonian captivity of the Church".

A radical reformer like Spinoza therefore found himself almost as much at odds with Protestant denominational practices as with Roman

Catholic ones and was a suspicious figure (if not a detested one) to dogmatic adherents of all denominations. The philosopher Kierkegaard memorably expressed the alienation of the true reformer by ironically contrasting the life of a pampered Lutheran Bishop with that of a "witness to the truth". The existence of the latter is a sad one:

> A witness to the truth is a man whose life from first to last is unacquainted with everything which is called enjoyment ... A witness to truth is a man who in poverty witnesses to the truth – in poverty, in lowliness, in abasement, and so is unappreciated, hated, abhorred, and then derided, insulted, mocked – his daily bread perhaps he did not always have, so poor was he, but the daily bread of persecution he was richly provided with every day. For him there was never promotion, except in the inverse sense, downward, step by step. A witness to the truth, one of the genuine witnesses to the truth, is a man who is scourged, maltreated, dragged from one prison to the other, and then at last – the last promotion ... crucified or beheaded, or burnt, or roasted on a gridiron, his lifeless body thrown by the executioner in an out-of-the-way place ...[33]

Spinoza did not know all the extremities to which Kierkegaard points, but enough that he would have recognized the description of a witness to the truth as applying to himself. Established Protestants welcomed tame reformers, but reformers of the Reformation they treated in the manner Kierkegaard describes.

Many of Spinoza's readers (then and now) interpret his attack on tradition as a rejection of the Christian Faith. It is better understood as a reformer's attempt to recapture its lost authenticity. For example, when Spinoza says to Oldenburg: "I hold an opinion about God and Nature very different from that which modern Christians are wont to defend", Lewis Feuer interprets his words as a confession that Spinoza is "spiritually excommunicate among the Christians".[34] But Spinoza's reference here is not to Christians in general. It is to "modern Christians" (*Christiani neoterici*). "Sectarian Christians" might better capture that quality of modern Christianity which Spinoza condemns. He goes on to say that he declines the opinions of these modern Christians in favour of views that are consonant with those of the apostle Paul and all the ancient philosophers.[35] I take Spinoza to mean by that claim that he regards his views as consonant with original (i.e., apostolic)[36] Christianity, as well as with ancient philosophy. These would be ways of commending his views to Christians, rather than of marking his separation from them.

Spinoza thus stands to Reformed Protestantism as it once stood to traditional Catholicism in the sixteenth century and as original Christianity stood to Judaism. Samuel Preus rightly sees Spinoza as trying to persuade his mainly Protestant readers that the religious outlook he is advocating is the next logical step in their tradition.[37] But as with all Protestant reforms, a real step forward must be, historically speaking, a step backward toward the recovery of an authentic core of faith that adventitious custom and inveterate dogmatism have obscured from view. Spinoza can thus be seen to be working and thinking at the radical fringe of what is called "the second reformation". Andrew Fix provides a description of the aims of the second reformation that applies closely to Spinoza as well:

> While the more moderate of the new reformers proposed to work within the established Protestant churches to carry out a further reformation of these churches that would build upon and extend the work of the first reformers, the radical new reformers rejected the work of the original Reformation as a failure and called for a reconstitution of Christian religious life on earth that went far beyond the reform of individual congregations or churches to encompass a complete reorganization of universal Christianity and of Christian society as well.[38]

Spinoza identifies his religious reforms closely with the religion of the apostles. Just how closely can be judged by the energy he devotes in the TTP to reconciling the views of three important apostles – Paul, James and John. Of the three he pays the most careful attention to Paul. As earlier noted his attitude towards Paul is sometimes deferential, but it is not uncritical. Spinoza is selective with regard to Paul's thought, as he must be to reconcile it with those doctrines he approves of in the writings of James and John.

Like Spinoza, Paul rejects the Old Testament propensity to portray human beings as able to resist temptation and God as prepared to change his mind, in accord with whatever they decide to do. Spinoza admires the moral determinism he finds in Paul, as well as the less anthropomorphic view of God:

> Paul teaches nothing more plainly than that men have no power over the temptations of the flesh except through the special calling and grace of God. ... [He] attributes justice to God and then corrects himself for having spoken after the human fashion and the weakness of the flesh.[39]

As Spinoza understands it, Paul's moral determinism leads him to say first, that we have no power over the inclinations of the flesh, unless it comes by the grace of God and, second, that we may nevertheless be guilty if we follow our inclinations. Paul thus seems to accept the view that some people could be condemned for doing what they could not resist or for omitting what they could not do.

It is not obvious at first why Spinoza would be in favour of such a view. His rejection of a similar position, which he imputes to Jews in general, and to Maimonides in particular, has already been discussed. He criticized them for believing that the Gentiles would be judged guilty of sins which they could only have avoided committing, if they had received revelations granted only to Jews. Spinoza was wrong in attributing this dogma to Maimonides, but quite categorical in denouncing it.[40] Why, then, does he agree with Paul that we can be guilty of yielding to inclinations we cannot resist?

A further reference to St. Paul helps to explain, though not to justify, what Spinoza means:

> [W]e must by no means neglect the passage in Paul's Epistle to the Romans (1:20) in which he says ...: "For the hidden things of God, together with their virtue and divinity, which are eternal, are observed by his creatures through the intellect from the foundation of the world. Therefore they are without excuse".[41]

The morally significant point for Spinoza seems to be that revelation be understood in Paul's way, as natural and therefore general, rather than as special and supernatural, as he thought Maimonides held. Spinoza makes this point explicit:

> [Paul] indicates clearly enough that everyone can get a clear understanding of God's power and eternal divinity by the natural light. From there they can know and deduce what to pursue and resist. Thus he concludes that no one is excused, and no appeal to ignorance will be received, as it might if the light in question were a supernatural one ...

It is not obvious that Spinoza is taking morally higher ground in the doctrine he accepts than he would have been in the doctrine he rejected. However I am not defending Spinoza's position at this point, but only tracing the different ways in which he presents it as a version of Christianity. In that regard it is significant that the only moral he draws from the passage just quoted is that it demonstrates "scriptural approval" for his own teachings regarding the Divine natural law and the natural light.[42]

Conformity with the "divine natural law" is a necessary, but not a sufficient condition for moral excellence, Spinoza thinks, once again in self-conscious agreement with St. Paul. He illustrates the point with the example of just action: "This I take to be Paul's meaning when he says that those who live under the law cannot be justified through the law, for justice, as commonly defined, is the constant and perpetual will to render every man his due".[43]

In distinguishing between obedience to the positive law and the doing of a moral act in this way, Spinoza echoes Paul's distinction between the letter and spirit of the law. But he also does something more. With this distinction Spinoza foreshadows his own signature theological doctrine that the saving power of mere obedience, that is, mere conformity to the law, can be known only from revelation, not from reason alone. Obedience to the two fundamental commandments – love of God and neighbour – is a good thing, and necessary for salvation. However only revelation could show it to be sufficient for salvation. Spinoza's innovation is to interpret this conceptual divide as cutting between those whose love of God and neighbour is based on a rational insight into the supreme moral significance of these commandments – that is, on rational or natural religion – and those whose acts of love derive from mere faith and obedience to a law they regard as revealed. It is a demonstrable from the meaning of the terms that those who do good for the right reasons are saved. But that those who do good because they are obedient can be saved, only revelation could disclose.

That Spinoza bases his religious intellectualism on St. Paul gives the TTP a Christian appearance. So does the favourable attitude he shows toward revealed religion. It is not obvious, however, that these two views are consistent. Once again, however, the focus here is on the religious character of his doctrine, rather than on its philosophical problems. The problems of the consistency of the doctrine presented in the TTP and also of its compatibility with the very different presentation of his thought in the Ethics are important ones, however, and will be considered at length in Chapter 7.

Though Spinoza is frequently favourable to St. Paul's doctrines, he is not always so. In fact he rejects the central Pauline teaching that faith is the sole key to salvation. Works, Spinoza says, are more significant than faith. Here again he draws attention to the agreement, if not the authority, of an apostle. This time, however, it is the Apostle James. Spinoza refers explicitly to James' Epistle to justify his position regarding this well-known crux of Christian theology. "Dismissing all those disputations of Paul", Spinoza says, "James sums up the whole doctrine of his religion in just a few words".[44] The few words Spinoza is referring to are these (James 2: 24): "You see that a man is justified by his works, and not by his faith alone".

In the Christian lexicon "works" means principally acts of charity towards other people. The concept of "works" provides a conceptual bridge to another of the key terms in Spinoza's religious vocabulary, namely "obedience". Spinoza makes the connection explicit while considering the implications of his definition of "faith" in Chapter 14. Faith, he defines as "believing those things about God which, if absent, destroy obedience to him, but are present whenever obedience is present". The first consequence of this definition, he says, is that "faith does not lead to salvation on its own, but only by reason of obedience, or, as James says in Chapter 2, Verse 17: 'faith alone without works is dead'".[45]

For Spinoza, then, obedience must always produce works. Implied in this first consequence of Spinoza's definition of faith is the further claim that obedience produces salvation. Thus for Spinoza, as for the apostle James, genuine faith expresses itself in works, understood as obedience to the rule of charity, that is, to the command to love God and neighbour. The obedient performance of such works is both sufficient and necessary for salvation, Spinoza holds, rejecting the Pauline idea that salvation arises through grace alone, without any consideration of works or merit.

My principal concern here has been to show how receptive Spinoza is to some of the principal teachings of James and Paul concerning salvation. Once again, however, it is certainly possible to doubt whether his selective adoption of their views gives rise to a consistent doctrine. In agreement with his own interpretation of Paul, he holds that salvation demands understanding the requirements of the Law. But he simultaneously takes from the apostle James the doctrine that mere obedience is sufficient. This may look more like inconsistency than reconciliation. It is far from obvious in a religious context, or indeed in any other, that all who obey understand why they are obeying.

Despite this tension, and the related ones discussed in the preceding paragraphs, Spinoza is not often accused of inconsistency. He is more frequently suspected of some kind of equivocal writing, as when Yirmiyahu Yovel warns readers that "Spinoza was a grand master of dual language and equivocation", a technique which he says "is manifest in those of Spinoza's writings published during his lifetime, especially the *Theologico-Political Treatise*...".[46] If Spinoza's intent was to equivocate, he might be thought to be doing so here in an effort to placate Dutch Calvinists with his references to St. Paul, and Arminians by borrowing from James. When I come to address this fundamental tension in Spinoza's religious thought I shall argue that there is no systematic equivocation here and no attempt to deceive Christian readers. But I have not yet completed my survey of his debt to the apostles.

Spinoza acknowledges a debt to the apostle John, for his doctrine of "love", another key term in Christian thought. Greek has at least four terms that can be translated as "love", and New Testament Greek appropriates one of them, ἀγάπη, to convey the specifically Christian meaning of the term. Older generations of English speakers reserved the word "charity" for this purpose.

Agapē-love, or charity, amounts to precisely those disinterested acts of kindness toward other people that Spinoza means by "works" and which are required for "obedience". He brings all these meanings masterfully together in commenting on 1John 4f: "whoever loves [his neighbour], is born of God and knows God; whoever does not love his neighbour does not love God, for God is love". Spinoza comments:

> From these words it follows once again that we must never judge anyone to be faithful or unfaithful except by his works. That is, if his works are good, however much he may dissent from other believers in matters of dogma, he is still a believer. Conversely, if his works are evil, however much he may agree with them in words, he is nevertheless an unbeliever. For where obedience is found, so necessarily is faith, and faith without works is dead. As John also expressly teaches in verse 13 of the same chapter, 'this is how we know that we remain in God and he in us: because he has given us something of his spirit', namely love. For John had said before that God was love, whence (that is, by his own already acknowledged principles) he concludes that truly having the spirit of God means having love. Furthermore, since no one has seen God, John concludes that no one can sense him or perceive him except through love to his neighbour and so likewise no one can know any other attribute of God except this love, insofar as we participate in it. These reasons may not be decisive, but they explain what John had in mind clearly enough. He is much clearer in Chapter 2 Verses 3 and 4 of the same Epistle, where he teaches expressly what we think him to mean: 'This', he says, 'is how we become aware (*novimus*) that we know (*scimus*) him: by obeying his commandments. Whoever claims to know him and does not obey his commandments is a liar and the truth is not in him'.[47]

Obedience, love and works thus involve participation in the divine nature through imitating the love we see God exhibit. This is a thoroughly Christian thought. It could be even more so of course, if obedience love and good works also involved the imitation of Christ. But would Spinoza go that far?

Simple logic would carry orthodox Christians from the imitation of God to the imitation of Christ, because they affirm the identity statement: Christ is God. Spinoza doesn't affirm it, at least not without reservations. The sticking point for Spinoza involves the doctrine of the Incarnation, according to which God assumed human nature in Christ. Spinoza tells Oldenburg that this doctrine is as incomprehensible to him as it would be to say that a circle assumed the nature of a square.[48] His categorical rejection of the Incarnation however seems to stem more from a Neoplatonic disdain for the capacity of the flesh than from heretical doubts about the divinity of Christ. Spinoza does not hesitate to say in the same breath to Oldenburg that the wisdom of God was manifest most of all in Christ. Elsewhere he goes even further, saying that God manifested himself to the fullest extent in Christ.[49] His rejection of the doctrine of the Incarnation would therefore be no obstacle to his accepting the idea that the love, obedience and works which we are called upon to exhibit are in fact an imitation of Christ.

The unpretentious phrase "religion of obedience", that characterizes the religion discussed in the TTP, thus contains an overwhelming amount of recognizably Christian doctrine. Spinoza means to convey by it an epitome of the teachings of the apostles, in which their differences are resolved. It is compatible with the traditional notion of Christian life as *imitatio Christi* and is meant to contain no dogmas which any Christian could reject.

The religion of obedience Spinoza discusses in the TTP he holds to have been introduced to the world through the unique, indeed miraculous, powers possessed by the disciples of Christ:

> If someone asks by what right were Christ's disciples, men of private station, enabled to preach religion, I reply that they did so by right of the power they had received from Christ against unclean spirits ... [but] no one may follow their example unless he likewise has the power of working miracles.[50]

Now if Spinoza thinks of his universal religion as the one that was miraculously introduced by Christ's apostles, it is hard to see it could be any other religion than Christianity. It is true that Spinoza only advocates what T.L.S. Sprigge has described as "a minimal state religion with a minimal creed".[51] But even to describe it as minimal is to imply the existence of a more elaborate original from which it has been taken. And the original can be nothing other than Christianity.

Spinoza's Christianity is also minimal for a reason. It is not the exhausted minimalism of which today's liberal Protestant churches are often accused, where traditional beliefs have been compromised or abandoned for the sake of social peace, or in pursuit of interfaith dialogue. It is instead the militant minimalism of the early Protestant reformers.

Politics, Piety and Providence

The closing five chapters of the TTP are devoted to demonstrating the proper relationship between religion and the state. But to say that the TTP's great ambition is "to liberate society from its religious restraints", as one study puts it,[52] is to make it more modern than it is. The idea that religion is principally a restraint arose during the Enlightenment. Spinoza does not approach it in that way. He gives no indication of wishing to release citizens from the obligation of living religious lives. On the contrary he tries to show them how to do so in a better way. His philosophy is not merely about escaping from bondage but also about achieving freedom in a more positive sense.

The TTP no doubt contributed to the process by which religion in Europe was liberalized and shorn of political power, but the desire to minimize organized religion is obviously compatible with a high regard for piety. The TTP envisions an ideal state in which simple piety would be the highest expression of freedom.

It is understandable, however, that Enlightenment ideas are sometimes read back into Spinoza. Knowing how things turned out can influence our understanding of what earlier authors meant. A case in point is Spinoza's assertion that religious questions are best decided by political authorities.[53] It could easily be interpreted as showing that Spinoza wants either to politicize religion or secularize the state. But neither of these views captures what Spinoza had in mind. For him political control of religious matters follows from the nature of religion itself.

Organized religion does not exist in a state of nature, but presupposes a social order of some kind.[54] Religion and politics must therefore cooperate with one another and there are, generally speaking, only a limited number of ways in which they can.

One way is theocracy (literally the rule of God) which can work under conditions like those that obtained in ancient Israel, but would not have been workable in seventeenth century Holland. Theocracy requires that we be able to establish God's assent or disapproval of human arrangements in a way that the ancient office of the prophets made possible, but which was no longer available in Spinoza's day. Furthermore theocracy is not suitable to a nation of traders, but rather to a closed, even introverted society. The main thing to be learned from Israel's theocracy is why it failed as a political system when

Israel tried to reestablish it during the period   called the Second Commonwealth or Second Temple (approximately the sixth century BC – 1st century AD). Its crucial weakness became apparent when political power fell into the hands of religious authorities who merely pretended to be the spokesmen of God.[55]

The same mistake was made when the Roman Empire was Christianized under Constantine and after. Because Christianity began as a clandestine religion the political rulers during the period of its establishment needed tutoring by religious officials. The latter, not wishing to lose their advantage, invented means of keeping politicians permanently in the dark about religious matters and so becoming indispensable authorities. This they did by introducing layer upon layer of impenetrable dogma, a technique that made theological training politically important throughout the middle ages. Religiously speaking, however, these priestly wiles did no more than lay the groundwork for the Reformation. Later reformers, with Spinoza in their wake, would dismiss the accumulated dogmas as inessential.

The imposing dogmatic superstructure inherited from the middle ages was seen by Spinoza as only a facade, an elaborate deception that hid from view the will-to-power from which it arose. Its real purpose, Spinoza thinks, was to guarantee that no one could become a religious authority without acquiring prolonged philosophical and theological training, and that none could acquire that except by leading a celibate life. Since political leadership demanded other qualities ecclesiastical power would always remain in ecclesiastical hands.

In Spinoza's eyes, however, these priestly successes made religion inefficient. They prevented political leaders from assuming the sovereignty over religious practices to which nature calls them.[56] To leave religious legislation in the hands of the Church, Spinoza insists, is also dangerous. It causes religious antagonisms to be played out in the public square, as religious strife since ancient times has made plain.

> If anyone wishes to remove this authority from the sovereign, he is only trying to sow division in the realm. From such division contentions and discord must necessarily arise, as once they did among the Hebrew kings and priests. And they can never be laid to rest.[57]

It is no surprise that Spinoza praises the Reformation for wresting away from the Pope the political authority usurped by Rome during the middle ages.[58]

To favour political sovereignty over religious affairs may have been a radical opinion, but it was far from unique to Spinoza. Hobbes had already written two decades earlier in his *Leviathan*:

> *The civil sovereign, if a Christian, is head of the Church in his own dominion*: From this consolidation of the right politic and ecclesiastic in Christian sovereigns, it is evident, they have all manner of power over their subjects, that can be given to man, for the government of men's external actions, both in policy and religion; and may make such laws as they themselves shall judge fittest, for the government of their own subjects, both as they are the commonwealth, and as they are the Church; for both State and Church are the same men.[59]

Opposition to religious rule was also a commonplace among the radical Protestants of Spinoza's day, many of whom believed that the true Church had disappeared with Constantine, when the persecuted Church acquired political power and itself became a persecutor.[60]

Perhaps Spinoza's endorsement of political rule in ecclesiastical matters makes Spinoza a "philosopher of secularization", as Yirmiyahu Yovel has called him,[61] but not if the epithet is understood as diminishing the religious character of his thought. Like the radical Protestants Spinoza believed that the different sects of the institutional church, with their distinctive forms of worship, did not need secularization because they were already, by their very nature, secular bodies. For them, "the religious community proclaims itself a secular institution, called to strengthen collectively its religious values, but deprived of any charismatic glory of a religious group in its ideas, activities and rituals".[62]

Radical Protestants distinguished, as Spinoza did, between outward and inward forms of worship.[63] Outward forms were human devices and, to the extent that they must be regulated, ought to be so by the sovereign power. However because even mere outward forms of worship are ultimately expressions of inward religion, Spinoza says that the degree to which the sovereign can regulate them is not absolute. The core message of the TTP in fact concerns this duality of outward and inward religion: freedom of thought and expression (outward religion) are essential to piety (inward religion) and can be withheld "only at great peril to peace and grave harm to the republic".[64] Also, "a sovereign who will not obey the revealed will of God ignores it to his peril and damnation".[65]

Inward religion cannot be secularized, if by that term is meant repressing every aspect of it that is not political. That cannot happen because inward religion is logically prior to the state. The state inevitably has inward religion at its core because it is inalienable from the individuals who make up the state.[66] Spinoza goes further. He says that where the laws of the state enter into conflict with piety, the state must give way and piety must prevail, provided a true revelation has been vouchsafed to the dissenter.[67] Spinoza makes it clear that he does not think such circumstances occur often. But he is committed to their having happened at least once, for it is only by such means that Christianity could have established its authenticity in the face of Judaism and pagan religions.[68]

On the other hand, though inward religion is not secular, it can rightly be called natural. It is because Spinoza regards inward religion as in some sense natural that he does not devote many pages to discussing it in the TTP.[69] Apart from outlining the fundamental dogmas of the Faith in Chapter 14 Spinoza touches on inward religion only in isolated remarks. The subject is important, but because it is rooted in human nature he thinks it more appropriate to a different kind of study.

At one point Spinoza calls inward religion a "divine law", which expresses itself as a certain manner of living (*ratio vivendi*). "The foundations of the best republic and the prescription for life in community are derived from it", he says. But because in the TTP Spinoza is concerned with this divine law only in general terms, he goes on to say that the place for a full treatment of it would be in a work of general ethics.[70] At the time of writing these words, Spinoza's own *Ethics* was still being written. It is surely not wrong to see an allusion to it here. Readers are referred to the *Ethics* for the critical exploration of inward religion they will not find in the TTP. That is the light in which I shall approach the *Ethics* in chapter seven of this book.

•   •   •

Lastly, Spinoza's treatment of *providence* can also be misread as a harbinger of Enlightenment atheism. He rejects the ancient Jewish conception of providence reflected in the Old Testament because in his eyes it included only what he calls "the external assistance of God". This form of divine assistance Spinoza says to be really nothing but good luck (*fortuna*).[71] The ease with which the Jews established themselves in the Promised Land and the level of prosperity they were able to attain there would be examples.

If there were no more to it, one could see here a masterful reduction of something supernatural (providence) to something natural (luck). Robert Misrahi, for example, thinks he is lifting the veil of Spinoza's language when he points out that the assistance of God is, for Spinoza, nothing other than "nature itself and its laws".[72] But identity statements are two-way streets. By the same token good fortune must involve the assistance of God and we must consider what is meant by calling it "assistance" (*auxilium*). Spinoza can just as well be read as finding in nature's fully deterministic laws evidence of God's guidance and design, a Christian doctrine of long standing.[73]

Spinoza does not leave the matter to depend on how we choose to understand identity statements however. He makes a religious interpretation of God's external assistance unavoidable. What is called good fortune can "rightly" be called miraculous, Spinoza says, when, as with the establishment of the Jewish people, it goes far beyond anyone's expectations.[74] As far as Spinoza is concerned, the limitation in the Old Testament conception of providence is not that it falsely attributes Jewish prosperity to God's assistance, but that there is a more important kind of divine aid which it overlooks.

Happy material circumstances are not the highest good of human life. They are neither what we should ultimately strive for nor what constitutes the best evidence of the providence of God. Our highest good is "the knowledge and love of God", Spinoza says.[75] God should therefore be the object of our striving, just as he is the natural object of our inward worship. Now whatever we can accomplish inwardly, out of our own resources is done through God's "internal aid". And that is the other and more important form of providence.[76] Thus for Spinoza, as for traditional Christian theology, God is both an efficient cause who equips us with our faculties and a final cause toward whom our faculties ought to be directed in love.

The Christian presuppositions that shape the TTP, its conception of the Bible and its affinity with the goals of the "second Reformation" make it very difficult to maintain the picture of Spinoza as a harbinger of Enlightenment secularism. I am conscious, however, of certain chapters of the book that many would count as completely resistant to a Christian interpretation. Foremost among them would be the TTP's chapters on miracles and the interpretation of Scripture. The Christian dimension of the TTP cannot be properly assessed until these chapters have been discussed.

Notes

1   Brykman [1972], 68; cf. Moreau [1992], 119.
2   Spinoza [1954], 8. See also her notes to the TTP, 1449-1485 passim. See also Spinoza [1989], 42; Seymour Feldman's introduction to Spinoza [1991], xviii; Misrahi [1977], 391.
3   Israel [1996], 5.

4   Mignini [1995], 64.
5   Spinoza [1925] 4, 166.
6   The word "concionator" I have translated in its classical sense as "rabble-rouser". I note, however, that the most prominent English, French and German translators agree in translating it as "preacher". Though religious authorities may well be the rabble-rousers Spinoza had in mind, to translate the term in this way appears to me an unwarranted restriction of its Latin sense. The context of letter 30 and letter 29 (to and from Oldenburg respectively) could easily have suggested this term to him, since both discuss the ferocity of the Anglo-Dutch war, then in its full fury.
7   Spinoza [1925] 3, 12.
8   For example, the Remonstrant theologian Philipp van Limborch saw Spinoza as a sly atheist, who simply wrote in a deceptive manner. Through him many of his English correspondents, such as Henry More, Henry Jenkes, and Ralph Cudworth came to hold the same opinion. See Coley [1957], 95f. In our own time the distinguished Spinoza scholar Robert Misrahi [1977], 387, says that Spinoza's philosophy amounts to "practical atheism".
9   van der Wall [1995], 206.
10   1 John 4: 13. In translating this and other Biblical passages I have paid attention to the Latin text that Spinoza uses. It is the Tremellius translation from the Syriac and Spinoza preferred it on two counts. First, he thought it likely that it was not a translation at all, but the original document of which the Greek text was a translation. And even if this were not so, he believed that Syriac (or Aramaic) was the language of the apostles. See Spinoza [1925], 262 = TTP, note 26.
11   Spinoza [1925] 3, 175f. = TTP 14.
12   See Spinoza [1954], 1454, note 4 and 1471: re 807, note 2.
13   Spinoza [1925] 3, 5-7 = TTP pref.
14   Spinoza [1925] 3, 8 = TTP pref.
15   Spinoza [1925] 3, 7 = TTP pref.
16   See Israel [1996], esp. p. 8.
17   These he outlines in Spinoza [1925] 3, 345 = *Tractatus Politicus* ch. 8, §46. I shall discuss the significance of these measures in Chapter 6.
18   Spinoza [1925] 3, 9 = TTP pref.
19   See Harrisville and Sundberg [1995], 22, 44. This useful synoptic study of "higher criticism" unfortunately accepts uncritically a number of views about Spinoza's place in it which it is the purpose of this book to refute.
20   Spinoza [1925] 3, 9 = TTP pref: "sedulo statui Scripturam de novo integro et libero animo examinare, et nihil de eadem affirmare nihilque tanquam ejus doctrinam admittere, quod ab eadem clarissime non edocerer".
21   Spinoza [1925] 3, 11 = TTP pref.
22   Spinoza [1925] 3, 11 = TTP pref: "sic ergo omnes integro et libero animo Deo obedire poterunt, et sola justitia et charitas apud omnes in pretio erit".
23   A number of scholars have taken this expression *not* to refer to the Christian Church. To take one example, Seymour Feldman writes of Spinoza's use of "fides catholica" in Chapter 14 (Spinoza [1925], 177 = Spinoza [1991], 161), "Spinoza's use of the term 'catholic' must always be understood in its original meaning as 'universal.' Spinoza in no way has in mind here the Roman Catholic Church". In one way the note is innocuous enough. Feldman is right that Spinoza does not have in mind the Roman Catholic Church in particular. But it in no way follows that he must therefore mean something as vague as simply a "universal church". Why can he not mean the Christian Church as a whole, which

customarily refers to itself as "the Catholic Church"? "I believe in ... the Holy Catholic Church" is one of the clauses in the Apostles' Creed, which Roman Catholic, Orthodox and nearly all Protestant denominations recognize in common. And all recognize that the Catholic Church and its various denominational expressions do not exactly coincide.

24 Spinoza [1925] 3, 179f = TTP 14.
25 Malet [1966], 304.
26 See Spinoza [1925] 3, 9 = TTP, pref.: "sedulo statui Scripturam de novo integro et libero animo examinare, et nihil de eadem affrimare nihilque tanquam ejus doctrinam admittere, quod ab eadem clarissime non edocerer". Cf. Walther [1994], 100f.
27 Harrisville and Sundberg [1995], 15f.
28 Spinoza [1925] 3, 160 = TTP 12.
29 Spinoza [1925] 3, 162 = TTP 12.
30 Spinoza [1925] 3, 163 = TTP 12: "nec ... quod religio catholica ... nova esset, nisi respectu hominum, qui eam non noverant".
31 Spinoza [1925] 3, 163 = TTP 12.
32 Calvin [1960] 1, 15.
33 Soren Kierkegaard [1944] *Attack on Christendom* Trans. by Walter Lowrie. Princeton, New Jersey: Princeton University Press.
34 Feuer [1966], p. 149.
35 Spinoza [1925] 4, 307 = EP 73.
36 The degree to which Spinoza identifies original with apostolic Christianity will be discussed below.
37 Preus [1998], 6.
38 Fix [1991], 115.
39 Spinoza [1925] 3, 42 = TTP 2.
40 Spinoza [1925] 3: 79f.= TTP 5.
41 Spinoza [1925] 3, 68 = TTP 4.
42 Spinoza [1925] 3, 68 = TTP 4.
43 Spinoza [1925] 3, 59 = TTP 4.
44 Spinoza [1925] 3, 157 = TTP 11.
45 Spinoza [1925] 3,175 = TTP 14.
46 Yovel [1989], 29.
47 Spinoza [1925] 3, 175f = TTP 14.
48 Spinoza [1925] 4, 309 = EP 73.
49 Spinoza [1925] 4, 316 = EP 65: "Deus sese maxime in Christo manifestavit". Cf. Malet [1966], 282.
50 Spinoza [1925] 3, 233 =TTP 19.
51 Sprigge [1995], 139. I shall be more critical of this characterization in Chapter 6.
52 Harris and Sundberg [1995], 47.
53 This is the subject of Chapter 19 of the TTP.
54 Spinoza [1925] 3, 198 = TTP, 16.
55 Spinoza [1925] 3, 221 = TTP, 17.
56 Spinoza [1925] 3, 237 = TTP, 19.
57 Spinoza [1925] 3, 235 = TTP, 19.
58 Spinoza [1925] 3, 235 =TTP, 19.
59 Hobbes *Leviathan* ed. Michael Oakeshott, New York: Collier, 1977, Pt. III, ch. 42, p. 398.
60 See e.g., van der Wall [1995]; Kolakowski [1969], 182.
61 Yirmiyahu Yovel calls Spinoza "a philosopher of immanence and secularization" and also "the first secular Jew" (Yovel [1989], x).

62   Kolakowski [1990a], 274.
63   "They were attempting to reduce religious life to religious form, that is, to free it from all admixtures of secular relations". Kolakowski [1990b], 404. Comp. Spinoza [1925], 229 = TTP 19.
64   Spinoza [1925] 3, 11 = TTP, pref.
65   Spinoza [1925] 3, 199 = TTP, 16.
66   Spinoza [1925] 3, 229 = TTP, 19.
67   Spinoza [1925] 3, 199 = TTP, 16.
68   Spinoza [1925] 3, 233f = TTP, 19.
69   I agree with Malet [1966], 214, that in such contexts Spinoza means by "natural" moral imperatives that can be satisfied out of our own resources.
70   Spinoza [1925] 3, 60 = TTP, 4.
71   Spinoza [1925] 3, 46 =TTP, 3.
72   Misrahi [1977], 406.
73   Thomas Aquinas (*Summa Theologiae* I, 116, 3, obj. 1) takes it from Boethius: *On the Consolation of Philosophy* IV, Prose 6, 78ff.
74   Spinoza [1925] 3, 47 = TTP, 3. This of course raises the question of what Spinoza means by miracles, which I shall discuss in the next chapter.
75   Spinoza [1925], 60 = TTP, 4.
76   Spinoza [1925], 46 = TTP, 3.

Chapter Five

Miracles, Meaning and Moderation

The chapters of the TTP which have contributed most to Spinoza's theological notoriety are the ones concerned with miracles and the interpretation of Scripture. Upon publication they were met with toxic levels of odium and rejection. To most of his contemporaries Spinoza seemed intent on discarding miracles and undermining the authority of the Bible and they saw in such attitudes an obvious danger to the religious and social order.

Most Spinoza scholars today would agree with that early reading of the texts, though the odium has evaporated and even turned to praise. For example, Manfred Walther has called the miracles chapter "a miracle of criticism" and Edwin Curley acclaims the TTP as "a neglected masterpiece", largely because of the hermeneutical method developed in Chapter 7.

Why does our age regard so positively texts that Spinoza's generation vehemently opposed? We see new things in them. We recognize contributions to questions of contemporary interest and are unconcerned with what seemed dangerous centuries ago. That is fair enough. But a change in attitude should not be mistaken for scholarly advance on the questions that interested the seventeenth century, for on those questions there has been no advance. Most contemporary readers understand Spinoza's position on the existence of miracles and biblical authority just as their ancestors did, differing only in their reaction to it. That is why the texts pertaining to these questions merit a second look today.

When they are consulted with these questions in mind, it becomes apparent that Spinoza neither dismissed miracles nor rejected biblical authority. He defends a Protestant outlook that emphatically includes miracles (at least up to the apostolic age) and also propounds dogmas. But it elegantly manages to embrace miracles without superstition and dogmas without dogmatism. That is one reason why Spinoza's appropriation of Christianity can be called a moderate one. Another is because it falls between scepticism and dogmatism. A third is that it finds a middle ground between unbelief and fanaticism. The remaining pages of this chapter will provide argument and textual warrant for the foregoing claims.

The view taken here of Spinoza's philosophy is distinctly minoritarian, but not without a pedigree. It is similar to that proposed by Spinoza's Collegiant friend, Jarig Jelles, who wrote the lengthy and important preface to the first edition of Spinoza's works, called *Posthumous Works*, cautiously attributed to "B.D.S.", and published in 1677. One of Jelles' chief concerns was to refute those who accused Spinoza of atheism and of trying to destroy all religion and piety in his readers. Jelles depicts Spinoza's teachings as "quite in conformity with what our Saviour and his apostles taught". Moreover the zeal Spinoza encourages us to have not merely to understand Christian doctrine but to live it "perfectly agrees with the Sacred Scripture and the Christian religion".[1] Throughout the preface Jelles portrays Spinoza as I intend to do: not as an extremist, but as a moderate advocate of Christian toleration.

There is no reason to think Jelles disingenuous. Spinoza was a radical, but did not necessarily think of himself as such regarding all religious questions. Neither did like-minded friends, such as Jelles, think it of him. In this chapter I shall explore the radicalism of Spinoza's chapters on miracles and biblical interpretation from the inside, from the point of view that makes them appear moderate.

Miracles

> No other element of Spinoza's philosophy provoked as much consternation and outrage in his own time as his sweeping denial of miracles and the supernatural. In fact, Spinoza stands completely alone among the major European thinkers before the mid-eighteenth century in ruling out miracles.[2]

So Jonathan Israel expresses the virtually unanimous verdict of contemporary scholarship. E.E. Harris puts it this way:

> Spinoza totally rejects belief in miracles as supernatural wonders. That the disciples believed in them and thought them to be evidence of Christ's divinity he had no doubt. But, he says, it would be no detriment to their teaching to hold that their belief in the miraculous was mistaken. As to what the churches have added in later times, most of this he finds unintelligible and ridiculous.[3]

Seymour Feldman agrees: "Given [Spinoza's] metaphysical infrastructure, the biblical doctrine of miracles, as traditionally understood, turns out to be an illusion".[4]

Manfred Walther devotes an interesting article to explaining how miracles represent a particular challenge for Spinoza's hermeneutics. On the one hand they occur in the Bible, which Spinoza has undertaken to expound "from premises accepted by those at whom it is aimed". On the other hand "belief in miracles represents a negation of the very principle of Spinoza's philosophy".[5] The biblical accounts of miracles are thus "the test of any philosophy or science that pretends to universal explanatory power".[6] Spinoza's ability to meet the challenge of miracles is what Walther calls "a miracle of criticism". But he takes the standard line of contemporary scholarship when it comes to Spinoza's view of whether miracles exist: "Miracles are concepts of reflection derived from a pre-scientific consciousness", he writes. "They denote nothing in the thing itself and are thus without cognitive content".[7]

There are some important differences in the sample passages I have quoted, beneath their surface unanimity. Some say Spinoza simply rejects miracles. Others that he rejects traditional, biblical or supernatural miracles. But none of the authors attributes to Spinoza any positive doctrine regarding miracles. For all of them the key aspect is rejection.

The controversial Spinoza commentator Leo Strauss is an exception to the rule. He detects what he calls uneasiness in Spinoza's critique of miracles.

> How little Spinoza finds himself at ease in this critique of miracles which is based on Scripture is made apparent by his remark that those passages in Scripture that unhesitatingly report on miracles as contra-natural or supernatural events must have been interpolated in the holy book by sacrilegious men. This remark directly opposes his whole principle of interpretation, that objective truth may not be used as the key for interpreting Scripture.[8]

Strauss believes he can explain the source of Spinoza's uneasiness. It arises, he says, because Spinoza has fortified his mind against miracles even though his method does not compel him to reject them. Spinoza therefore must override his own method in order to make rejection of miracles possible.

> Reason devoid of faith, engaged in the pursuit of scientific inquiry, shows itself as immune to miracles. The assertion of miracles, as trespassing beyond the bounds set to strict experience that can be tested, is rejected as asserting too much. ... So it is not the advancing positive method, proceeding from point to point, but only the reflection of the positive mind on itself, the recognition by the positive mind that it represents a progress beyond the previously prevailing form of consciousness (a finding that first takes the form of the crude antithesis between superstition, prejudice, ignorance,

barbarism, benightedness on the one hand, and reason, freedom, culture, enlightenment on the other) which creates a position impregnable to proof by miracles.[9]

Strauss's characterization of the anti-miraculous turn of mind is most perceptive, but its target is wrong. It is not Spinoza who rejects miracles out of hand. It is his readers, a long succession of them stretching back to the Enlightenment and including Strauss himself. The text that Strauss presents as indicative of Spinoza's uneasiness can be explained without difficulty in another way. What Spinoza rejects are biblical texts that depict miracles as defying the natural order. His warrant for rejecting them is provided by that very "principle of interpretation" to which Strauss refers, namely the proposition that the Bible is self-interpreting. Texts depicting supernatural miracles are disqualified, Spinoza thinks, by more and better biblical texts saying the opposite.[10] Spinoza's mind is not hardened against miracles as such, though his readers' minds often are.

What Spinoza says about Miracles

The miracles chapter concerns an error to which common people (*vulgi*) are prone. Common people, both Jews and Gentiles, misunderstand nature, because they think of it as force and impetus and of God as controlling it with the majesty of a ruler in his realm.[11] This misunderstanding leads to others. People think they see most evidence of God's majesty amid apparently unnatural events, for they imagine that in them God seizes control of nature's forces. This in turn leads them to believe God's sole purpose in taking control of events must be to compel nature to gratify the wishes of his human subjects.[12]

It is possible that the word "vulgi", which I have been translating as "common people", really aims at, or at least includes, another target. The seventeenth century sometimes used the same term to refer to the scholastic philosophers. Scholastics were responsible for what is called the "traditional" understanding of miracles. So it will also be worth investigating to what degree Spinoza's account of miracles contradicts theirs, once Spinoza's own position has been ascertained.

Against the common, but erroneous, view of nature Spinoza sets out four propositions that he aims to demonstrate:

1) That nothing can happen against nature, but that nature keeps to a fixed and immutable order (*fixum et immutabilem ordinem*).

2) That miracles teach us nothing about God's essence, his existence or his providence, while the natural order does.

3) That Scripture means by providence nothing but nature's order.

4) That the miracle stories found in Scripture require a new interpretation.

Of these the first is the only one that could be thought to endorse the flat denial of miracles alleged by the Spinoza literature. But does it? In support of that proposition Spinoza advances a more general one which I will call "the Miracle Axiom", abbreviated "MA".

> MA: Nothing happens that does not a) agree (*convenit*) with nature's laws or b) follow (*sequitur*) from them.[13]

Spinoza attaches to MA a note on the word "nature" that is of crucial importance. It is meant to ward off a potential misunderstanding. He tells us that nature includes "infinitely more than merely matter and its affections". The practised reader of Spinoza will see here an allusion to his theory of the infinite attributes of God. Thus MA does not say that we must explain miracles exclusively in terms of extended things, but rather in terms of God, that is of extension plus thought plus all the other unnamed (and to us incomprehensible) attributes of the divine being. True, God is nothing more than nature, according to Spinoza. But it is no less true that nature can be understood as divine. And so understood MA cannot reasonably give offence to religious readers.

Next Spinoza proposes two definitions of miracles, a weak one and a strong one. The weak one (WM) runs as follows:"a miracle is a deed (*opus*) whose natural cause *we* (or the narrator) cannot explain by appeal to the example of some everyday thing".[14] (My emphasis). The strong definition (SM) is more restrictive: "a miracle is that whose cause can never be explained with reference to natural principles known to us by the natural light".[15]

WM is weak because it allows for something being miraculous to one person, but not to another. SM guarantees that an event is miraculous for one person only if it is miraculous for all.

Miracles of the weak sort obviously abound. WM allows us to describe as miraculous any event for which we have no explanation. And the existence of such things in no way contravenes the Miracle Axiom, MA. You or I may be unable to explain many events that are fully in agreement with nature's laws. We may simply be ignorant of the natural laws which were operating in bringing that event about.

The strong definition (SM) envisages the possibility of events that are beyond any human intellect to explain. But they do not for that reason become unnatural or supernatural events. Events that satisfied SM would in no way contradict the Miracle Axiom. Therefore miracles, as Spinoza defines them, are possible.

Possible, yes. But are there any miracles of the SM variety in fact? If so, they must be events of such subtlety, depth or complexity as to be beyond the scope of a human intellect. But Spinoza commits himself to the existence of such things when he reminds us that "nature is not confined by the laws of human reason ... but by an infinite number of others, which pertain to the eternal order of the whole of nature, of which man is but a small part".[16] More concretely, he implies that the establishment of the Jews in the Promised Land was miraculous[17] and states plainly that the apostles worked miracles when they established the Christian faith.[18] The purpose of the chapter on miracles is not to deny the existence of miracles at all, but only to explain what they are.

Someone might of course argue that to understand the force of Spinoza's attack on miracles, it must be contrasted with the traditional scholastic conception of them. What would St. Thomas, for example, say to Spinoza's Miracle Axiom, MA?

The surprising answer to that question is that St. Thomas would endorse it. He writes: "If the order of things is considered from the point of view of its primary cause, then God can do nothing against the order of natural things".[19] What Thomas means by the "primary cause" is of course God himself. He distinguished between "primary causality", which flowed out of God into his creatures, and "secondary causality", causal relations of creatures among themselves. In the light of this distinction, causal transactions wholly dependent on secondary (i.e., creaturely) causality would be called "natural". Those in which God, the primary cause, intervenes directly, would be called supernatural, or miraculous. On the Thomistic picture the natural order, that of secondary causes, functions for the most part autonomously. But its creator, the primary cause, is capable of intervening in it at his discretion. Such interventions are called miracles and may be divided into three grades depending on how much interference with secondary causes is necessary in order to bring them about.

The least remarkable miracles are those in which God merely hurries natural processes along, as in a speedy recovery from an illness. A higher grade of miracles are those in which natural processes are made to operate in unnatural places, as when the dead are brought back to life. It is not miraculous for new life to appear, but it is miraculous when it appears in people who have been dead. Most miraculous of all are those events in which wholly unnatural things are accomplished, as when two bodies are made to occupy the same place at the same time.[20]

The Thomistic conception of nature as a realm of "secondary causes" had about it an undeniable charm and is still most people's unofficial picture of how the world works. It sees the universe as an extended, inorganic structure housing a community of organic creatures, including plants, animals and human beings. These creatures possess characteristic powers some of which can be exercised or not at their discretion. And since they help compose the realm of secondary causes, they ensure that it is essentially unpredictable because of the latitude they enjoy in exercising their powers. The dog may or may not chase the rabbit; the rabbit may run or dive for his hole. The Thomistic world is far from the ideal of predictability sought in early modern physics. Future states of the world are not uniquely determinable on the basis of prior ones, even if God does not intervene. But since God could intervene, the realm of secondary causes is not even "closed", in the sense of being immune to interference from outside.

This scholastic picture of nature was rejected scornfully and *in toto* by Spinoza, as by all the other major modern philosophers with the exception of Leibniz[21]. They thought of nature more simply: as inanimate matter in motion. It is true that an echo of the doctrine of secondary causes exists in Spinoza's distinction between the causality of finite modes and that of God.[22] But finite modes have no spontaneity, no power that they can either exercise or not. They are not secondary causes in the scholastic sense.

Miracles do not go away just because the modern picture of the universe is adopted. They return in the form of purely epistemic notions. They no longer have to do with whether or not events have mechanical explanations – they always do. Whether something is a miracle or not depends on whether we human observers know what the explanation is. Miracles become fundamentally things which astonish *us*, just as they are in Spinoza's weak and strong definitions.

Once again, however, this would come as no surprise to St. Thomas. He traces the root of the word "miracle" to the original meaning of "admiration", namely "wonder". "It should be noted", he writes, "that the word 'miracle' derives from 'admiration'. But admiration arises when an effect is manifest, but the cause is hidden". And since what is hidden to one observer may be apparent to another, "something is a miracle to one that is not a miracle to another".[23] This is precisely the possibility for which Spinoza's weak definition of miracles, WM, allows.

If St. Thomas had become convinced that there was no realm of secondary causes in his sense, that is, if he had adopted the early modern conception of nature, he could still have preserved his theory of miracles. Lower grades of miracles would be explained as those events whose causes were unknown to us; higher grades would be explained as those which were unknowable by us. Had they agreed about nature St. Thomas and Spinoza would also have agreed about miracles.

Leibniz, who prided himself on his religious orthodoxy approaches miracles in a way little different from Spinoza's. Leibniz distinguishes between ordinary events which are in conformity with the "subalternate maxims of nature" and miraculous events, which are not. The latter, however, are still in conformity with what Leibniz calls the general order of things (*l'ordre général*).[24] Commenting on Spinoza in another place he says "I believe it is possible to reconcile miracles to philosophy, provided we understand miracles not as supernatural events, but as events that are above the nature of sensible bodies".[25] Whether Leibniz realizes it or not, he is merely adopting a version of Spinoza's own solution.

Leibniz leaves open the possibility of miracles occurring at any time. So do both Spinoza's Miracle Axiom and his strong and weak definitions. As a matter of personal belief, however, Spinoza seems to think that there have been no miracles (at least in the strong sense) since the apostolic age. But if that is his view he is doing no more than flashing his Reformation credentials.

"The gift of healing, like the rest of the miracles, which the Lord willed to be brought forth for a time, has vanished away in order to make the new preaching of the gospel marvellous forever", says Calvin.[26] He resented the fact that his Roman Catholic detractors reproached the reformers for their lack of miraculous confirmation. "In demanding miracles of us", Calvin writes, "they act dishonestly. For we are not forging some new gospel, but are retaining that very gospel whose truth all the miracles that Jesus Christ and his disciples ever wrought serve to confirm".[27] And Luther, in his commentary on Galations 4:6 says that the visible signs of the Holy Spirit ceased once the Church had been established and properly advertised by such miracles.

Of Spinoza's four goals in the miracle chapter only the first, that of showing that nothing happens contrary to nature, seemed likely to be in conflict with the common or scholastic view of miracles. But upon examination there turns out to be no conflict at all, not even when Spinoza's Miracle Axiom or his strong and weak definitions are added to the mix. The presumption of conflict derives from the many generations of readers who have approached Spinoza in the expectation of finding a refutation of miracles and allowed their expectation to shape their reading of the texts.

The Meaning of Scripture

The novelty of Spinoza's account of the meaning of Scripture was immediately noticed, and it received no more approval than had his treatment of miracles. It was denounced as harmful, vile, blasphemous, diabolical, and, of course, as atheistic.[28] But it was Leibniz, reading the TTP as soon as it appeared, who pronounced what can be said to have become the conventional understanding. The TTP, he says, contains criticisms whose tendency is to overthrow the Christian religion.[29]

Today's readers seem in basic agreement about both its novelty and its subversive tendency. David Savan calls Spinoza the founder of a new "scientific hermeneutics".[30] Harris and Sundberg, in their history of the historical-critical method of biblical exegesis, add an evaluative note that brings them close to Leibniz's view. They say that in the TTP for the first time "the Bible is treated like any other text. It is shorn of *a priori* religious authority."[31]

As with Spinoza's treatment of miracles so here: the dispassionate assessment of the TTP by recent scholars contrasts starkly with the apprehensive or even hysterical comments of many of its early readers. But the striking difference in tone from one generation to another does not alter the underlying agreement in substance. And any agreement of such longevity can profit from renewed scrutiny.

I shall argue that the conventional view is wrong about the relationship between Spinoza's hermeneutic and Christianity. Spinoza asserts rather than denies the Bible's a priori authority. Even Leibniz's usual acuteness may have deserted him when it came to Spinoza. His judgement that the TTP tends to undermine Christianity is only true if we suppose that he means by Christianity the various denominations and sects that were dominant in Spinoza's time and place. The TTP may well be calculated to undermine them, particularly their political pretensions, without threatening Christianity as such.

Those who take the conventional view will have trouble accounting for what Spinoza says near the beginning of the chapter on interpretation, where he castigates hermeneutical innovators:

> If men were serious in what they profess about Scripture, it would make a difference in the way they live ... They would not be gripped by so blind and rash a lust for interpreting Scripture and thinking up novelties in religion. On the contrary they would not dare to include among the teachings of Scripture anything that was not most clearly taught by it".[32]

It may be said of course that my interpretation of the TTP also raises a difficult question. If Spinoza's approach was as innocuous as I say, how has he come by his reputation for subversiveness? But that question is surprisingly easy to answer. Spinoza's notoriety among his Christian contemporaries of all denominations is comparable to that of Luther among Roman Catholics. When one attacks what people believe to be scriptural, one appears to be attacking Scripture. Strike at a denomination and the members of that denomination will judge it to be an assault on Christianity. The Church may seem to issue a blank cheque when it proclaims itself to be always in need of reformation (*semper reformanda*). But it never welcomes those who try to cash that cheque.

Spinoza incurred the wrath of the Reformed Church because he deployed its own weapons against it. They agreed that the meaning of Scripture ought not to be decided by appeal to tradition, without considering that they too had a tradition.

They also failed to perceive an important difference of focus. Spinoza's interest in the Scripture is for the most part epistemological rather than theological or pastoral. Priests may be concerned with what people ought to believe about Scripture; Spinoza is raising the Cartesian question of what they can know. And he is also trying to answer it in Cartesian style – through a *method* of interpretation. Few of Spinoza's contemporaries would have understood the methodology of the TTP. It is therefore not surprising that they mistook its intent.

The method Spinoza proposes is not simple. To know the meaning of a biblical text one must first establish what Spinoza calls its "history" (*historia*). This includes mastering as far as possible the original language and social context of the book in question, uncovering the links in its transmission and reception, and investigating the life of its author or authors. This history, if achieved, can furnish us with the doctrines which are "most univeral and the basis of all Scripture".[33]

In setting out the requirements for such a history, Spinoza does not imply that they can easily be met. The concrete conditions under which biblical scholars must operate may preclude the completion of a fully satisfactory history for any book of the Bible. For some books, particularly those of the Old Testament, it may be largely unachievable.

In the first place classical Hebrew was understood even less perfectly in Spinoza's day than it is today. Spinoza informs us that neither dictionaries nor grammars were available, a point that Spinoza took so seriously that he undertook to supply a Hebrew grammar. This lack of scholarly aids, together with the peculiar complexities of the Hebrew language and the ambiguities inherent in its classical written form, mean that Hebrew texts of any length will be replete with insoluble grammatical cruxes. Next, our biographical knowledge of the authors of some books may range downward from sketchy to non-existent. Finally, Spinoza says, we lack original language manuscripts of some books that seem to have come down to us only in Hebrew translation.[34]

Now even if in some cases histories could be established in a satisfactory way, they would not by themselves constitute interpretations. Completed histories do no more than mark the place where interpretations begin. But given the difficulty of establishing a history even in ideal conditions, together with the fact that conditions are never ideal, it can hardly come as a surprise that "in a number of places the true meaning of Scripture is unknown to us".[35]

The great Reformers, such as Luther and Calvin, knew no method of scriptural interpretation of comparable scientific sophistication. Yet if they could have learned of Spinoza's method, nothing would have prevented them from endorsing it. They would have shared Spinoza's interest in determining how great the gap is between our knowledge of a text's history and the original intention of the authors. But unlike Spinoza they would have been unconcerned, whatever the size of that gap turned out to be. They believed they had an intermediary capable of bridging the widest chasm. To fill the void between our deficient scholarly histories and the meaning of Scripture they would invoke the assistance of the Holy Spirit.[36]

For those who accept what Spinoza says about the limitation of our histories, it might seem that the only alternative to the doctrine of the Holy Spirit would be agnosticism about the meaning of Scripture. But Spinoza teaches a different lesson. It is possible to learn the meaning of parts of Scripture without supernatural assistance. The obstacles we face do not affect "those things which the intellect assents to and of which we may easily form a concept".[37] He means that there are some things which we can recognize as taught by the Bible because they are also confirmed by our own intelligence.

In so saying Spinoza is not making our intellect or our conceptual ability a measure of what the Scripture teaches. He means only that if his method detects a certain proposition as taught by Scripture, and our intellect concurs, then we may be sure that it is indeed scriptural. But on the other hand we cannot discount a candidate proposition, just because our intellect rejects it. Even passages flagrantly in defiance of reason might count as scriptural. "If we wish to know whether or not Moses believed God to be a fire, the matter cannot be decided by its congruity or incongruity with reason. The only way to decide it is by appeal to other stated opinions of Moses".[38] In other words, intellectual assent is proposed by Spinoza as a sufficient, but not as a necessary condition for recognizing a scriptural proposition as one of Scripture's authentic teachings.

On the other hand intellectual assent imposes no limit on what Christians may choose to believe about the meaning of a scriptural passage. If his critics had considered Spinoza more carefully they would have seen that his method did not put in peril any of their beliefs. He is only trying to circumscribe more narrowly what can be proclaimed as a dogma and supported by reference to the Bible. With an eye to the political dimension of religious belief, Spinoza is concerned with what faulty interpreters might impose on all people as dogma.

Spinoza's solution is that only those things can be affirmed dogmatically as universally obligatory which are susceptible of verification by his own exegetical method. This will include things not independently ascertainable by reason, but very few. What the Bible will mainly be found to teach is "doctrines (*documenta*) of true piety" and "things salutary and necessary for blessedness".[39] In the event, as will shortly be seen, Spinoza will reduce the revealed teachings of the Bible to one main axiom and its consequences.

Having outlined his own method of interpretation, and drawn some general conclusions from it, Spinoza briefly sketches and rejects two alternative approaches. To the first he attaches no name, but it is the generic outlook of the Reformation and would have been endorsed by the Reformed Church of Holland in Spinoza's day.[40] The second he calls after Maimonides, but there can be little doubt that the real referent was his friend Lodewijk Meyer, whose *Philosophia Sanctae Sripturae Interpres* (*Philosophy: the Interpreter of Holy Scripture*) had been published four years before the TTP and had often been attributed to Spinoza.[41] Not wishing to offend a friend, but wanting to distance himself from what he regarded as a wrong-headed method of Bible interpretation, Spinoza discussed it under another name.

The Reformed Church, following Calvin, appealed to the Holy Spirit or the "supernatural light" to close any gaps between what Scripture said and what they assumed it meant. The question Spinoza puts to them is a challenging one. If, as they also hold, such supernatural light is only granted to those who read with faith, must it not follow that only those who already believe can understand the Scripture? And if that is so, what would be the point of putting Bibles into the hands of unbelievers?

Rationalists, like Lodewijk Meyer do not have this problem. They make reason the arbiter of scriptural meaning. But Spinoza rejects Meyer's alternative as well and for motives any reformer would recognize and applaud. If reason is allowed to determine meaning a new priestly caste will be called into being. Ordinary people will once again be separated from that direct relationship with God on which the Reformation had insisted. They will not be able to understand the Bible but will require experts – philosophers – to interpret it for them. Unable to resist a touch of irony here, Spinoza points out that such a solution to problems of interpretation would require common people to treat philosophers as "incapable of error", which presumably surpasses even the vast gullibility with which Spinoza credits the uneducated.[42]

Spinoza's critique of the Reformed Church and that of Meyer do not amount to refutations and there is no reason to believe that Spinoza thought they did. What he is objecting to are rival *approaches* to the Bible, which cannot be dignified as methods, at least not when compared to the sophistication of the TTP. He therefore does no more than indicate some ways in which these approaches are deficient.

Spinoza takes the view that the message of the Scriptures is simple. It consists mainly of revealed moral truths that can also be known by the natural light, together with one in particular that can't. Like the first reformers Spinoza favours biblical literalism. The surface meaning of the text is assumed to be the true meaning unless weighty textual arguments can be made to the contrary. Literalism is the remedy for rash innovation in religion and untenable subtleties in interpretation. His motto is this: "Never accept as the doctrine of Scripture anything which is not very clearly taught by it".[43] Insofar as Spinoza's method leads to a view intermediate between Meyer's rationalism and the Reformed Church's pneumatology (reliance on the Holy Spirit) it may said to be a moderate doctrine.

He is also moderate in a second way. He has found a means of recognizing religious dogmas without giving way to dogmatism. Spinoza's conception of religion certainly includes dogma. His method entitles us to affirm a number of general religious truths all of which derive from one that is revealed. About these we may be dogmatic, as he will show in Chapters 14 and 15. About the rest we ought to exhibit restraint in endorsing them and tolerance toward those who do not. But it is not dogmatism to claim to know what we know.

Dogmatic claims are opinions asserted as undeniable truths. The Church Fathers may have been over-dogmatic in asserting the sometimes fanciful interpretations they derived from the Bible by applying their fourfold method of interpretation.[44] Likewise, Protestants who claimed to know propositions by the intervention of the Holy Spirit may have illegitimately asserted them as dogmas. But since Spinoza's method is scientific, any dogmas it established could be asserted with the same confidence as the findings of any other science would be.

Meyer's rationalism is also a form of dogmatism, though a negative one. Its proponents are prepared to reject bona fide revelation, if it does not agree with the pronouncements of their reason. Like pneumatology, rationalism invites Bible readers to unwarranted dogmatism. Spinoza's method alone restrains them. That is how it can both allow for dogma and yet not be dogmatic.

Avoiding dogmatism is very good, but it is not sufficient by itself to make one moderate. There are, after all, immoderate ways of avoiding dogmatism. Spinoza would not qualify as moderate if, to escape dogmatism, he had taken refuge in its opposite, scepticism. But the dogmatic basis he supplies for religion, which will be discussed in detail in the next chapter, is proof that Spinoza is not a sceptic. In this respect also then, he is moderate.

There is a third aspect to his moderation. Spinoza can be accused neither of unbelief nor fanaticism. If the only dogmas admissible in what he calls "true religion" were those knowable by unaided reason, he might be suspected of thinking their biblical origin inessential. But the Bible is more important to Spinoza than that. He allows for at least one fundamental article that cannot be derived from reason, but depends on Scripture alone, namely "that simple obedience is sufficient for beatitude" and "leads to salvation".[45] But he goes further. He acknowledges as dogma whatever can be validly deduced (*legitime possunt deduci*) from that assumption.[46]

Of the fundamental principle itself, however, Spinoza says there can be no mathematical (i.e., logically compelling) demonstration. Why then should we believe it at all? Spinoza's answer is that we can have what he calls "moral certainty" about the efficacy of obedience. He elaborates as follows:

One would have to be stupid not to embrace what is confirmed by so much prophetic testimony, what is so great a consolation to those who are weak in reason, what is to the state of no small utility, and what can be believed without danger or damnation, for the sole reason that it could not be demonstrated mathematically. As if nothing should be admitted as true in wisely ordering our life unless no reason for doubting could ever cast doubt upon it. Or as if many of our actions were not uncertain and full of contingency.[47]

The subtle combination of epistemological and pragmatic justifications for this principle has been the object of intense study.[48] But even a casual reader can see that no one who endorses as dogmas propositions he admits to be logically contingent can be accused of unbelief. Yet Spinoza is not fanatical either, since he bases his acceptance of the dogmas on what he thinks is such reasonable evidence that it would be a lapse of reason to reject any of them.

Finally, Spinoza can rightly see himself as a moderate interpreter of the Bible. On the one hand there are Roman Catholics who interpret the Bible in the light of their long and distinguished tradition of interpretation. On the other hand are the great reformers who impute no authority to that tradition, vesting all authority instead in the guidance provided by the Holy Spirit. And Meyer occupies a third position, claiming that reason is both sufficient and necessary as an authority.

According to Spinoza all three of these approaches to interpreting Scripture are too extreme. The first two mistakenly introduce something contingent (not even morally necessary) into their interpretations – tradition in the case of the Roman Catholics; subjectivity in the case of the reformers. Meyer's error lies in making the Bible irrelevant. Since reason is both sufficient and necessary, the consultation of the Bible becomes an unnecessary step in knowing the will of God. Spinoza acknowledges the Bible without exalting either tradition or subjectivity.

The point upon which both his seventeenth century detractors and his present day admirers largely agree is that Spinoza, in applying his method, undermined the authority of the Bible. But there are several good reasons for contesting this claim. It is true that the hermeneutical method Spinoza proposes confines itself mainly to what can be corroborated by reason. But that is because of the difficulties in knowing the exact meaning of what the Bible says, not because that meaning, when known, should be doubted. On the contrary when the meaning of Scripture is known, as Spinoza says above, "one would have to be stupid not to embrace it". Everything he says in Chapter 7 and throughout the TTP attributes to the Bible precisely the "a priori religious authority" Harris and Sundberg accuse him of abolishing. He does reject unwarranted dogmatic inferences from the Bible, but that puts him in the company of all religious reformers.

If the argument of this chapter has been correct, Spinoza must be understood as a reformer, rather than as a foe of Christianity. Abundant further evidence of this interpretation is provided by Chapter 14 of the TTP, which will be the subject of the next chapter.

Notes

1 Akkerman and Hubbeling [1979], 135, 133.
2 Israel [2001], 218.
3 E.E. Harris [1992], *Spinozas's Philosophy: An Outline*, Atlantic Highlands, N.J./London: Humanities Press, 1992, p. 111.
4 Spinoza [1991], xv.
5 Walther [1994], 100f.
6 Walther [1994], 102.
7 Walther [1994], 103.
8 Strauss [1965], 129. The passage Strauss is referring to is found at Spinoza [1925] 3, 91 = TTP, 6.
9 Strauss [1965], 136.
10 Spinoza [1925] 3, 82 = TTP 6: "Ex aliquot Scripturae exemplis ostendam ipsam Scripturam per Dei decreta et volitiones, et consequenter providentiam nihil alium intelligere quam ipsum naturae ordinem, qui ex ejus aeternis legibus necessario sequitur".
11 Spinoza [1925] 3, 81 = TTP 6.
12 Spinoza [1925] 3, 82 = TTP 6.
13 Spinoza [1925] 3, 83 = TTP 6.
14 Spinoza [1925] 3, 84 = TTP 6.
15 Spinoza [1925] 3, 84 = TTP 6.
16 Spinoza [1925] 3, 190f = TTP 16.
17 Spinoza [1925] 3, 47 = TTP 3.
18 Spinoza [1925] 3, 233 = TTP 19.
19 *Summa Theologica* I, q105, a6, resp.
20 *Summa Theologica* I, q105, a8, resp.
21 See "Leibniz and Secondary Causes", in *Leibniz: Tradition und Aktualität. Proceedings of the V. International Leibniz Congress* Hanover: Leibniz-Gesellschaft, 1988, 374-380.
22 See 1Ep16 and corollaries, 1Ep33 and 2Ep9.
23 *Summa Theologica* I, q105, a7, resp.
24 Leibniz [1978] 2, 12.
25 Leibniz [1978] 1, 124.
26 Calvin [1960] 2, 1467.
27 Calvin [1960] 1, 16.
28 Spinoza [1991], vii.
29 Leibniz [1970] *Sämtliche Schriften und Briefe* Reihe 1, vol. 1, p. 148. Hildesheim: Olms.
30 Savan [1986], 97.

31   Harrisville and Sundberg, [1995], 44.
32   Spinoza [1925], 97 = TTP 7.
33   Spinoza [1925] 3, 102 = TTP 7
34   Spinoza [1925] 3, 108-110 = TTP 7
35   Spinoza [1925] 3, 111 = TTP, 7.
36   Cf. Harrisville and Sundberg [1995], 18, 20f.
37   Spinoza [1925] 3, 111 = TTP, 7.
38   Spinoza [1925] 3, 100f = TTP, 7.
39   Spinoza [1925] 3, 111 = TTP, 7.
40   See Malet [1966], 190, note 1.
41   As Edwin Curley suggests [1994], 78.
42   Spinoza [1925] 3, 114 = TTP 7.
43   Spinoza [1925] 3, 97 = TTP 7.
44   See e.g., Thomas Aquinas, *Summa Theologica* I, q1, a10.
45   Spinoza [1925] 3, 184, 188 = TTP 15.
46   Spinoza [1925] 3, 175 = TTP 14.
47   Spinoza [1925] 3, 187 = TTP 15.
48   See Mathéron [1971], Chapter 4.

Chapter Six

Christian Pluralism

In Chapter 14 of the TTP Spinoza brings to the forefront his concern with the Christian Church, and how to reform it:

> The many dissensions in the Church (*tot dissensiones in Ecclesia*) oblige me to show, even though it is most obvious (*manifestissimum*), how from the foundation already laid bare [i.e., obedience as the love of neighbour] all the dogmas of the faith (*fidei dogmata*) can be discovered.[1]

The fact that the word "Church" is written with a capital "C" is in keeping with the longstanding convention of capitalizing it when it is meant as the proper name of the Holy Catholic Church, that is of the body of all believers spread through the various denominations and around the world. However, no important inference could be based on so small a point, especially when the TTP's most recent editors have concluded that capitalization is an unreliable guide to Spinoza's intentions.[2]

But in this case, whether or not capitalization indicates the presence of a proper name, the context demands it. There can be no mystery about which church it was that suffered from the "dissensions" Spinoza is proposing to heal. In the opening pages of the TTP's preface, he indicated that he would be criticizing "men who style themselves Christians" yet who "daily struggle with one another in the most bitter hate".[3] He could hardly address that problem by discussing any other church or faith or by discussing church or faith in abstract terms.

Finally, Spinoza could not reasonably expect those of faiths other than Judaism and Christianity to be much impressed by dogmas derived, as are those he will present in this chapter, from the Old and New Testaments. And it is doubtful that there were many Jews so liberal in their outlook that they would tolerate the normative role played by the New Testament in these derivations. I shall therefore take the question of what religion Spinoza means to reform in Chapter 14 to be settled.

In Chapter 14 Spinoza sets out to answer one of the questions that tore apart the seventeenth century Christian Church: how much is it necessary to believe in order to be Christian? Spinoza will put forward a subtle answer which, if it had been accepted, would indeed have ended the hostilities in the Church to which it was addressed.

Although Spinoza's proposal for religious peace went unheeded Chapter 14 remains of capital importance for understanding what that proposal was. It contains, Spinoza says, the main points he intended to establish in the TTP.[4] It would also be a mistake to assume that because the particular sectarian disagreements Spinoza was addressing are largely forgotten, the solution he proposed must itself be obsolete. Spinoza was alive to the deepest aspects of his subject and their ramifications extended far beyond his particular time and place. His proposal may still have something to teach us about how to face the clash of world religions today, or to work out a basis for multiculturalism.

When groups of people are living together in unbearable tension, there are, generally speaking, only three possible remedies. A given group can flee the situation; it can fight its rivals, with the purpose of annihilating or at least subduing them; or it can compromise with them.

All three responses were tried by different Christian sects during the sixteenth and early seventeenth centuries. There were wars of Roman Catholics against Protestants and Protestants against each other. Some religious communities fled Europe in order to live in peace. But there were also thoughtful individuals in different confessions who began to understand the advantages that might come from compromise.

The challenge of compromise lay in the difficulty of finding a way for religious communities with incompatible but deeply held beliefs to coexist. Spinoza's proposal involved defining first a core of beliefs to which all parties agree (*fundamentalia*, as he sometimes calls them). That core should be as small as possible. Next, he would try to stretch the limits of religious freedom to admit as much as possible of what transcended core beliefs without contradicting them.[5] A minimum of dogma, a maximum of freedom: that is the basic recipe. However it is very basic, really little more than an acknowledgement of what peaceful coexistence logically entails. It is not surprising, therefore, that others had come up with versions of it before Spinoza, even if they had not articulated it with the same clarity.

Jaroslav Pelikan, in his study of the early modern period and the many "reformations of church and dogma" it proposed, cites one of Spinoza's predecessors in irenic theology, the Lutheran divine Georg Calixtus (1586-1656). Pelikan describes his work as the period's "most noteworthy doctrinal consideration of the question of unity". Calixtus had sought to foster Church unity by returning to the "consensus of the first five centuries" that culminated in the Apostles' Creed, on the assumption that every form of worship compatible with the Creed could then be tolerated.[6]

Spinoza's advantage over Calixtus and other ecumenists lies in his method. Calixtus' approach to the sectarian problem is theological and historical, following the received paradigm of his age.[7] Spinoza's sharply different approach is scientific, logical and analytic. By the scientific method of determining the meaning of Scripture, which Spinoza develops in Chapter 7 of the TTP, he discovers the Bible's fundamental revealed teaching on obedience. Taking that teaching as axiomatic, he then uses logical analysis to identify a set of consequences which will be jointly sufficient to define the Christian faith and severally necessary to it.[8] These he will call the dogmas of the faith. The result is an epitome of Christianity which, if accepted, would be maximally tolerant, enabling the greatest number of different sects to recognize one another as Christians.

Spinoza's scientific and logical approach was superior to Calixtus' in the way rationalism sometimes is to empiricism. Where Calixtus' solution took for granted a good deal of the religious agreement it was supposed to guarantee, Spinoza's was more economical in its assumptions and therefore in theory more generally acceptable. Where history supplied Calixtus' fundamental dogmas, Spinoza's were guaranteed by logic. They were derived rigorously from a teaching that could be scientifically demonstrated to belong to the Christian faith.

Rationalism, so excellent in theory, is sometimes less successful in practice, however. In practice people may prefer the familiar, no matter how many questions it begs, to the logical minimum which takes nothing for granted yet has the appearance of novelty. This predilection for what we know is no doubt part of the reason why Spinoza's solution won so few converts among religious people and continues to be perceived as subversive by many scholars today. To appreciate the depth and subtlety of what Spinoza proposed it is necessary to look at it in some detail.

The first thing to note is that Spinoza does not use logic as deists do, who try to derive their dogmas from human reason alone. He bluntly tells his friend and correspondent Jakob Ostens that he considers deism to be false.[9] Spinoza's proposal is not deism because he puts a revealed teaching at its core, the very thing that deism rejects. Spinoza's dogmas are indebted to human reasoning only insofar as they are logically derived from a primordial revelation. The brief text of that revelation, already discussed in the previous chapter of this book, is that salvation can be won through obedience to God.

From that revealed truth, or at least from a version of it, Spinoza derives by logical analysis seven "fundamentals" or "dogmas". These are what he will propose as the basic Christian creed. They are assertions covering the matters to which all Christians are logically obliged to give their assent. Beyond them of course lie optional beliefs that Christians may or may not hold, because they are neither entailed nor excluded by the seven dogmas. The technical name for inessentials of this kind is adiaphora. To affirm or deny adiaphora may determine one's membership in a particular Christian sect, but it does not make one more or less a Christian. Spinoza goes on to consider a number of adiaphora immediately after presenting his dogmas.

There is in principle no limit to the number of adiaphora there can be, since they could potentially include any religious proposition that is neither a dogma nor in conflict with a dogma. Spinoza is fully aware that the ones he discusses are merely examples.[10] But he has good reasons for choosing to discuss the ones he does, as will be seen below.

Sects and Heresies

The first step Spinoza takes toward his prescription for religious toleration is to give a clear account of the origin of militant sectarianism and the polemical use of the term "heresy". They result, Spinoza says, from an undisciplined search for the official teachings (*documenta fidei*) of Scripture. He might have said, less modestly, that they result from theologians having attempted to read the Scriptures without the benefit of the scientific method of interpretation Spinoza develops in the TTP. Unskilled readers (*vulgi*) come nowhere near the standard set by such a scientific approach to Scripture. They are content to impose human inventions and whims (*commenta et placita*) as truths upon believers.[11]

Objectionable and dangerous sects arise when large groups of people embrace such unfounded doctrines. Sectarianism of this kind is superstitious and that is bad enough in itself. But it is worse when those who accept these figments brand as heretics those who do not.

Spinoza does not offer a definition of what he means by heresy and sectarianism, but it is not difficult to supply an appropriate one, provided we recall the limitations definitions always have. They inform the user of what distinguishing marks will characterize all the individuals that fall under them, but no definition can equip the user to recognize those distinguishing marks. That is the work of human judgement and even the best definition cannot guarantee that those who know it will apply it properly. Reformation history is filled with examples in which A's sect can be B's heresy. Indeed that is a part of the problem Spinoza is addressing. But the disagreement of A and B is at the level of judgement rather than definition. They can agree on what it would be like for something to be a heresy or a sect.

Sectarian beliefs, then, can be defined as those which Christians may receive or reject and still be Christians. Heretical ones would be those which all Christians must reject in order to remain Christians.[12]

Strictly speaking these definitions leave it open whether or not there is a core of positive Christian belief, neither sectarian nor heretical, a core that all Christians must embrace. Spinoza will argue that there is and his seven dogmas are meant to be a sufficient statement of it.

Because core Christian dogmas are not a requirement of logic alone, it is significant that Spinoza includes them in the TTP. If there were none, there would be no positive criterion for calling oneself a Christian and any appearance of Christian commitments in the TTP would only be a facade. However Spinoza's insistence on the seven dogmas shows that minimalistic Christianity of the TTP is no facade.

The fact that there are core Christian dogmas also helps to illuminate Spinoza's understanding of the nature of sectarianism. Sects arise when people embrace adiaphora in addition to dogma. As already mentioned some adiaphora are based on human invention and whims. They are superstitious and objectionable. But not all adiaphora are that way and sects need not be so. They may arise from the deep human will to believe and Spinoza, far from condemning it, actually encourages it: "Each man is expected", Spinoza says, "to adapt the faith to his own opinions".[13] This he clarifies as follows: "I do not accuse sectarians (*sectarios*) of impiety when they adapt Scripture to their own opinions, but only when they do not wish to extend the same liberty to others".[14] Thus sectarianism is wrong when it tries to impose its distinctive teachings on those unwilling to accept them.

It is not hard to see the danger in sectarian militancy. First, many propositions stated in the Bible are unsuitable for being made into doctrines. Consider, for example, the recorded utterances of the Devil. To venerate words simply because they come from the Bible, without any scientific proof of their being meant by it as doctrines, runs the risk of being superstitious. To force such beliefs on others is, in addition, odious.

Sects can also go wrong by mistaking adiaphora for dogma. The adiaphorous teachings in favour with a given sect may be right, but because they cannot be scientifically proven from the Bible, none should be imposed. The sectarian error is really the mirror image of the heretical one. Sects make adiaphora into dogma; heresies make dogmas into adiaphora, either by dismissing what are properly dogmas or by embracing teachings incompatible with them. The way to overcome both sectarianism and heresy is therefore to make the true dogmatic basis of the Christian faith clear. That is why Spinoza demonstrates his seven dogmas and surrounds the demonstrations with affirmations of their importance.

As mentioned above, what distinguishes Spinoza's treatment of Christianity from deism is that Spinoza begins with revelation. He has discovered a unique moral teaching which can be scientifically documented as Biblical, using his method of scriptural interpretation. In Chapter 14 he expresses that teaching in these words: "The highest purpose of the whole of Scripture" – by which Spinoza means, as he later adds, both Testaments – "is to teach obedience".[15] In other places, as has already been seen, Spinoza describes the revelation of the Bible more fully, as including the fact that salvation arises through obedience and that obedience involves works of kindness to other people. Here he is more concise, probably because he wishes to present those supplementary properties of obedience as deducible from the core revelation presented here: namely that Christians must obey God. I shall call it in its concise form the Obedience Axiom (OA).

Because it is not derived from reason alone OA does not possess the mathematical certainty it would have if it were. But, as discussed in the previous chapter of this book, it nevertheless retains the high degree of probability that Spinoza calls moral certainty.[16] As it happens OA is also very fruitful, in that it entails a number of other propositions, both practical and theoretical. Logical analysis will reveal that the consequences of OA include all the fundamentals of what must be believed (*fides ejusque fundamentalia*), if one is to be a Christian.[17]

Before he names and proves the seven dogmas entailed by OA, Spinoza wants to clarify its connection to the proper Christian conception of faith and practical life. Although for present purposes the dogmas are of greater interest, there are two reasons for following Spinoza patiently through this detour. First, he uses it to establish the contextual meaning of OA in a way that permits him later to deduce his seven dogmas with greater ease. Secondly, two of the practical consequences he deduces make it possible to clear up in advance certain misunderstandings of the dogmas that have occurred in the secondary literature.

From Obedience to Faith

There is some variability in how Spinoza spells out OA's practical implications. On occasion he will say that the chief law of Scripture is to "love God above all things and your neighbour as yourself". In other places he will shorten the command to only love of neighbour.[18] These discrepancies are reconciled, however, when Spinoza says that the worship of God and obedience to him consist only in justice and charity or love toward one's neighbour.[19]

Such semantic looseness is not a departure from orthodox Christian teachings, but an echo of them. The same inconsistency is found in the New Testament and is there resolved in precisely the same way, most famously when Jesus says that in the last judgement service to one's neighbour will be reckoned as equivalent to service to God.[20] OA charges Christians with believing and doing whatever is necessary for exhibiting this neighbourly love (charity).[21]

Scripture may of course excite us to believe and do many things in excess of what it *requires* of us. But Spinoza's concern here is only with what is required. His minimalist focus and practical emphasis carry over into the definition of Christian faith he proposes. Christians, he says, must "have such sentiments (*talia sentire*) as necessarily produce obedience to God when they are present and destroy it when they are absent".[22] Texts from the apostles James and John are then cited to confirm this.

There is a direct, clear connection between the obedience this definition enjoins and the works of charity we are to perform. The emphasis on works is recurrent because it expresses one of Spinoza's bedrock convictions. In Chapter 1 it was noted in connection with Spinoza's continuing friendship with Juan de Prado, after Prado's excommunication, contrasting sharply with the formalistic treatment Prado received from his other friend, Orobio de Castro. In Chapter 4 the same disposition appeared again in Spinoza's clear preference for the teachings of the apostle James over those of St. Paul, when it came to the relative value of faith and works. The same conviction accounts for Spinoza's characteristic definition of piety in Chapter 13 of the TTP:

> The piety or impiety of opinions cannot be determined by considering them in themselves, apart from works. The only reason for saying that a man's belief is pious or impious is the degree to which he is either moved by it to obedience or licenced by it to sin and rebellion. This is so much the case that if believing a truth causes someone to be obstinate, then his faith is impious, and it is pious if it makes him obedient, even though it be based on a false belief.[23]

The definition of faith proposed here is so obviously a consequence of what has already been established, Spinoza says, that it needs no comment. But Spinoza is far from thinking that the definition exhausts what can be said about Christian faith. On the contrary it is intended to be minimalistic. Christians will believe by faith a good deal in addition to what it teaches. The function of Spinoza's definition of faith is to allow Christians to disagree on the greatest possible number of subjects. Its success as a definition depends only on its ability to capture those beliefs that must be accepted and exclude any that are incompatible with them.

From Faith to Practical Life

Satisfied that the definition he has proposed of Christian faith has been properly derived from OA, Spinoza is now ready to deduce five practical implications from it. Of these the first three require no comment, for they merely reinforce the connection between faith and good works.[24]

The fourth consequence, however, is more significant. It states that the real antichrists are those who persecute upright and justice-loving men on the grounds that the latter disagree with them on principles touching faith.[25] What Spinoza has in mind is the offence discussed earlier, in which sectarians attempt to force on other people the adiaphorous beliefs which distinguish their sect, but for which there is no compelling proof.

The interesting question however is whether this critique of religious dogmatism can be extended to include even the seven dogmas Spinoza will later derive logically from OA. Would the attempt to force *them* on someone who did not agree also qualify the enforcer as an antichrist? No matter which way Spinoza answers, it will be in tension with other things he wants to say. If coercion is disallowed the importance of the seven dogmas is lost – they are reduced to the status of adiaphora. But if they can be coercively imposed, it seems to limit Spinoza's religious tolerance.

Neither answer may be wholly pleasing, but it is at least clear which one represents Spinoza's opinion. In the first place he would say that one can legitimately employ the power of the state to encourage, and sometimes even to enforce, belief in the seven dogmas. But he would deny that this places him among the antichrists, because he would say that it does not constitute persecution of upright and justice-loving men. What would account for his taking these positions?

Spinoza never deals explicitly in the TTP with the question of whether it would ever be right to coerce people into accepting the seven dogmas. But elsewhere he reveals why he did not. In his unfinished work, *Tractatus Politicus*, he writes:

About religion we went on at sufficient length in the *Tractatus Theologico-Politicus*. However we omitted certain matters which did not need to be discussed there. Chiefly, that all patricians must be of the same religion, namely a very simple and supremely Catholic (*maxime Catholica*) one such as we described in that treatise. For above all it is to be feared that patricians become sectarian, one showing favour to one group, another to others until at last, a prey to superstition, they strive to limit the freedom of their subjects to say what they feel.[26]

Spinoza supplies a plausible reason here for forcing the patricians to uphold the seven dogmas: only the dogmas provide for unity of religion in a way that is consistent with the greatest freedom. If no restriction were placed on the sects to which patricians were permitted to belong, they might end up using their political power to impose the adiaphora of superstitious sects on the people they rule. If that happened the combination of true piety, freedom and peace which the TTP has set out to prove achievable would become impossible. Therefore patricians must only be permitted to belong to tolerant sects, those whose dogmatic basis does not exceed the seven dogmas.

Immediately following the passage just cited Spinoza continues in the same vein, outlining what the state should do with religions that do not subscribe to the seven dogmas at all – that is, with non-Christian religions. He suggests that they be tolerated, but only as long as they remain politically marginal.

Thus there are clear limits to the religious diversity Spinoza is prepared to tolerate. But he can still argue that the religious constraint he allows falls short of persecution. The "antichrists" he denounces are fanatics who persecute "upright and justice-loving men". But the just and upright, if they are Christians, do not deny the seven dogmas, since these contain "nothing upright men could quarrel about".[27]

People who are neither Christians nor Jews may deny the dogmas of course, but if they do there might be prudential grounds for a Christian state to marginalize them. The dogmas are logically derived from the exhortation to act obediently, and therefore in charity to one another. Those who deny them are thus a danger, not because they are not Christian, but because they do not agree to act in a way that favours the type of inclusive community Spinoza is hoping to build. Moreover his intolerance toward them is only slight. It goes only as far as assuring that they do not attain such power that they would be able to divert the state from its tolerant Christianity. One cannot reproach Spinoza for intolerance unless one is also prepared to criticize the intolerance of political liberals toward extremists who would upset the liberal order.

Spinoza can therefore escape the charge of being himself an antichrist. A small amount of coercion is necessary in order to give the seven dogmas a favourable place in society. There is even mild religious repression. But the enforcers of it are not persecutors of just and upright men, and therefore no antichrists – at least, not in Spinoza's eyes.

The fifth practical consequence of the definition of Christian faith also contains some important lessons. Spinoza says that faith does not so much require true dogmas, as pious ones, dogmas which move the soul to obedience.[28] Once again it is essential to ask whether Spinoza means to include in that statement even the seven dogmas he is about to derive. If so, it would seem to empty Christianity of all content, since none of it would have to be true.

Some have taken this to be exactly Spinoza's meaning. For example Seymour Feldman writes: "Spinoza makes clear that these seven principles of the universal religion, which define faith, need not be literally true".[29] However there are four good reasons why Spinoza must regard the dogmas as true.

First, because right after the derivation of consequence five Spinoza says that if anyone were to embrace as dogmas propositions he knew to be false "he would necessarily be a rebel. For how could anyone who loved justice and sought to please God worship as divine what he knew to be alien from the divine nature"?[30] Secondly, Spinoza wants to make these dogmas "universal",[31] which surely means non-optional. Thirdly, each of the dogmas is meant to be a logical consequence of the principle of obedience, which itself is morally certain. Logic demands therefore that they also be morally certain. Finally, Spinoza claims that his dogmas will leave no room for controversies in the Church.[32] This boast could hardly be made of dogmas that need not be true. Thus we are safe in thinking that only adiaphora are such that they need not be true.

The Seven Dogmas

These five reflections on faith and practice play an important role in the transition to the seven dogmas. First, they assist the reader in understanding some of what is entailed by OA. In its austere form the bare proposition that God must be obeyed would not seem capable of generating the complete dogmatic structure necessary for Christian faith. Therefore in amplifying it before beginning his deductions Spinoza is following the requirements of demonstration, which he knows so well from his simultaneous work on the

Ethics. The trick of demonstration, as Spinoza understands it, lies in finding the proper order. You must establish first whatever you will need to draw on later.

That being said, it must be acknowledged that the TTP does not attempt to rival the *Ethics* in demonstrative rigour. In the TTP the proofs are usually left sketchy, as the first dogma illustrates:

> God exists, that is a supreme being, perfectly just and merciful, which is to say an exemplar of true life. Whoever does not believe that he exists cannot obey him nor acknowledge him as judge.[33]

The point of Dogma 1 is not to prove God's existence from first principles, as the first sentence might suggest. He is not looking for the kind of proof he will construct at the beginning of the *Ethics*. Here the goal is only to show the connection between accepting the Obedience Axiom and recognizing the existence of a God. The proof sentence offered (sentence two of the quoted passage) makes this clear. It points out that belief in the existence of God is a precondition of obeying him or acknowledging him as judge.

The same pattern of proposition and proof is found in the second dogma, except that the reason for accepting the dogma is given in more detail:

> God is unique. For no one can doubt that uniqueness is absolutely required by the supreme devotion, admiration and love we owe to God. For devotion, admiration and love arise solely from the singular excellence of one above the rest.

Next Spinoza shows that "God is everywhere present and everything is manifest to him". For this dogma he offers the following indirect proof:

> If we believed there were things that eluded him, or if we did not know that he sees all things, then we might have doubts about the fairness of the justice with which he regulates everything. We might not even recognize his justice at all.

The structure of this proof is unusual. Spinoza focuses on the moral dimension of God's ubiquity and all-seeing character. The moral governance of the universe can only depend on him if he sees things correctly. Otherwise there would be room for doubt about his justice. The connection to OA is unstated, presumably because Spinoza thought it obvious. If we suspected

God's right to be called just, reason could reject the revealed claim that we owe him a debt of obedience. However, since OA is by hypothesis true, God must be ubiquitous and all-seeing.

The fourth dogma runs as follows: "God has supreme right and dominion in all things; he is forced to do nothing but always acts by his absolute good pleasure and singular grace. For all are bound to obey him; while he himself is bound to obey no one". Here, as in Dogma 1, the proof is laconic, limited to what is essential. It adds to OA the complement that the obligation to obedience is ours and only ours. God himself has none. This is understood, but not explicitly stated in OA. Once it is made explicit, Dogma 4 is proven.

Dogma 5 requires no proof and none is offered, for it is simply a version of OA itself, as understood in the light of the practical consequences deduced from it above. It states that "worship of God consists in justice and charity or love of neighbour".

The sixth dogma once again requires proof. It says: "All who obey God by living in obedience are saved. The rest however, who live under pleasure's sway, are lost".[34] Spinoza offers the following consideration as proof: "If men did not firmly believe this dogma, there would be no reason why they should submit to God rather than to their own desires". Once again the unstated premise is that OA is certain and therefore that men must submit to God rather than to their own desires. That being the case, however, Dogma 6 must be true.

The reader who is familiar with Spinoza's other writings may already have noted points of dissonance between them and these dogmas. In the final dogma tensions of that kind become almost impossible to overlook. It states that "God forgives the sins of those who repent". Dogma 7 seems then to recommend repentance, whereas in the *Ethics* Spinoza categorically declares it not to be a virtue.[35] Given the strong inclination that exists among contemporary readers of Spinoza to treat the *Ethics* as the canonical text, one can understand the temptation that arises to view this dogma – and if this one, why not the others as well? – as concessions to unenlightened Christian readers.[36] But those who yield to this temptation will have even more to explain away when Spinoza comes to the dogma's proof:

> For there is no one who does not sin. Therefore if anyone were not convinced of this dogma he would despair, nor would he have any reason to believe in God's mercy. On the other hand anyone who firmly believes that God forgives sin by the mercy and grace with which he directs all things truly knows Christ according to the spirit and; Christ is in him.

No comparable discussion of sin, mercy, forgiveness and grace can be found in the *Ethics*. That such seemingly eccentric passages should occur right at this point in the TTP raises a serious question about interpreting Spinoza. These seven dogmas are the focus of Chapter 14 and Chapter 14 is the centrepiece of the TTP. A reader who made his first acquaintance with Spinoza's thought through the TTP could hardly fail to notice its distinctly Christian dimension, though sectarian Christians would likely judge it unorthodox or even heretical. And yet the idea that Spinoza might have been advocating any type of Christian thought barely registers in the secondary literature. Why?

To that intriguing historical question I offer this answer: even careful readers have been systematically prejudiced against such a reading, though not always wilfully so and not always by the same things. To trace the development of this prejudice would be in itself a worthwhile study in historiography, but it would also be long, complex and different from what is here intended. A brief outline can however be given without difficulty.

Seventeenth century readers were frequently prejudiced against the Christian dimension of Spinoza's philosophy by their own sectarianism. In an age in which Leibnizian ecumenism earned for that philosopher the Low German nickname of "Lövenix" ("believes nothing"), Protestant leanings as radical as Spinoza's were easily seen as atheistic and antithetical to Christianity in general. Christians of an undogmatic turn of mind, however – men like Jarig Jelles – had no difficulty in acknowledging the Christian dimension in Spinoza's writing.

In the Enlightenment many influential readers allowed their own hostility to Christianity to prejudice them. It taught them to read Spinoza between the lines, in order to see him as one of themselves.

> Via an amazing process of transmogrification, no sooner was [Spinoza] dead than he became a cult figure, a secular 'saint' and an object of hagiography in the eyes of disciples and followers, some of whom initiated a deliberate campaign to heroicize his image, deeming this an effectual means of advancing the radical intellectual program to which they were committed.[37]

Readers today are often prejudiced for another reason. They read the TTP as none of its original readers could – in the light of the *Ethics*. The status they attribute to that later work, in which explicitly Christian turns of phrase are rare, leads them to discount the TTP in places where the two works appear to be in conflict. And since this prejudice agrees in its outcome with earlier ones, a spurious sense of historical consensus arises that seems to preclude acknowledging the radical Christian dimension of Spinoza's thought.

It would help to have an example of this contemporary prejudice at work. The best one for present purposes is the otherwise irreproachable investigation of the Christian dimension of Spinoza's work by Alexandre Matheron: *Le Christ et le salut des ignorants*. Matheron is consistently and conscientiously faithful to the *prima facie* sense of the TTP, and exemplary in his command of the text of both it and the *Ethics*. But his exposition of the TTP is weakened on those occasions when he presents it as only a deficient form of what is stated more exactly in the *Ethics*. In his account of Spinoza's seven dogmas, for example, he treats them as popularizations of a moral philosophy contained in its definitive form in the *Ethics*. He will sometimes depict the *TTP* as tolerating less rigorous statements of religious principles suitable to the understanding of non-philosophers, whom he refers to, following Spinoza, as "the ignorant".

> Each of the seven dogmas, taken in its true sense, refers back to a proposition or to a group of propositions from the *Ethics*. Let us go further: the set of these propositions and groups of propositions constitutes an exhaustive summary of the theoretical foundations of Spinoza's moral philosophy. Let us go further still: each of these foundations, taken in itself entails according to Spinoza the same consequences as the article corresponding to it entails for the ignorant.[38]

Matheron argues plausibly that the seven dogmas can be aligned with like-minded doctrines from the *Ethics*. The seventh dogma is the most resistant to this treatment, though even here the connections Matheron makes are plausible ones. It is not outrageous to connect Dogma 7 with the doctrine that the idea of God as it exists objectively in our souls can be understood to free us from our sins in the sense that it rescues us from the passions on which sin depends. By similar means Matheron is also able to find in the *Ethics* counterparts of the other Christian elements in Dogma 7 and its proof.[39]

But it is possible to welcome Matheron's ingenious correlation of doctrines between the two texts without accepting the unproven claim that the *Ethics* contains the "true sense" of the TTP in general or of any of the dogmas in particular. Why should anything said in the TTP require any sense different from the one it appears to have? Why should the TTP not be self-contained when its explicit aim has been to derive everything it puts forward by a scientific method from the Scripture? The long-established habit of seeing the *Ethics* as normative for the TTP should not be permitted to blind us to the difficulties it entails, or to the benefits that might arise from putting it aside.

Spinoza was a good writer and good writers do not publish books that require their readers to consult some other book for their interpretation. This is especially true when the required book has not yet even been written, much less published. If the TTP really required the *Ethics* in order to be properly understood, its meaning would have been lost on its original readers, since the *Ethics* did not appear until seven years after the publication of the TTP. Yet the TTP's theological importance was recognized without any such assistance.

No one would deny that the *Ethics* may be of assistance in understanding unclear passages in Spinoza's other works, including the TTP. Comparison of different writings is a standard way of becoming familiar with any author. Nor is there any objection in principle against treating some particular work – usually a later one – as definitive of an author's thought. An argument can even be made for saying that the *Ethics* occupies such a place among Spinoza's works. In that case, however, discrepancies between the TTP and the *Ethics* would be explained by saying that the author had changed his mind or at least refined his ability to articulate it by the time he finished the later text.

To such standard exegetical postures there can be no objection in principle. What is objectionable, and quite a different thing, is to pretend that the TTP has somehow been written in code and requires the *Ethics* if it is to be deciphered. If a book is thought to contain only cryptic teachings, it can neither be read nor interpreted, but only decoded. Philosophical interest must reside in the other book in which the "true senses" are supposed to be contained.

The alternative proposed here is that the two texts are self-contained expositions of Spinoza's thought, each able to be understood independently of the other, but also coherent with one another . To think of them this way does not disqualify Matheron's mapping of the seven dogmas into the *Ethics*, it merely reveals what it means. The seven dogmas have counterparts in the *Ethics* because the *Ethics* embraces the same radical Protestant outlook as characterizes the TTP. The mapping shows how a fastidious philosopher like Spinoza, who may have preferred the seven dogmas in the form they take in the *Ethics*, might still be putting forward a minimal Protestant Christianity, whether or not he countenanced any further doctrines or any rituals. Since the TTP was written in part to prepare the way for the *Ethics*, it should not be surprising to discover in the later work particular versions, variants or applications of the general doctrines of the earlier one.

Treating the two books as independent is simpler and more plausible than attributing to Spinoza devious stratagems of coded writing. But one can go further. Since they are works by one author written during roughly the same period of his life one should expect the fundamental doctrines of each to be compatible with those of the other. It would therefore be interesting to attempt something more than was done by Matheron. He has shown that something he calls the "true sense" of the dogmas can be found in the *Ethics*. But that leaves open the question of whether or not the apparent sense of the dogmas is really in conflict with what is said in the *Ethics*. The assumption that it is in conflict is what leads people to interpret the TTP as a coded writing. Yet two independent observations by Spinoza would lead one to think that the apparent sense of the TTP is an appropriate guide to what is meant in the Ethics. One observation is made about the TTP, the other is made in it.

A letter of Spinoza's to Oldenburg in 1665 was discussed in Chapter 3. In it Spinoza revealed his motives for interrupting his work on the *Ethics* in order to write the TTP. It is implied that he wrote it in part to prepare the minds of potential readers so that they could more easily understand the *Ethics* when it was finally published. Thus if we had to treat one of these two books as code and the other as key, the *Ethics*, not the TTP, would have to be the one regarded as code.

But code and key are really no use in this context at all. The *Ethics* needs an introduction not because it has a secret teaching and not only because it is controversial. A major reason is because it is so austere – theorem upon theorem, each justified with rebarbative formalism. The TTP has the merit of introducing many of Spinoza's most controversial ideas in a form that is more easily accessible. It should be possible then to take its major teachings for granted and find them, stated, perhaps, with greater logical rigour, but in no way deformed in the *Ethics*.

A remark made within the TTP goes further and suggests that the earlier text might even be definitive in some cases, if it appeared to disagree with the *Ethics*. Spinoza is anticipating the criticism that the TTP takes too lofty and abstract an approach to the question of how we ought to live. Without dismissing the criticism, he says that the particulars and applications the critic rightfully seeks would belong to a different sort of work. The critic should look for them in a book on ethics.[40] Assuming he has his own *Ethics* in mind, and is discreetly doing a little advance publicity for it, this remark implies that the *Ethics* relates to the TTP as the particular does to the general. But in that case perceived conflicts between the two texts ought normally to be resolved in such a way as to preserve the more general theory. In that sense, then, the TTP might have a normative role to play in interpreting some doctrines of the *Ethics*.

Such cases, however, would be the exception. Spinoza devotes all of Chapter 15 of the TTP to pointing out that neither religion nor philosophy are handmaidens to one another, each being equipped with its proper object and method. Philosophers are not encouraged to take things scriptural at face value, but neither are theologians dependent on philosophers for explaining what scriptural doctrines mean. Insofar as the TTP is regarded as a religious text then, and the *Ethics* as philosophical, we should expect each to be for the most part at least independent of the other, though without conflict.

Although recognizing the independence of philosophy and religion is useful in accounting for broad differences in the tone and style of these two works, that principle would not be enough to resolve all their points of difference. It would be unsatisfying, even if it were logically defensible, to resign ourselves to an interpretation of Spinoza according to which he defends simultaneously a philosophy and a theology which appears to contradict it, but doesn't, simply because it is theology. The interesting question clearly is the degree to which seeming incompatibilities of dogma between the two texts can be resolved without denying the surface sense of either text. If the TTP is treated as self-contained, and the "true sense" of what it says is assumed to be available in its own pages, can its surface religiosity be preserved in the face of the apparent naturalism of the *Ethics*? The task of the next chapter is to show the remarkable extent to which it can.

A step toward it can be taken already, however. It can be shown that the surface meaning need not be in any way superficial. No text could offer a better illustration of that point than the passage immediately following Spinoza's treatment of the seven dogmas, in which he considers non-necessary teachings, or what I have called adiaphora.

Adiaphora and Freedom

At the beginning of Chapter 14 Spinoza promises to talk first about what must be believed and then about religious freedom. Most of the chapter is subsequently spent working up to his discussion of the seven dogmas – the things that must be believed. The discussion of religious freedom is a terse, but important one, confined to a meaty section immediately following his treatment of the dogmas. The concluding sentences of the chapter are devoted to tying up loose ends. Brief though it is, that single section on religious freedom is of great importance for Spinoza's argument. It repays close study and indeed requires it, for it contains a dense and subtle discussion of what I have called adiaphora.

Only the seven dogmas are necessary to the faith (*necessaria*). They are all that believers are required to acknowledge. It follows, therefore, that all the distinctive doctrines of every sect are, from a religious point of view, unnecessary (*nihil ad fidem*).[41] There could be any number of such unnecessary doctrines, and innumerable permutations of them in different sects, both real and imaginable.

Because the adiaphora are logically distinct from the dogmas, one easily comes to think of them as distinct also in subject matter. But Spinoza's treatment of them soon teaches us that things are not so straightforward. Nothing prevents the two types of belief from overlapping in content. For reasons which will soon become clear Spinoza is particularly interested in cases where dogmas and adiaphora approach one another as closely as possible. In fact all the examples of adiaphora Spinoza supplies involve interpretations of elements of the seven dogmas or even of the dogmas as a whole. There must of course be scores of potential adiaphora that are wholly independent of the dogmas. Sectarian teachings dealing with sacraments and liturgy would be examples. It is therefore significant that Spinoza concentrates entirely on adiaphora related to the seven dogmas.

The first of the dogmas is that God must exist and the first group of adiaphora discussed by Spinoza concern how he exists. It is adiaphorous, he says, whether we imagine God to be fire, spirit, light, thought or something else.

Another dogmatic proposition is that God rules all things. But we are told that it is adiaphorous whether we believe that he does so freely or by the necessity of his own nature.[42]

These two examples illustrate Spinoza's method throughout this section of the text. In each case a dogma is contrasted with permissible, but non-obligatory (i.e., adiaphorous) extensions of its meaning.

The choice of examples shows that religious freedom, as Spinoza conceives it, includes the right to interpret even the dogmas themselves and to believe whatever goes beyond them without contradicting them.[43] Taken together the list of adiaphora Spinoza mentions includes conventional and orthodox teachings of the Church (e.g., that God is good and just); matters of scholastic disputation (e.g., whether God is potentially or essentially omnipresent) and epithets for God in favour with radical Protestants (e.g., God as light, spirit, fire). The list's very heterogeneity illustrates Spinoza's expansive conception of what is tolerable.

Other adiaphora on Spinoza's list come from a more surprising source. They are pivotal teachings of his own philosophy. The example dealing with God's government of the universe is a good illustration. That

God directs all things not freely but out of the necessity of his own nature will later become one of the signature doctrines of the *Ethics*.[44] In the *Ethics* it will figure among the things which must be believed. How, then, can it appear here among the adiaphora?

Nor is it alone. In six of the seven cases in which Spinoza gives examples of adiaphora, he inserts a teaching that is recognizably his own or will be such at least once the *Ethics* is published. What are they all doing listed as adiaphora in the TTP, as if they were merely religious opinions which could, in principle at least, be rejected by Christians in favour of more traditional teachings of the Church?

The purpose of including them is neither to win the reader over to philosophy nor to prejudice him against the more traditional alternatives. If his motive were to discredit traditional beliefs it would be counterproductive to call them permissible. What is far more likely is that Spinoza is engaged here in pre-emptive damage control. He is helping clear the way for his *Ethics*, by showing that its key doctrines are religiously acceptable. In placing some of his own theological and philosophical views among the adiaphora Spinoza is preparing his readers to see that the philosophy presented in the *Ethics* can be counted as a Christian philosophy, just as his friend Jelles would claim it could in his preface to the *Posthumous Works*.

The list of obviously Spinozistic adiaphora includes:

A) that God is the exemplar of true life because all things are and act through him and because we for that reason also understand through him and see through him how to recognize what is true, just and good.

B) that God is essentially omnipresent

C) that God directs all things from the necessity of his own nature

D) that God teaches his laws as eternal truths

E) that man obeys God due to the necessity of a divine decree

F) that the rewards of virtue and the punishments of vice are natural.

In the context of the TTP, A-F are being considered religiously instead of philosophically. While philosophically they may be a priori certainties, there is no religious reason to believe them unless they are logical consequences of OA which, by hypothesis, they are not. Which particular adiaphora we believe is insignificant to the faith (*nihil ad fidem*). Religiously speaking what counts is the tendency of a given belief to induce piety and justice in the believer. If some people need more traditional adiaphora to have that effect, that is well and good, but a place is also prepared here for others whose inclinations are philosophical.

Another significant fact about this discussion of the adiaphora is that they are not drawn from all seven dogmas. Spinoza offers no comment on Dogmas 2, 5 or 7. Why not?

There is a simple reason why Spinoza did not comment on Dogma 2. God's uniqueness does not lend itself to multiple interpretations. But Spinoza's silence about 5 and 7 is more puzzling. The reason cannot be that there are no counterparts to 5 and 7 that Spinoza could have offered, had he so chosen. Matheron has shown quite convincingly that philosophical versions can be found in the *Ethics*. But Dogmas 5 and 7 deal with obedience, sin, repentance, forgiveness and the spirit of Christ, the essential parts of the Christian message as Spinoza understands it. Offering no philosophical counterparts for them underlines the Christian character of the TTP.

Pluralism

Spinoza classifies among the adiaphora some of the doctrines most cherished by sectarian Christians. It is not essential to Christianity, he tells us in Chapter 14, whether or not we think of God as just, merciful or free. In his correspondence he goes further still, treating as adiaphorous – and admitting that he personally does not believe – the literal interpretation of the two most important Christian teachings, the Incarnation and the Resurrection of Jesus Christ.[45]

In the light of such admissions it is not difficult to explain why orthodox sectarian readers condemned Spinoza as a heretic. As was earlier pointed out, Christian dogma has traditionally been determined by theological reflection on the historically transmitted creeds. On that criterion a literal acceptance of the Incarnation and Reformation would be non-negotiable. But however predictable the widespread sectarian condemnation of Spinoza's views may have been, it begged the very question Spinoza was trying to raise: are sects entitled to pronounce non-members heretical? One intention of the TTP is to show that they usually are not.

In his history of scepticism Richard Popkin makes an important point concerning the Reformation which also applies to the TTP. The Reformation was not just another of the many dissident movements of the past which the

Roman Catholic Church was able first to digest and then to evacuate as heresies. Popkin explains why. Earlier attempts to change the thinking of the Church had accepted the Roman Catholic criteria for determining Church doctrine, and therefore could not refuse whatever decision the Church ultimately rendered regarding their views. The genius of the Reformation lay in successfully challenging the criteria themselves.

> Once a fundamental criterion has been challenged, how does one tell which of the alternative possibilities ought to be accepted? On what basis can one defend or refute Luther's claims? To take any position requires another standard by which to judge the point at issue.[46]

The same argument can be made about the more radical reformation Spinoza advocates in the TTP. In place of historical and theological criteria for determining dogma Spinoza has proposed first an analytic treatment of Scriptural revelation, the fruit of which is OA, and then a logical analysis of OA, yielding the seven dogmas. To condemn Spinoza's criteria – logic and analysis – from the traditional sectarian point of view simply does not settle the issue. For that reason the present study has dismissed those condemnations as based on prejudice.

It is also interesting to note that while the sects were bound to condemn Spinoza, the converse did not hold. Instead the TTP is a tract for Spinoza's times. Jaroslav Pelikan describes the times in these words:

> On the foundations – or from the debris – of the sixteenth-century Reformation and its doctrinal definitions, the separated churches of Western Christendom, already in the sixteenth century but especially in the seventeenth, constructed their several systems of confessional dogmatics, each a simulacrum of the 'one, holy, catholic, and apostolic' tradition to which in one way or another, they all still pledged allegiance.[47]

The TTP is an attempt to break free of this futile pattern in which each new creed lifts its fanatical cry of battle and wins over an ever smaller portion of fragmented Christendom. Spinoza puts forward as non-negotiable only those statements to which Christians are logically committed in virtue of calling themselves Christians. To these minima they are entitled to add as much adiaphorous doctrine as they please, provided it is consistent with the seven dogmas. Such additions are not only permitted, but expected.[48] In the republic Spinoza envisages, a plurality of sects will therefore arise, all equally entitled both to the respect of the state and to the title of Christianity. Each will build a different structure of faith on the same seven pillars of dogma.

Thus it is important to qualify what T.L.S. Sprigge says about the seven dogmas forming "a minimal state religion with a minimal creed". Spinoza's idea is indeed along those lines, but it is bigger. There would be no one state religion in the republic he envisions. Instead the state would be host to a plurality of Christian sects, each of which would centre upon a common core of dogma. Sprigge also underplays or misstates Spinoza's generosity toward other religions. He writes that "with certain qualifications, any religions should be allowed to flourish, which incorporated [these] basic principles, with whatever extra teachings suited them".[49] But this way of putting it does not distinguish sects from religions. Spinoza's republic would offer almost no restriction to sects that embraced the seven dogmas, but it would also tolerate (non-Christian) religions that did not accept these dogmas, as long as none of them acquired significant political influence.

One great contribution of the TTP to religious thinking lies in the way it eludes the trap of sectarianism. It articulates for the first time in Church history how the logically inescapable dogmas of the Christian faith could be represented in indeterminately many sects.

Spinoza's proposal is also successful in avoiding heresy to this extent at least, that it cannot be found to be heretical on its own terms. It denies no dogma and affirms nothing contrary to dogma.

Spinoza's main concern in the whole of the TTP is to show how a non-heretical, non-sectarian pluralism of this kind is possible. Beginning in the subtitle of the work itself, Spinoza stresses again and again that a pluralistic order of this kind is his goal:

> Liberty of thought can not only be permitted without injury to piety and to the peace of the republic, but it is impossible to suppress it without likewise suppressing the peace of the republic and piety itself.

Pluralism, Spinoza in effect is saying, is not only conducive to piety and peace in itself, but even indispensable to them. He does not accuse sectarians (*sectarios*) of impiety because they interpret Scripture after their own fashion, but only when they do not allow others the same liberty. He goes on to say that there is nothing more wicked (*nihil scelestius*) or more destructive of the state (*reipublicae magis perniciosum*) than this latter attitude.[50] On the pluralistic solution he proposes, dogmatic fundamentals can be supplemented with as little as the Collegiants found necessary to add or with as much as the Calvinists or Lutherans did. This attitude helps explain why Spinoza could have been perfectly sincere in telling his Lutheran landlady that she could be saved within the framework of her own faith.[51]

But Spinoza's pluralism goes further. He tells the Collegiant Jakob Ostens something still less conventional for that age, namely that "even Turks and other heathens" can have the spirit of Christ.[52] The seventh dogma explains what he must mean. One can be obedient to OA, thus sharing the mind of Christ, without recognizing Christ's revelation as the source of the axiom. The connection with the *Ethics* shows how this can be possible. One can realize that the ethical equivalents of the seven dogmas are good things in themselves, and act accordingly, without knowing that they can lead to salvation, which can only be discovered through revelation.[53]

It is important to notice the limits as well as the generosity implicit in Spinoza's recognition of outsiders to the Christian faith. They may be saved through the conformity of their minds and actions to the fundamental teaching of the Christian Bible. No concession is made to the teachings of their own scriptures. Christian teaching therefore remains the measure of salvation, even for those outside the Christian Faith.

Spinoza and Catholicism

Among Spinoza's surviving letters is one that seems strangely out of keeping with the pluralism and toleration of the TTP. It contains a blistering attack upon the Roman Catholic Church. Catholicism's distinctive doctrines are said to be founded upon superstition. Roman Catholics are said to propound absurdities about the devil and the Eucharist, to dress ridiculous errors up as mysteries, and to relate many falsehoods in their "pontifical books".[54]

Of these charges the first is the hardest to reconcile with Spinoza's pluralism. Stated in full it alleges that "whatever distinguishes the Roman Church from others is absolutely superfluous and consequently founded solely upon superstition".[55] It is difficult to see what exactly Spinoza could mean by such a charge. Could he think that Roman Catholicism fails so dismally as a sect that every one of its beliefs going beyond the seven dogmas is actually in conflict with them? Could he imagine that Roman Catholics have not succeeded in establishing a single legitimate adiaphoron?

To such a silly charge his correspondent could easily point out that Catholicism embraces many teachings in common with other Christian sects, such as those of the three great creeds. But surely that would have come as no surprise to Spinoza.

One might instead understand Spinoza to be making an even simpler charge. Perhaps he only accuses Roman Catholics of embracing more beliefs than those contained in the seven dogmas. This accusation has at least the merit of being true, but it is ineffective as criticism. All the sects Spinoza treats as legitimate go beyond the seven dogmas and, as has repeatedly been pointed out, are expected to do so.

If the letter had to be taken as a serious part of Spinoza's religious philosophy, one would have to construe his charge somewhat along the following lines: some central Catholic doctrines are not legitimate adiaphora because they turn out to be inconsistent with the seven dogmas. That charge would be weighty and interesting if it could be shown to apply to the Roman Catholic Church in some way that at the same time exonerated the main Protestant sects. It would show that Spinoza understood Catholicism to occupy a no man's land between legitimate Christian sects and other religions.

But the letter does not justify such a reading either. His charges are not followed up by documentation and analysis and no thought is given to the degree to which Protestants would be exempt from similar charges. The letter therefore must either reveal that Spinoza was a bigot, lacking personal commitment to the religious pluralism he advocates in the TTP, or else that this letter is not a serious reflection on religious questions. The circumstances of the letter's composition suggest that the latter conclusion is the right one to draw.

The context of letter 76 (in the standard numbering) shows it to be polemical and personal, rather than academic and objective. It is a reply to a letter Spinoza received from Albert Burgh, a young man who may at one time have been one of his students. During a trip to Italy he was converted to Catholicism and exhibited thereafter the tactless zeal that sometimes animates new converts. Spinoza tells Burgh that he was not originally intending to dignify the young man's provocative letter with any reply. He was apparently only persuaded to do so by the insistence of Burgh's father, a high-ranking official in the Dutch Republic.[56]

Spinoza mentions the "bitter grief" into which Burgh's conversion plunged his parents.[57] In the heated religious atmosphere of seventeenth century Holland conversion to Catholicism was a religious, social and political *faux pas* that would have embarrassed the convert's family and close friends. To his former teacher, i.e., Spinoza, Burgh's conversion would come as an intellectual rebuke, both to his philosophy and to his radical Protestantism. It is understandable then, that when Burgh senior implored him to reply to his son, Spinoza chose to write in a polemical, rather than scholarly, tone of voice. He hoped no doubt to shame the young man out of his dogmatic extremism.

The letter's internal inconsistency may also be regarded as evidence of its polemical intent. After singling out Roman Catholicism for criticism, it more than once implies that Catholicism is no less acceptable a sect than any other, not because the others are also bad, but because Catholicism is good. For example, Spinoza admits that many Roman Catholics are known for the holiness of their lives, denying only that holiness is a monopoly of the Roman Church.[58]

Spinoza may or may not have shared the visceral dislike of Catholicism common in the surrounding Dutch community. At least he was not above exploiting it a little to carry a polemical point. But his anti-Catholic outburst in the letter to Burgh gives no grounds for thinking him a bigot, or for supposing him hypocritically uncommitted to the religious pluralism he advocates in the TTP.

His pluralism, by contrast with the letter to Burgh, is a theological tour de force. Founded on a bedrock of Christian dogmas, it is tolerant of Christians of all persuasions. It even envisions how non-Christian religions could be smoothly integrated into a fundamentally Christian state. What Spinoza offers in the TTP is thus a most original interpretation of the religious crisis of the seventeenth century and how to resolve it. And as was mentioned at the outset of this chapter, it is not without implications for religious and inter-cultural conflicts today.

Even if it is granted that this kind of pluralism makes good sense of the TTP, however, questions will remain concerning the exact relationship of that text to the *Ethics*, published seven years after the TTP and just after Spinoza's death in 1677. No one can fail to notice how different the two books are in form, content and tone. The big question will be whether or not the distinctive religious doctrines defended in the TTP can be shown to be compatible with the teachings of the *Ethics*. In the next chapter I shall argue that they can.

Notes

1   Spinoza [1925] 3, 175 = TTP 14.
2   For other capitalized uses see, e.g., Spinoza [1925] 4, 321 = EP 76: "Ecclesia Pharisaeorum"; 322: "Ecclesia Mahumedana". In their "Notice on the Latin Text" in Spinoza [1999], 25, the editors explain why they did not retain the text's capitalization in their edition: "Pour ce qui est de la ponctuation, des majuscules et des acents, le groupe de Recherches Spinozistes a décidé de moderniser le texte. ... Pour les majuscules ... apparemment elles ont été placées au hasard". I, however, have retained it where it seemed not to be random.
3   Spinoza [1925] 3, 8 = TTP pref.

4   Spinoza [1925] 3, 180 = TTP 14.
5   Spinoza [1925] 3, 173f = TTP 14.
6   Pelikan [1984], 337f.
7   Cf. Pelikan [1984], 332.
8   Cf. Spinoza [1925] 3, 178. See also the discussion of these points below.
9   Spinoza [1925] 4, 220 = EP 43
10   Spinoza [1925] 3, 178: "Haec et similia, inquam, nihil refert in respectu fidei, qua ratione unusquisque intelligat, ...".
11   Spinoza [1925] 3, 173 = TTP 14.
12   The Rev. Chris Criminger has pointed out to me that some Christians today, especially those from strong liturgical or sacramental traditions, might object to the weight these definitions place upon dogma. However the emphasis is appropriate at least to Spinoza's time and place. Pelikan ([1984], 4) quotes "the Anabaptist theologian Balthasar Hubmaier who was speaking for all the Reformers when he wrote 'A Christian life must begin first of all with doctrine, from which faith flows'". Later on the same page he quotes "the axiom of the German-Swiss reformer, Henrich Bullinger, 'Doctrine is the most important thing, which stands out above all others'".
13   Spinoza [1925] 3, 179 = TTP 14.
14   Spinoza [1925] 3, 173 = TTP 14.
15   Spinoza [1925] 3, 174 = TTP 14: "Summum totius Scripturae intentum ... esse tantum obedientiam docere".
16   Cf. Spinoza [1925] 3, 187 = TTP 15.
17   Spinoza [1925] 3, 174 = TTP 14.
18   Spinoza [1925] 3, 165, 174 resp. = TTP 12. 14 resp.
19   Spinoza [1925] 3, 177 = TTP 14.
20   Matthew 25: 40.
21   Spinoza [1925] 3, 174 = TTP 14: "quod ad hoc ipsum mandatum exequendum absolute necessarium sit".
22   Spinoza [1925] 3, 175 = TTP 14.
23   Spinoza [1925] 3, 172 = TTP 13.
24   Spinoza [1925] 3, 175 = TTP 14: The first three consequences are 1) Faith is not in itself sufficient for salvation but only by reason of our obedience... i.e., faith without works is dead; 2) Whoever is obedient necessarily has a true and saving faith; 3) we can judge no one to be of the faith or outside it except by his works.
25   Spinoza [1925] 3, 176 = TTP 14.
26   Spinoza [1925] 3, 345 = TP 8, § 46.
27   Spinoza [1925] 3, 176 = TTP 14.
28   Spinoza [1925] 3, 176 = TTP 14.
29   Spinoza [1991], 177, note 3.
30   Spinoza [1925] 3, 176 = TTP 14.
31   Spinoza [1925] 3, 177 = TTP 14.
32   Spinoza [1925] 3, 177 = TTP 14: "nullum locum controversiis in Ecclesia". Note once again the capitalization of "Ecclesia".
33   Spinoza [1925] 3, 177 = TTP 14.
34   Spinoza [1925] 3, 178 = TTP 14.
35   E.g., Spinoza [1925] 2, 250 = 4Ep54: "Poenitentia virtus non est ...".
36   Cf. Spinoza [1954], 1471f = Note to p. 809.
37   Israel [2001], 296.
38   Matheron [1971], 103.

39   Matheron [1971], 111-114.
40   Spinoza [1925] 3, 60 = TTP 4.
41   Spinoza [1925] 3, 178 = TTP 14.
42   Spinoza [1925] 3, 178 = TTP 14.
43   Spinoza [1925] 3, 178 = TTP 14: "Haec et alia similia, inquam, nihil refert in respectu fidei".
44   Spinoza [1925] 2, 73 = 1Ep33dem: "Res enim omnes ex data Dei natura necessario sequutae sunt, et ex necessitate naturae Dei determinatae sunt ...".
45   Incarnation, see Spinoza [1925] 4, 309 = EP 73; Resurrection, Spinoza [1925] 4, 313f = EP 75.
46   Popkin [1979], 3.
47   Pelikan [1984], p. 332.
48   Spinoza [1925] 3, 179 = TTP 14.
49   Sprigge [1995], 139.
50   Spinoza [1925] 3, 173 = TTP 14.
51   In other words, Spinoza's pluralism is part of the answer to the fascinating question posed by J.Thomas Cook [1995]: did Spinoza lie to his landlady? Cook thinks that Spinoza lied in telling her she "could be saved" in her Lutheran faith and required no other. However Spinoza's treatment of the adiaphora shows that her Lutheranism is no doctrinal barrier to her salvation. Cook thought Spinoza was lying because he must have known that she was not capable of the mental attainments necessary to rise to the "intellectual love of God", from which true blessedness comes (p. 35). In the next chapter I shall show why this is not necessarily so.
52   Spinoza [1925] 4, 226 = EP43.
53   Spinoza [1925] 3, 184 = TTP 15. I shall develop this point further in the next chapter.
54   Spinoza [1925] 4, 318-324 = EP 76.
55   Spinoza [1925] 4, 318 = EP 76.
56   Nadler [1999], 336.
57   Spinoza [1925] 4, 318 = EP 76.
58   Spinoza [1925] 4, 318 = EP 76.

PART III
ETHICS RECONSIDERED

Chapter Seven

Providence, Obedience and Love

In the foregoing chapters I have argued that the importance Spinoza accords to the obedience axiom (OA) and the seven dogmas of Chapter 14 of the TTP reflects his commitment to a form of radical Protestantism. Yet even someone prepared to read the TTP that way might still hesitate to say it discloses Spinoza's real relationship to Christian tradition. The hesitation would arise from uncertainty about the status of the TTP among Spinoza's writings as a whole. Few Spinoza scholars would be prepared to identify anything in the TTP as an official doctrine of the mature Spinoza before they had tested it against his other writings, particularly the *Ethics*. And the tendency in the secondary literature to resolve conflicts between Spinoza's two great texts in favour of the *Ethics* has been a subject of comment.[1]

In the previous chapter I questioned the appropriateness of simply preferring the *Ethics on principle*. I argued that the two works ought to be read as independent treatises of equal integrity, partially overlapping in subject matter, but differing in approach. Insofar as my proposal is directed only against unconscious and uncritical bias in favour of the *Ethics*, it is hard to see why anyone would resist it.

It would be nice if all the conflicts between the two texts could be passed off as minor ones, mere effects of mood or style. But what happens when the two texts appear to express logically incompatible views? The revealed religion of the TTP, for example, appears to be in conflict at several points with the natural religion of the *Ethics*. Merely to insist on calling the conflicting passages independent would be tantamount to attributing what Henry Allison calls "Averroism" to Spinoza. It would imply that Spinoza had endorsed some version of the paradoxical doctrine of "double truth" conventionally associated with Averroes' name, according to which one and the same proposition can be true in religion while being false in philosophy, or vice-versa.[2] Allison does not shrink from attributing this view to Spinoza, though he softens it by denying that it leads to outright contradiction:

> [With the seven dogmas] we are far from the intellectual love of God of the *Ethics* and it is only Spinoza's Averroism that can reconcile such a creed with the basic principles of his metaphysics. The God of religious faith, unlike the God of philosophy, is decked out in human attributes and functions

as a lawgiver and judge. Moreover, the religious person views salvation as a reward for virtue, rather than virtue itself and requires a belief in the mercy and forgiveness of God, without which one would despair of this salvation. The point, however, is that such faith does not contradict, but rather operates on an entirely different level from, philosophical truth. Its articles are necessary to inculcate piety, or virtue, not in the free individual or philosopher, who lives according to the dictates of reason, but in the multitude, who can never rise above the first level of knowledge.[3]

There is also a passage from TTP 15 that it is tempting to read Averroistically. Spinoza argues there that neither theology nor philosophy is a handmaid to the other discipline, but that each reigns supreme, so to speak, in its own kingdom.[4] Allison says that such passages advocate some kind of Averroism without contradiction, though he does not show how to get the one without the other.

In addition to the support lent it by some texts, a full-fledged Averroistic reading of Spinoza would be attractive for another reason. It would make short work of reductive readings of the TTP of the kind I have complained of in Matheron, Misrahi, Francès and others. There is no need to reduce one text to another, if inconsistency is no barrier to embracing both.

Inconsistency is, however, a formidable barrier, as Allison implicitly recognizes when he opts for a guarded form of Averroism. What he suggests is very close to what is wanted – Averroism without contradiction – but he does not explain how it is possible. It would be liberating to read the TTP without having to look over one's shoulder at the *Ethics*, but that freedom is purchased too dearly if it turns out to involve Spinoza in outright contradiction or in the obscurity of "double truth". In the present chapter I intend to show how it is possible to read the *Ethics* and the TTP as independent texts of the same author, without attributing to him any contradictory views.

Even with the narrow focus on Spinoza's religious doctrines adopted here, comparing these two texts is a large task. It would be beyond the scope of the remaining pages of this monograph were it not for Spinoza's extraordinary theological conciseness in the TTP. His entire Christian theology, as he himself stresses, is fully expressed in OA (the Obedience Axiom) and its consequences, most importantly the seven dogmas. I shall refer to the combination of OA and its consequences as OA+. The work of the present chapter will consist then in arguing against the reductionists that OA+ is fully compatible with what is taught in the *Ethics*, and with supplying a textually based justification for reading them as independent texts of equal value.

The Seven Dogmas Revisited

Can the theology of the TTP be understood as the work of the same author who wrote the *Ethics*, without attributing any inconsistency to that author? To say that it can is not to deny that there are large-scale differences between the two texts, including differences of mood, approach or style. But such dissimilarity does not amount to logical inconsistency.

There are disparities of greater significance, however. Beginning with the least threatening, there are small scale, but important, differences at the level of terminology. A number of expressions used in the TTP have a contextual meaning there which cannot be taken for granted when the same expression occurs in the *Ethics*. If the TTP meaning of an expression were attached arbitrarily to an occurrence of the same expression in the *Ethics*, it could render the *Ethics* inconsistent. For example, great importance is attached in the TTP to the fact that God is just, though justice is treated as an "extrinsic" property in the *Ethics*.[5] But since nothing is extrinsic to God,[6] we cannot suppose Spinoza to mean that the sort of justice he attributes to God in the TTP is extrinsic to him. To suppose that would be to render Spinoza's teachings inconsistent. I shall call expressions of this kind, whose meaning may change from one text to another, non-transferable.

However, non-transferable expressions are not necessarily indicative of contradictory teachings. Where A and B are works of a single author, the mere existence of expressions in text A that are not transferable to text B need not imply any inconsistency between A and B. If A discusses galley proofs and B mathematical proofs the word "proofs" will likely occur in non-transferable contexts. But the non-transferability of the word "proof" does not necessarily signal any contradiction in A or B or in the thought of their author. Confusion could easily be sown by transferring sentences dealing with galley proofs into a context dealing with mathematical proofs, but only the appearance of contradiction could be created in this way. And that appearance could be dispelled simply by putting the different occurrences of the terms in context.

The moral is that the existence of non-transferable terminology in text A or B of the same author is innocent unless it is associated with non-transferable *doctrines*. What needs to be considered in the present case is whether or not among Spinoza's non-transferable expressions there are some that are linked to non-transferable doctrines.

As already indicated, the present study restricts itself to expressions from the TTP involved in the teachings of OA+. Some of them are certainly not transferable to the *Ethics*. However I shall argue that none of these expressions gives rise to a non-transferable doctrine. The first step in establishing that conclusion is to reconsider the seven dogmas, taking note of any expressions that might be non-transferable. In the list of the dogmas that follows all such terms have been flagged in bold print.[7]

Dogma 1:   God exists, that is a supreme being, perfectly **just and merciful**, which is to say an exemplar of true life. Whoever does not believe that he exists cannot **obey** him nor acknowledge him as **judge**.

Dogma 2:   God is unique. For no one can doubt that uniqueness is absolutely required by the supreme **devotion, admiration and love** we **owe** to God. For devotion, admiration and love arise solely from the singular excellence of one above the rest.

Dogma 3:   God is everywhere present and everything is manifest to him. If we believed there were things that eluded him, or if we did not know that he sees all things, then we might have doubts about the **fairness** of the **justice** with which **he regulates everything**. We might not even recognize his justice at all.

Dogma 4:   God has supreme right and dominion in all things; he is forced to do nothing but always acts by his absolute good pleasure and **singular grace**. For all are **bound to obey** him; while he himself is bound to obey no one.

Dogma 5:   **Worship of God** consists in **justice and charity or love of neighbour**.

Dogma 6:   All who **obey** God by living in this manner are **saved**. The rest however, who live under pleasure's sway, are **lost**. If men did not firmly believe this dogma, there would be no reason why they should **submit to God** rather than to their own desires.

Dogma 7:   God **forgives** the **sins** of those who **repent**. For there is no one who does not **sin**. Therefore if anyone were not convinced of this dogma he would despair, nor would he have any reason to believe in God's **mercy**. On the other hand anyone who firmly believes that God **forgives sin by the mercy and grace** with which he **directs all things** truly **knows Christ according to the spirit and; Christ is in him.**

As already indicated, it will be no cause for concern if there should be expressions among those flagged that are not transferable to the *Ethics*. The TTP is chiefly a theological work, not a philosophical one; its tone is religious, rather than naturalistic and it is a well-known fact that expressions can have different meanings in such different settings. We do not normally find it confusing that amazing grace is attributed to God, ballerinas and tactful letters. Confusion only arises when we interpret a given occurrence of a non-transferable term in a way not suitable to its context, that is, when we treat non-transferable expressions as if they were transferable.

The seven dogmas depict God as just, fair, merciful, forgiving, gracious and as directing all things. The *Ethics* extols justice and fairness (*aequitas*) but at the human level.[8] The word for grace, *gratia*, occurs in the *Ethics*, but in the sense of "reciprocal love" or gratitude.[9] Spinoza does not speak of forgiveness in the *Ethics* and when he does speak of mercy (*misericordia*) often indicates disdain for it by attaching to it the epithet "womanish".[10] Repentance is called for in Dogma 7, while in the *Ethics* it is said not to be a virtue.[11] But then in the *Ethics* virtue is not understood in normative but descriptive terms, as what involves or enhances our power.[12]

Though the terminological ambiguities indicated in these examples would make it easy to draw from the two texts apparently incompatible claims, that is no proof of there being anything more at issue here than non-transferable terminology. The essential thing is to find out whether the TTP contains any *doctrines* that are not transferable to the *Ethics*? To discover that it will be necessary in the first place to progress beyond the terminology to the essential teachings of the seven dogmas. Spinoza helps by supplying his own summary. (Again the terms suspected of being non-transferable are flagged in bold print):

> All [the dogmas] point in the same direction, namely to the existence of a supreme being who **loves justice** and charity, whom **all must obey if they are to be saved**, and whom they must **worship by cultivating justice and charity** toward their neighbours.[13]

This summary suggests that the doctrinal thrust of the seven dogmas can be captured under three main headings, having to do with God's commitment to justice, the necessity of human obedience and the necessity that our obedience to God involve worship of him that is expressed in acts of justice and charity. The categories chosen below are the three Spinoza suggests in his summary, but widened to subsume beneath them all the other expressions flagged above in the seven dogmas. The teachings of the TTP that appear to be in conflict with the *Ethics* are thus the following three:

1) *God is Providential.* To call God providential is to say that he is just and also something more. The "something more" is necessary to capture

the claim in Dogma 7 that God "directs all things" and in Dogma 3 that he "regulates everything". The heading chosen also reflects the descriptions of God as a judge (Dogma 1), and fair (Dogma 3). If he is providential he is more than merely fair. He also has the other qualities of mercy, grace and forgiveness of sins, attributed to him in Dogma 7.

2) *Obedience is required of all.* Human beings according to OA and several of the derived dogmas are bound to obey or submit to God (Dogmas 1, 4 and 6). Obedience is said to save those who act accordingly (Dogma 6) and to cause those who do not, but who pursue their own pleasure instead, to be lost (*perditi*).

3) *The Path to Salvation is through Love.* Finally our obedience is to be shown and our salvation achieved through acts of love. These must have a dual focus. They must be love of God (Dogma 2), but expressed not only in worship, devotion, admiration of God and acknowledgement of our sin (Dogma 7) but especially in charity toward our neighbour (Dogma 5). Those who manifest this twofold love may be said to have Christ within themselves and to know him according to the spirit (Dogma 7).

When the different doctrines of the dogmas are gathered together under these three headings the real difficulties involved in reconciling the TTP and the *Ethics* comes at once into sharper focus. The points of tension between the two texts cannot be explained away through any combination of nontransferable terminology and large-scale differences of mood and style. Each of the TTP doctrines of providence, obedience and love looks as if it might prove to be logically incompatible with the teachings of the *Ethics*.

First, how can the view of God as directing all things, saving mankind and acting justly and mercifully in our regard, be reconciled with the naturalistic and necessitarian understanding of nature developed in *Ethics* 1?

In the second place, if human salvation lies in obedience, which demands only the lowest kind of knowledge (imagination) and requires us to act at the behest of an external authority, what shall we make of the *Ethics'* identification of salvation with knowledge of the third kind and the requirement that we act out of our own internal spontaneity?

Thirdly, the TTP links human salvation to the expression of love both to God and to man. However Dogma 5 makes it clear that love of neighbour, or charity, is the most significant. How can this be so when the *Ethics* equates the intellectual love of God with salvation? To quote Henry Allison once again, in the TTP we seem far from the intellectual love of God.

These are the three central points of conflict between the two texts. The attempt to answer them in order will therefore provide an appropriate agenda for this chapter. If they can be answered, then the radical Protestant outlook I have attributed to Spinoza in previous chapters will have been shown to be compatible in its main lines at least with the teachings of the *Ethics*. If so, then the impetus for reducing the TTP to the *Ethics* will be undercut, since there will be no reason not to read the two texts as independent of one another. Finally, the *Ethics* will have been shown to supply no reason for doubting Spinoza's sincerity in defending the doctrines which figure powerfully in the TTP.

Providence

If the TTP depicts a God who "governs all things with justice, grace and mercy" and therefore in the interest of mankind, how can it fail to be in conflict with the *Ethics*, which repudiates both the everyday conception of what is in our interest and our attribution of purposes to God? The entire Appendix of *Ethics* 1 is devoted to itemizing the ways in which everyday opinion involves an erroneous view of providence. Through further reflection on what was taught in the sequence of demonstrated propositions that makes up the body of *Ethics* 1, the Appendix attempts to uproot the "prejudices" (*praejudicia*) that lead untutored persons to hold a number of false opinions about themselves and God. The Appendix, then, is the best place to begin exploring whether or not the *Ethics* contradicts the providential outlook adopted by the TTP.

  In the Appendix Spinoza aims at the prejudices and false conceptions of God which he says arise when we do not take account of the (necessary) linkage of things (*rerum concatenatio*) as explained in the demonstrated theorems of *Ethics* 1.[14] Although the Appendix may catch a number of prejudices in its net, they all are said to derive from a primary one (*pendent ab hoc uno*):

> Men commonly suppose that all natural things are goal-directed, as they themselves are. Indeed they even suppose that God directs all things to some certain end, ... for they say that God made all things because of men and made men to worship him.[15]

It is not obvious how to reconcile this passage with the providential picture of God found in the TTP in general and OA+ in particular. Not once, but twice – in Dogmas 3 and 7 – Spinoza explicitly says that God directs all things (*omnia dirigit*), the very Latin words that the *Ethics* puts in question at this place.

Notwithstanding the words they have in common, however, the *Ethics*-criticism does not fit the TTP-dogmas exactly. The dogmas stop at saying that God directs all things. They do not explicitly attribute any purpose to him, towards which he directs all things. Yet the attribution of purposes is what the Appendix actually objects to. It criticizes the view that God directs things to "some certain end" (*certum aliquem finem*). It denies that there is anything in God resembling human goal-directedness.

The addendum regarding purposes is not just an incidental part of Spinoza's criticism, for he repeats it in different words a couple of pages later, reminding the reader that no preconceived goal (*nullum finem praefixum*) can be ascribed to nature, and that final causes are all human inventions.[16] But does the absence of any reference to purposes in the dogmas really except them from the critique found in the Appendix?

I think so, though it is easy to imagine an argument to the contrary. The dogmas do not need to be specific about God's purpose, it could be urged, for he cannot avoid having one if he is directing things at all. To direct things to no end in particular would be the same as not directing them. Therefore when Spinoza says that God directs all things he should be understood to imply that they are directed to particular ends. Thus the TTP doctrine of providence falls under the scope of the critique found in the Appendix.

The difficulty with the counterargument is that it begs the question. It illustrates the very prejudice about the necessary goal-directedness of things which Spinoza is trying to uproot. God (or nature) can direct all things merely by being their efficient cause, Spinoza thinks. Final causes (ends) need never enter into it.[17]

But Spinoza's imagined interlocutor would not be silenced by this reply. He would next ask how God can be thought just, gracious and merciful, as OA+ depicts him, if he is merely the efficient cause of things. The simplest reply open to Spinoza would be that these qualities can be derived, if not from the "eternal necessity" with which all things proceed, then at least from God's "supreme perfection".[18]

However, this reply would be more likely to cause a new misunderstanding. Spinoza's critic would next ask why there are so many imperfections in nature, if God is absolutely perfect, illustrating once again the anthropocentric prejudice Spinoza's appendix is trying to expose. Spinoza's answer would be to deny that such imperfections really exist. Perfection cannot be reckoned, Spinoza insists, according to what is delightful or offensive to human sensibilities, or what furthers or inhibits human nature.[19]

This imagined sequence of counterarguments and replies summarizes Spinoza's critique of the everyday view of providence in the Appendix of *Ethics* 1. It also shows how Spinoza's rejection of purposes can be defended without ever putting in question the TTP claim that God directs all things. Yet it would be premature to conclude that the TTP and the *Ethics* are therefore compatible on this point. Spinoza's critique of providence goes deeper than the foregoing sketch indicates. And something incompatible with TTP-providence might lurk in its deeper structure. It is therefore desirable to examine his critique of providence at greater length.

The fundamental weakness of the everyday view of providence is that it depends on a false understanding of ourselves. We attribute to ourselves a freedom we do not possess and then project it onto God, who doesn't possess it either. This happens as follows: we are conscious of our appetites and wishes, but ignorant of the causes that dispose us to have them. Our limited self-consciousness permits us to imagine ourselves (wrongly) to be free.[20] Yet even if we were correct about our freedom, we would make a second error in ascribing a similar freedom to God or nature. Thus what we say of God compounds self-deception with anthropomorphism.

The latter error conceals further subtleties within it. No doubt we pursue what we find useful to ourselves, whether we do so freely or otherwise. But to attribute the same tendency to God falsely elevates human psychology into a standard, as if the law governing a part of nature can be assumed to apply to the whole. We take our final step into error when we suppose that because nature in fact furnishes us with much that is useful, such as hands, eyes and teeth, nature must set out on purpose to make itself useful to us. Once again we uncritically make our human good, as we conceive it, into a pattern for the government of the whole of nature. The majesty of God's being, infinite in an infinity of ways, is reduced to the level of a genie, bent on pleasing and gratifying his human creation.[21]

These criticisms are illuminating and effective, but they demolish only one conception of providence, the one that is based on human confusions and anthropomorphic projections onto God and nature. Spinoza's critique would be inconclusive against anyone prepared to admit that God's ends are inscrutable, far surpassing our understanding, and that they procure the good of all his creatures in ways that creatures do not necessarily fathom.

More firepower is needed to deal with this more sophisticated view of providence. But Spinoza is not out of ammunition. The error of this subtler view of providence lies in attributing ends to God that are distinct from what he does. "I will show", Spinoza says, "that nature has no foreordained end and that all final causes are nothing but human fictions".[22]

Consider how he argues against the view that God has foreordained purposes in what he does. In the Appendix he draws attention in particular to proposition 16 of part 1, which demonstrates the infinite fecundity of God's nature, and proposition 32, in which Spinoza shows that the will (including God's will[23]) is not a free cause, but a necessary one.[24] When 16 and 32 and their corollaries are put together they imply that God accomplishes all that lies in his power and does so out of the necessity of his own nature. Thus since God does everything in his power and does it necessarily, he requires no preordained purposes to guide his actions, whether such purposes are knowable by us or not.

Imagine now a defender of providence won over by considering propositions 16 and 32. He might continue to uphold a version of the doctrine of providence, but would have to admit that God can entertain no purposes distinct from or antecedent to those on which he acts. But even that concession is not utterly fatal to the view that connects providence with purposes. God can still have had a purpose in creation, as long as it is the one he acted on. In a way it even makes sense to say that God could have had different purposes, provided those other purposes were the ones he acted on. In other words, if the world had turned out differently, God's will and purpose would also have been different from what they are now. That could all be granted while still admitting that purpose and act are one. But if they are one, Spinoza cannot deny purposes without also denying acts. We might grant that God could have done nothing differently, given the will that he has, and still hold it possible for God to have had a different will, and therefore to have done differently. We would then be attributing what Spinoza calls "an absolute will"[25] to God.

Spinoza does not attack the idea of God's having an absolute will in the Appendix, because he has already refuted it to his own satisfaction in proposition 33 of Part 1. In that proposition he argues that "things could have been brought into being (*produci*) by God in no other order than the order in which they have been brought into being". The proof turns on showing that the actual order of things is intrinsic to the nature of God and that God's nature can be no different from what it is.

Spinoza is aware that his demonstration will provoke philosophical objections, and he addresses them in the proposition's second scholium. However he views his replies there as strictly speaking superfluous. Anyone who meditates on *Ethics* 1, weighing carefully the propositions proven there, should be able to answer such objections for himself, he says.[26]

Spinoza's confidence that only those who have not understood proposition 33 or its predecessors will differ from him appears to me to be misplaced. There is still a loophole through which the notion of providence can reappear. Uncovering it leads from the everyday conception of providence, of which Spinoza is rightfully critical, down to philosophical roots that are not so easily eradicated.

As Spinoza concedes, the proponents of providence "will ask us to suppose that God had made another universe (*aliam rerum naturam*) or that he ruled otherwise concerning the present universe". They will then assert that "no imperfection in his nature would follow from that".[27]

That God might have made a different universe or dealt differently with the one he has made are two separate objections, as Spinoza recognizes. To name them by the defenders of them Spinoza likely had in mind, the first is Thomistic (or possibly Leibnizian[28]), the second Cartesian. Spinoza devotes a separate counter-argument to each in the second scholium of proposition 33. The first of these positions, the Thomistic one, is the trickier of the two. Indeed, for Spinoza to imply that it can be refuted by any careful reader of the demonstration of proposition 33 is probably an indication that he himself never fully understood the motivation from which it comes. What the first objection really raises is the possibility of God's having multiple choices before him. This possibility simply cannot be excluded by proposition 33, which focuses on the way things follow necessarily from the nature of God.

No matter how conclusive the proof of proposition 33 a gap will always remain between its thesis and the objection it needs to answer. Proposition 33 appeals to the immutability of God's nature to prove that God can choose nothing but what he chooses. Let it be so. But the interlocutor will say that God could have had an immutable nature and still chosen something else, provided he chose that other thing immutably. There would then be a different series of events that God could not have avoided choosing. To meet that objection fully Spinoza must prove not only that God is immutable, but that he could have had before him no alternative he did not choose.

It is not always easy to see what divides Spinoza and his imagined interlocutor, because they appeal to different intuitions about the nature of possibility, and hence about modality in general. One conception of possibility, the one that is Spinoza's, links it to an agent's power;[29] the other, that of Spinoza's unnamed interlocutor, expresses possibility in terms of the choices an agent has.

To illustrate the difference in simple terms, a train with sufficient fuel, if put in gear and unobstructed, will cover every inch of the track on which it is set. It will pass necessarily through each town and village on its route until it reaches the end of the line. Like the God of *Ethics* 1, the train's course of action is immutable. It does whatever is in its power to do. But how does that exclude the possibility of there being alternative routes the train might have covered with the same exhaustiveness and inexorable necessity? No proofs dealing with the train in isolation will suffice to exclude that possibility. What is required in addition is a proof that there is only one track.

In his *Quaestiones disputatae de potentia* Saint Thomas endorses something like the position Spinoza is trying to refute:

> The natural end of the divine will is therefore its goodness, which God cannot fail to will. But creatures are not commensurate with that end to such a degree that without them the divine goodness that God intends to achieve through creatures could not manifest itself. For just as the divine goodness is manifest through those things which now are and through the present order of things, so it could have been manifest through other creatures, ordered in a different way. And so the divine will can take a different course from what it takes in fact without prejudice to God's goodness, justice or wisdom.[30]

To refute a position of this kind successfully Spinoza must not simply reiterate his proof of the immutability of God. He must show how that immutability entails the absence of any options for God. And that is what he attempts unsuccessfully to do in his response in the second scholium of proposition 33.

After reiterating his own position he contrasts it with four arguments that would support different versions of a providential God. The first and third assume (with St. Thomas) that God might have had different worlds to choose from. The second and fourth assume (with Descartes) that God might have done something different with the present world. Since the first objection is also the most difficult one for Spinoza, it should be investigated first.

"Suppose God had created a different natural order (*aliam rerum naturam*)", Spinoza's unnamed interlocutor objects, "no imperfection in his nature would follow from that". Unfortunately, Spinoza sees in this counterfactual only a confusion which needs to be cleared up. He shows no awareness that his interlocutor might be operating with an alternative conception of possibility, one that is capable of coherent expression. (Leibniz expressed it in his doctrine of possible worlds, for example.) Spinoza's strategy is to show that his own notion of possibility, derived from God's immutable nature, excludes all of the choices the interlocutor imagines to be possible. In order to understand what it is about and where it fails it will help if the steps of Spinoza's refutation are numbered and considered individually:

1) By their hypothesis, Spinoza says, God is able to change (*mutare*) his decrees.[31]

Though this way of stating the interlocutor's objection misses its point, it at least hits on the right translation of the objection into Spinoza's preferred terminology. The interlocutor's real claim is that there are different ways things could have been. For Spinoza it becomes the claim that God has the power to make things differently. But, Spinoza pursues, he could not have decreed differently without understanding and willing differently, hence:

2) If God had decreed otherwise concerning nature and its order, then he would necessarily have had a different intellect and will.

With that inference Spinoza is already proceeding toward the *reductio*:

3) But if it is permissible to attribute a different intellect and will to God, without any change in his essence or perfection, why could he not change his decrees concerning created things without any loss of perfection?

The implication of Spinoza's question is that the interlocutor, having already conceded the possibility of God's willing, understanding and decreeing differently, will be forced to admit that God could equally well change his mind right now, and cause events to take a totally new course.

There can be little doubt that this is what Spinoza means,[32] though it does not seem to follow. It is easy to imagine someone holding that God could have chosen a wholly different world while denying that he had the option of altering the chosen world in mid-course. Nor does the subsequent justification Spinoza gives for attributing the opposite view to his interlocutor make the attribution any more plausible.

4) For in respect of God's essence and perfection, his intellect and will and their relation to created things and their order remain the same however they are conceived.

It is hard to see why someone could not hold 4) to be true respecting God's initial choice but false respecting any subsequent amendments of it. In other words, what is wrong with saying that God can make up his mind, but not change it? It is one thing to send an engine running down a particular track, quite another to make it hop onto a new track in mid-course.

Spinoza is stretched thin here because, to repeat, he is trying to destroy a rival view without first acknowledging, and perhaps before even recognizing, its strength. He misses the different understanding of modal terms to which the rival view is indebted by first massaging it into his own terms before setting out to refute it (see premise 1). That the interlocutor's position in that mangled form should turn out to be incompatible with Spinoza's of course reveals nothing about its merits on its own.

Enough has been said about the weakness in Spinoza's refutation however. The object of examining it in this context is not to evaluate its soundness as a critique of its rival, but only to see whether it indicates inconsistency with the views he defends in the TTP. For present purposes, then, step 4 may be conceded and, with that granted, Spinoza can then pull the rabbit he has been reaching for out of the hat:

> 5) Yet all philosophers acknowledge that there is no potential intellect in God, but only an active one.

The significance of 5) becomes clear when the next step in the argument is added to it:

> 6) For his intellect and will are not distinct from his essence, as they also all acknowledge.

Now if the intellect and will are entirely active and both part of God's essence then:

> 7) It follows therefore [i.e., from 5 and 6] that if God had had a different active intellect and a different will, his essence would also necessarily have been different.

And

> 8) Therefore it follows [from 2, 3 and 7] that if things had been otherwise, God's intellect, will and essence would all have been different, which is absurd.[33]

Having reached this conclusion Spinoza at last accomplishes what he has been trying to do all along. He ties the particularity of creation to the essence of God and in that way defeats the idea of a plurality of worlds. If God cannot be otherwise than he is, neither can the world. But the entailment will not seem to be a logically strict one to those who understand modality in terms of possible worlds.

Spinoza returns to the attack a little later, pointing out another flaw in the rival position. It errs by setting up God's choices as if they were "exemplars", he says. Exemplars would be models of creation independent of God to which, in choosing one or the other, God would subject his will. But this Spinoza rejects as the height of absurdity, because it subjects God to fate.[34] Though this attack does greater justice to the rival position and has the merit of underlining once more Spinoza's rejection of particular independent purposes in natural events, it once again stops short of recognizing the rival interpretation of modal language.

The other view Spinoza criticizes is the Cartesian one that attributes to God arbitrary powers to change the course of events in mid-stream. It is a variant of the strange Cartesian doctrine that God's omnipotence is not constrained even by eternal truths. For several reasons Spinoza's critique of these arguments can be dealt with more quickly than could his arguments against the Thomistic/Leibnizian position.

In the first place, being Cartesian, this rival position has more in common with Spinoza's general outlook than had the other one, as he indicates at the close of his critique of it.[35] But in the second place he attacks it by appeal to the same premise as the previous argument, namely that God's nature cannot be other than it is. In the third place, and most importantly, the chief concern in the present context is with understanding Spinoza's own position, rather than with his success in proving its superiority to other positions.

Briefly then, to combat the Cartesian ascription of arbitrary power to God, Spinoza first establishes what he takes to be its underlying assumption: "that God, who necessarily understands (*intelligit*) what he wills (*quod vult*) can bring it about by his own will that he understands things in some other way than the way he understands them in fact".[36] Spinoza then rejects that assertion on the basis of having "just shown" its absurdity, that is, on the basis of step 8) of the previous argument.[37]

When the Appendix of part 1 is considered in conjunction with the arguments of proposition 33 at least this much becomes clear: the *Ethics'* contention that God's essence is immutable and that only one world is possible is in no way incompatible with God's directing all things within the actual world. It is debatable whether Spinoza has successfully refuted the philosophically subtle conceptions of providence in which purposes are attributed to God. But it is certain that the refutations in no way conflict with the TTP account which does not attribute any purposes to him.

A significant textual confirmation of the unity of Spinoza's thought on providence can be derived from the TTP alone. If the TTP were not compatible with the view of providence taken in the *Ethics*, it would not even be consistent with itself, for in addition to saying that God directs all things, the TTP stresses the immutability of God's decrees, just as the *Ethics* does. The TTP states unequivocally "that God acts and directs all things solely out of the necessity of his nature and perfection and that his decrees and volitions are eternal truths, always involving necessity".[38] But since, logically speaking, TTP-providence is compatible with the immutability of God and the uniqueness of the world, it follows that it is both self-consistent and consistent with the *Ethics*.

Unlike those philosophers who believe that God chose among different possible worlds, Spinoza acknowledges only one world. However in his eyes uniqueness, instead of being an obstacle to this world's perfection, is the confirmation of it. The world derives its perfection not through comparison to other possible worlds, but directly from God. "Things have been produced by God in the highest perfection, when indeed they follow necessarily, as is granted, from his most perfect nature".[39]

Since God contains all perfections and can act in no other way than he does, it follows that all his works are also as perfect as they can be. Therefore nature has perfectly provided for us, as for all its creatures, even if it does not always appear to be so to minds clouded by the confusions criticized in the Appendix. So Spinoza argues, at least, when it suits him to make concessions to the terminology of his interlocutors.

In his own terms, Spinoza could state the same point more briefly and forcefully: God is perfect and God is nature; therefore nature is perfect. If nature is perfect, to understand nature is to be content with it, or, in Spinoza's technical term, to *acquiesce* in it. Our true happiness, even our salvation, consists, Spinoza says, in arriving at this true acquiesence of soul.[40] The Thomistic and Cartesian notions of providence seem to him, in different ways, to diminish the perfection on which our acquiescence must be based. That is why Spinoza rejects them. He also rejects the view of the vulgar regarding final causality, good and evil. But none of that commits him to denying the view of the TTP, that God directs all things with justice, mercy and grace. There is no evidence to suggest that in writing the Appendix Spinoza was targeting views he elsewhere defends. But if that is so, the first of the apparent conflicts between the TTP and the *Ethics* can be declared to be no conflict at all. As far as that apparent conflict is concerned, the TTP and the *Ethics* are independent texts of equal authority.

Obedience

A second point of possible disagreement concerns the relationship of salvation to obedience. The TTP teaches that all are required to obey God (Dogma 4) and that all who obey God are saved (Dogma 6). It is a revealed doctrine, and therefore true, though it can be known only with moral, never with apodictic, certainty. What Spinoza calls simple obedience occurs when the source of one's actions lies outside oneself. It consists in executing someone else's commands solely because of the authority of that other person.[41] How can this teaching be reconciled with what is said in the *Ethics*, where Spinoza equates salvation with freedom and spontaneity?[42] Freedom, in the rigorous sense given it in the *Ethics*, demands spontaneity: the agent himself must be the unique determining source of his action.[43] Can salvation simultaneously involve freedom and yet be attainable through obedience that is not free?

The *Ethics* and the TTP also give different accounts of salvation. In the *Ethics* Spinoza describes it in strictly intellectual terms. He makes it depend on what in his own technical terminology he calls "knowledge of the third kind",[44] which he says is a form of knowledge accessible only to the few who are wise (*sapientes*), and therefore neglected by almost everyone.[45] It is difficult to see how the author who makes these claims in the *Ethics* could be the same one who says in the TTP that obedience is required of all and a reliable route to salvation, though it presupposes only the lowest kind of knowledge, imagination.

One way of making these teachings consistent would be to suppose that Spinoza recognized two different kinds of salvation and envisioned different ways of achieving each kind. On this view he would have an exoteric philosophy according to which obedience leads to salvation and an esoteric one in which it does not. In the esoteric philosophy salvation would be reserved for philosophers, in the exoteric one all people would be eligible, but the salvation made available to them would be of a lower order.

Such an interpretation is implicit in the justification Thomas Cook gives for thinking that Spinoza lied to his landlady when he told her she could be saved in her own religion (Lutheranism):

> Did Spinoza lie to his landlady? Well, it seems to me that he certainly misled her in answer to her question. He led her to believe that she could be saved (in *her* sense of 'saved'), whereas in fact she could not. Not only could she not be saved in *that* sense, but in the sense of 'salvation' that is most important to Spinoza, she cannot be saved 'in her religion' at all.[46]

An alternative to attributing duplicity to Spinoza would be to attribute to him the doctrine of double truth. On this view he would not have to lie to his landlady because things could be true in religion that are not true in philosophy. The difficulty in this tolerant position, as seen earlier, is to avoid seeming to embrace contradictions.

Self-contradiction is the worst thing that can be attributed to a philosopher. Faced with that as the only alternative commentators prefer to believe that Spinoza was a deceiver. That thesis also combines well with reductivism, allowing Spinoza to deceive in one place and tell the truth in the other. He can equivocate or even lie about salvation or obedience, for example, provided he only intends half of what he says seriously. Nor is there much debate about where to find the serious half. It is of course the esoteric doctrine of the *Ethics*. Thus Victor Brochard believes that Spinoza's words cannot be taken entirely at face value when he speaks of salvation in religious terms. "[Spinoza] puts faith below reason, in that he considers revelation to be a transposition of the truth to put it within reach of simple people. Faith is inadequate knowledge and by the spirit as well as by the letter of his doctrine, inadequate ideas differ little from false ones".[47]

The most lengthy and significant study of the obedience problem, however, is Alexandre Matheron's *Le christ et le salut des ignorants chez Spinoza*. Although, as mentioned in the previous chapter, he subscribes there to the view that the *Ethics* contains "the true sense" of the seven dogmas of the TTP, he proposes a solution to the obedience problem that is independent of that assumption. His solution is also a *tour de force*, for it shows how Spinozistic salvation in the fullest sense could be available to those who merely obey God in the most deferential sense of that term.

Matheron's account of the obedience problem is the strongest point in a strong book. However, it is also more complex than it needs to be. His conclusion – that the accounts of salvation given in the *Ethics* and the TTP are compatible – can be reached more efficiently than he realizes, and in a way that stays closer to the surface sense of both the TTP and the *Ethics*. It is also possible to dispense with both of the hidden doctrines which Matheron finds it necessary to postulate – with scant textual evidence – in order to justify his conclusion. A more direct and textually motivated route to Matheron's correct conclusion is mapped out below.

The task Matheron takes on is a challenging one: to show that there is some sense in which the simple obedience spoken of in the TTP can be connected with salvation as it is understood in the *Ethics*. He interprets the task with the utmost rigour, recognizing that to be fully convincing he must begin with the type of obedience furthest from the spirit of the *Ethics* and finally arrive at the *Ethics'* most demanding conception of salvation, the one remotest from the obedience with which he began. Any less ambitious undertaking would show at best a limited compatibility between the two texts.

It is possible to arrive at Matheron's conclusion by a less circuitous route than he takes. Some of his terminology is badly chosen and in fact hinders and complicates his progress. For that reason it is important to make clear from the outset the alternative terminology that will be employed here. Matheron rightly recognizes that simple obedience to commands, what I shall call deferential obedience, is not the only kind Spinoza discusses. One may also obey because of the actual rewards of obedience. Since we try to accomplish whatever conduces to our joy (*laetitia*),[48] obedience can sometimes be voluntary. And if we saw those rewards as flowing from God, that would cause us to love God and increase our desire to obey his will.[49] When obedience is sought in this way, rather than imposed, I shall call it preferential obedience.

Some of what Matheron says about obedience is less useful than his division of it into two kinds. His assumption that deferential obedience will "almost inevitably" involve constraint[50] seems to me gratuitous. His reasoning is as follows: most non-philosophers, he says, will never obey a law, even a good one, unless forced to do so. So far he is in agreement with Spinoza. He goes beyond Spinoza, however, when he infers that therefore constraint of some kind will need to be introduced in order to ensure universal obedience.[51]

The difficulty lies in Matheron's unwarranted assumption that all must be saved, the doctrine that theologians call "universalism". But they also call it a heresy.[52] Spinoza does not endorse universalism in the TTP and, in the last words of the *Ethics*, speaks forcefully against it: "If salvation were ready to hand and could be found without much effort, what would account for its being neglected by almost everyone? But everything noble must be as difficult as it is rare".[53]

Spinoza's position concerning salvation is the traditional Christian one: distributive rather than collective. He holds that anyone who obeys can be saved, not that everyone will obey and will be saved. But if universalism is not attributed to Spinoza then there is no reason why obedience needs to be conjoined with constraint. Conjoining them leads Matheron to use the term "strong obedience" (emphasizing force exerted from outside) for what I have preferred to call "deferential obedience", meaning obedience which conforms to Spinoza's TTP definition: activity in which the authority of another is followed (whether or not by constraint).

Matheron's analysis of salvation, on the other hand, gets everything right. Salvation is intellectual, because it involves what Spinoza calls "knowledge of the third kind" or "intuitive science".[54] It is connected with joy[55] or even intense joy,[56] and involves an everlasting activity of the soul which is unmixed with passion, and therefore free.[57]

One can find instances even in the TTP itself in which Spinoza understands salvation in this strong sense. Matheron points out the place where Spinoza says that "we are saved when we love God in true liberty, constantly and with the whole of our soul".[58] I shall call this eternal salvation. It needs a name because, as Matheron argues, there is room in Spinoza for a weaker notion of salvation which I will call temporal salvation.

Salvation in the weaker sense would be a passionate joy that arose from obedience to God but lasted at most for one's lifetime. Only in unusually fortunate circumstances could passionate joys last for a whole lifetime of course, because they are normally only aroused by transient objects. But as Matheron argues there is no reason in principle why, through obedience, one could not take steps that would associate a passionate joy with a multiplicity of objects. It would then return more frequently and occupy the mind more fully.[59] And so by extension it is not inconceivable that such passionate joy might be prolonged for the whole of one's life[60] and lead to what I am proposing to call temporal salvation.

The two kinds of obedience combine with the two kinds of salvation to produce four different propositions that the obedience axiom might express. The strongest would be that people who are deferentially obedient to the revealed law of God could acquire the kind of sophisticated intuitive knowledge necessary for eternal salvation. It would claim, in other words, that someone for whom the law appears only as a burden and who pursues a good course only because driven to it by hope of reward or fear of punishment might nevertheless achieve salvation of the highest kind. If that can be shown to be Spinoza's intended thesis, then OA+ will be understood in the sense most difficult to reconcile to the teachings of the *Ethics*. If OA+, so understood, could be shown compatible with what the *Ethics* says of salvation, then the motivation for attributing duplicity, Averroism or reductionism to Spinoza would vanish.

Before attributing this strong interpretation of OA+ to Spinoza, however, it must first be shown that he did not intend some weaker sense of salvation or obedience or both. He might, for example, have meant that preferential obedience, which may involve love of God, can produce eternal salvation. Alternatively, he could have meant that deferential obedience produces only temporal salvation, to which it is closer. The weakest possible thesis would be that preferential obedience can produce temporal salvation.

There are thus four pertinent questions to answer. In order of strength, beginning with the weakest, they are: 1) Can preferential obedience lead to temporal salvation? 2) Can deferential obedience lead to temporal salvation? 3) Can preferential obedience lead to eternal salvation? 4) Can deferential obedience lead to eternal salvation?

In addition to these four possibilities (expressed in his own terminology) Matheron finds it necessary to consider a dozen others. It is worth pointing out briefly why they are not pertinent before returning to examine the four that are.

Because eternal salvation is strongly intellectual Matheron argues that it would not, in the ordinary course of things, be attainable by everyone. It would only be universally attainable if a thoroughgoing social transformation took place along the lines of the liberal and pious political order envisioned in the later chapters of the TTP. Though even such a utopian social climate would not guarantee that each person would achieve salvation, it would at least maximize each individual's chances for self-improvement and be a necessary step on the way to universal salvation. Accordingly Matheron adds a new pair of terms to the four already in place. He considers whether or not the obedience is practised by individuals or by the whole community.[61]

That question becomes irrelevant, however, once we realize that there is no reason to attribute universalism to Spinoza. Remove the theological requirement that all people be saved and the logical requirement for a perfect community to facilitate their salvation also falls away. Without it the new pair of terms – individual/community – can also be dropped together with the additional questions it generates when its two elements are introduced and combined with the other four. Universal salvation will always be desired by virtuous persons because it is in the interest of all concerned,[62] but for Spinoza it remains a desideratum, not a dogma.

It has already been mentioned that Matheron distinguishes between what he called strong and weak salvation. He also distinguished between salvation enjoyed in the present life and that which is eternal. But these terms overlap. Strong salvation must be eternal and weak salvation must be temporal even as he defines the terms. Thus my single pair of terms, eternal and temporal salvation, do the work of Matheron's two pairs: present life/next life, and strong salvation/weak salvation.

So streamlined, only four of Matheron's sixteen questions remain for consideration. But more has been eliminated here than needless questions. The unmotivated assumption of universalism, which generates some of the redundancies, also drives what Matheron proposes as a solution. For universalism to be true, everyone would have to attain to knowledge of the third kind and its accompanying intellectual beatitude. For this to happen a social transformation would have to occur in which every person found himself in social circumstances favourable to attaining the condition of beatitude. But circumstances so utopian would require a social transformation that could only be achieved with great effort over many generations. Left to their own resources, few people will achieve beatitude or salvation during their present lives. And if they have not achieved it by the time they die they will not get there after death either. For notwithstanding Spinoza's doctrine that we are still something after death, i.e., that there will remain of us the idea of a certain essence in the mind of God, there can be no change to that idea after our death. "For eternity", as Matheron reminds us, "by its very non-temporality excludes all progress".[63]

Thus universalism is impossible unless two conditions are fulfilled: First, it must be possible for a utopian society to be realized as indicated above. Second, individuals must be able to be reincarnated, so that they get a chance to live in an environment that would make possible for them the attainment of beatitude. There is not much evidence for Spinoza's having believed either of these propositions, but what there is of it Matheron discusses, including a suspicion once voiced by Leibniz that Spinoza believed in Pythagorean transmigration of souls.[64] Matheron freely admits that the evidence he presents for his two postulates falls short of proof. He will be content merely to establish that the postulates are logical preconditions of the claim that obedience leads to salvation and that they are at least consistent with Spinoza's teachings.[65]

However if Spinoza is not committed to the doctrine of universalism, none of the extended series of questions and neither of the postulated preconditions is necessary. When they are put aside, only two matters need to be resolved. Which among the four possible theses did Spinoza intend to defend in the TTP and is that thesis consistent with the teachings of the *Ethics*?

To begin with the weakest of the four candidate doctrines, then, can OA+ be understood to mean that preferential obedience gives rise to temporal salvation? That question is easily answered in the affirmative. Preferential obedience is the kind that arises through obedience to God and finds its rewards in passionate joy, the type of joy that is lost with the death of the body. As Matheron points out, once we understand the terms of this, the weakest of the four possible interpretations of OA+, we can have no further doubt about its truth. Preferential obedience naturally gives rise to temporal salvation, because it *is* temporal salvation. "Causality", as he says, "is resolved in identity".[66]

This first possible interpretation of OA+ is thus part of what it means. But not all. The salvation promised to the obedient in the TTP also includes beatitude.[67] And Spinoza explicitly denies – even in the TTP – that true beatitude can be reduced to the passionate joy of any individual. Passionate joy is unique to the individual who has it and "whoever counts himself happier because he is doing well and others not so, or because he is more blessed and fortunate than they are, is bereft of true happiness and beatitude".[68] But if this reasoning holds against the first interpretation of OA+, it will also disqualify the second, that deferential obedience can lead to temporal salvation. For here again the type of salvation on offer is simply not strong enough to meet the expectations created by the TTP.

To think that Spinoza's notion of salvation stopped with temporal salvation would also mean conceding Thomas Cook's claim that the faith of Spinoza's landlady would not have been able to save her in the fullest sense of the term. Spinoza would therefore have told her a lie. But the TTP clearly says the opposite: salvation in the fullest sense is available even to ordinary people.

To capture the meaning of Spinoza's claim in OA+ we must hold him to something at least as strong as thesis 3), that preferential obedience gives rise to *eternal* salvation. But it is easy to see that this will also be insufficient, since preferential obedience is only a special case. The usual case, the one by which Spinoza repeatedly defines what he means by obedience, includes what I have called deferential obedience, that is, action in conformity with a command.[69] And in the thirty-first of Spinoza's own notes to the TTP he explicitly links this form of obedience to salvation, saying that "it is sufficient for salvation or beatitude that the divine decrees be understood (*amplecti*) as laws or commands (*jura seu mandata*)".[70] The universality of the ability to obey is what justifies Spinoza in believing that everyone is capable of salvation. They must be because "absolutely everyone is capable of such obedience".[71]

This cursory examination of the four possible meanings of OA+ is sufficient to show that Spinoza intends OA+ to be construed in the strongest sense its words can bear, those of the fourth possible thesis. In other words he is claiming that deferential obedience can give rise to eternal salvation. It is significant that Spinoza is defending a recognizably orthodox Christian idea of salvation, not the intellectualistic gnosticism with which he is sometimes credited.

The more challenging task is to determine whether or not this strong claim about deferential obedience is compatible with the intellectual form in which salvation is understood in the *Ethics*? They do not appear compatible. In the TTP Spinoza teaches that:

1) Simple obedience is the way to salvation.[72]

In the note accompanying this statement, cited above, Spinoza draws attention to the key feature of simple obedience as he understands it. To be obedient, he says, it is sufficient to embrace divine decrees as divine laws or commands.[73] Thus "simple obedience" here is what I have been calling deferential obedience. The person who is deferentially obedient to commands is not capable of the highest kind of knowledge, however. He is incapable of what Spinoza calls the intellectual love of God. In a later note Spinoza writes: "Love of God is not obedience but a virtue, which is necessarily part of the man who knows God in the right way. For obedience heeds the will of the one giving the commands and not the truth and necessity of the matter".[74] Thus

2) Obedience is not the way to the intellectual love of God.

TTP doctrines 1) and 2) are perfectly consistent with each other. The difficulty arises when a doctrine from the *Ethics* is placed alongside them. In the scholium of 5Ep36, Spinoza clearly states:

3) Salvation = intellectual love of God.[75]

Propositions 1) - 3) appear to form an inconsistent triad. 1) and 3) together entail the negation of 2).

When TTP teachings are juxtaposed with *Ethics* teachings in this way it is easy to see why some careful readers of Spinoza have believed them inconsistent. If they are inconsistent, then there is no choice but to admit what I have hitherto denied: that there are fundamental doctrines in the TTP that are not transferable to the *Ethics*.

From that admission one or another of the unappealing interpretations of Spinoza that I have tried to reject would also have to be adopted. One could think that Spinoza contradicts himself in an effort to placate or entice his Christian readers, or for fear of persecution, or because of a deceptive style of writing derived from the Marrano tradition, or because he believes in double truth or is simply devious. The only way in which to accept Spinoza's inconsistency and deny his duplicity, would be to accuse him of self-contradiction and hence of philosophical incompetence.

Of the interpretations of Spinoza's two major texts examined so far, the only one that allows Spinoza both to mean what he says and be consistent in saying it is Matheron's. Although he never confronted the problem of propositions 1) - 3) in its simple logical form, his interpretation can certainly accommodate it. Matheron would simply deny the contradiction by mentally adding one word to each of propositions 1) and 2). We must understand proposition 1) to mean that simple obedience is the way to salvation *eventually*, and proposition 2) to mean that obedience does not lead *immediately* to the intellectual love of God. Though obedience cannot lead directly to salvation, the gap between them can be overcome with mediating steps taken over sufficient time through a sufficient number of consecutive lifetimes.

Though logically possible, Matheron's interpretation still remains unsatisfying, however, because he admits that the two postulates on which it rests have only weak textual support. What if it is possible to interpret propositions 1) - 3) in a way that has the merits of Matheron's position, without its textual deficit? I claim it is possible. In other words, Spinoza's consistency and competence can be defended without appeal to any arbitrary postulates.

The interpretative principle I shall invoke is best introduced through an example from another context. The example is particularly useful because it does not involve any attempt to transfer doctrines from the TTP into the *Ethics* setting, and yet, from a logical point of view, is isomorphic to 1) - 3). Thus it not only suggests a way of dealing with 1) - 3), but also treats as separate issues the general question of Spinoza's consistency on the one hand and the particular question of whether or not major TTP doctrines are transferable to the *Ethics* on the other.

The example I shall use is composed of doctrines all of which are found within the *Ethics* itself and concerns Spinoza's well-known solution to the mind-body problem of Descartes. Early in Part 2 of the *Ethics* Spinoza proves what is often referred to as the "parallelism" of mind and body. "The order and connection of ideas is the same as the order and connection of things", Spinoza says.[76] In the scholium to the same proposition he anchors that parallelism in something stronger, numerical identity. There he says:

> that thinking substance and extended substance are one and the same substance, which is comprehended first under the one attribute and then under the other. In the same way a mode of extension and its idea are one mode, but expressed in two ways.[77]

Now although Spinoza admits that physical events and mental events unfold on parallel lines and also that the two are, in the last analysis, identical, he nevertheless forbids crossover explanations. Modes of thought may be explained with reference to God, considered under the attribute of thought, or with reference to other modes of thought, but never with reference to the attribute of extension. And modes of extension may be explained with reference to God, considered under the attribute of extension, or to other modes of extension, but never by reference to the attribute of thought. In Spinoza's words: "Neither the body can determine the mind to think, nor the mind determine the body to motion or rest or anything else (if there is anything else)".[78] To use one of Spinoza's own examples, a mental decision and a bodily appetite may be one and the same thing, but the decision must be explained as the result of earlier thoughts and the appetite as a result of earlier conditions of the body.[79]

Now this elegant way of avoiding Cartesian problems with mind-body interaction creates a difficulty at the level of explanation resembling the one just encountered in his religious philosophy. Let M be our mind at the present time. There must therefore also be a physical state, P, such that P is our body at this time, and M=P. And finally there must be prior states M* and P*, such that M* is integral to explaining how M came to be and P* is integral to explaining how P came to be and M*=P*. But this solution to the mind-body problem commits Spinoza to three claims that seem inconsistent:

i) M* is integral to the explanation of M
ii) P* is not integral to the explanation of M
iii) M*=P*

Propositions i) - iii) are logically isomorphic to the problematic 1) - 3) presented above,[80] even though i) - iii) involve no transfer of doctrines from outside the *Ethics*. This example of the consistency problem has the additional advantage of having received careful critical attention from which its theological counterpart can benefit.[81]

The most useful study of this aspect of the mind-body question in Spinoza is that of Michael Della Rocca [1996], who accounts for the apparent inconsistency of i) - iii) in a way that has important implications for the understanding of Spinoza's philosophy in general. Della Rocca argues that the doctrines represented by i) - iii) are not really inconsistent at all. Instead they reflect Spinoza's implicit recognition of what contemporary philosophers of logic call "opaque contexts",[82] that is, contexts in which terms with identical referents cannot always be treated in identical ways. Logicians call a context opaque when there is no guarantee that terms with identical referents can be substituted for one another in that context without affecting its truth-value.

Ordinary beliefs furnish familiar examples of opaque contexts. I may believe a) that my wife is a careful driver, b) that the woman in the next lane is a reckless driver, and not realize c) that the woman in the next lane is my wife. If the opacity of belief-contexts were not taken into consideration, then from b) and c) it would follow d) that I believe my wife to be a reckless driver, which I do not. The conjunction of d) and a) would show me to have inconsistent beliefs, which I am unaware of having. We seem to be forced by logic into accepting highly counterintuitive statements about our own beliefs.

Accepting them is however not the only way of dealing with a) - c). An alternative is to recognize that belief-contexts are opaque and that identicals may therefore not always be validly substitutable within them. If substitution is restricted, my beliefs can be understood to be consistent after all. I believe a) and b). Though c) is true, I am not aware of its truth and it therefore does not follow that I believe d). When opacity is recognized, the apparent inconsistency of a), b) and c) is explained and the entailment of d) is blocked.

Della Rocca finds an implicit recognition of opacity in Spinoza's account of mind-body parallelism: if modes of thought must be explained exclusively with reference to other modes of thought, and modes of extension with reference to other modes of extension, that is tantamount to declaring the context of explanation opaque, like that of belief. It means that P* is not integral to the explanation of M even though P* is identical to M* and M* *is* integral to the explanation of M. In other words it can be said that M-explanations are of a kind that must involve only states with M-descriptions and P-explanations must involve only states with P-descriptions. Della Rocca does not confine the role of opacity in Spinoza's metaphysics to the level of explanation.[83] However to recognize the existence of opacity at that level is sufficient for proposing an alternative to the apparent inconsistency of 1) - 3), to which I now return.

If the consistency of propositions i) - iii) can be defended because i) and ii) belong to different explanatory contexts, the consistency of propositions 1) - 3) should be defensible on analogous grounds. Proposition 1) affirms the possibility of progressing from "simplex obedientia", what I have called "deferential obedience", to salvation. It is a religious teaching. Spinoza even calls it the unique teaching of theology,[84] not in the sense that it is the only one, but rather the source of all the others. From OA are derived all the religious dogmas that make up OA+.[85]

Several considerations suggest that Spinoza regarded theology as defining its own context of explanation. First, theology has a different subject matter from reason. It deals with what is revealed: "By theology I mean precisely revelation", Spinoza says.[86] Secondly, revelations cannot be rational in Spinoza's sense, i.e., demonstrable, because, if they were, theology would be reducible to philosophy. And it is one of the fundamental contentions of the TTP that "philosophy must be kept separate from theology ... neither being a handmaid to the other".[87] Thirdly, theological explanations are explicitly said to be both universal in scope and yet compatible with those of reason.[88]

It is not difficult to see why any religious account of the ascent from obedience to salvation must fall short of necessity. Proposition 3) affirms that salvation is the same thing as the intellectual love of God. Proposition 2) implies that no proposition or set of propositions connecting obedience with the intellectual love of God could meet reason's standard (apodictic necessity). But propositions 2) and 3) together do not exclude the possibility of an explanation of the path from obedience to salvation meeting a lower standard. It could provide the moral certainty Spinoza associates with proofs of this kind.

Thus if 1) and 2) are assessed with respect to different contexts of explanation, and if these contexts are sensitive to the ways in which things are described, i.e., if they are opaque, then the fact that salvation and the intellectual love of God are co-referential does not mean that anything provable by theological standards is also demonstrable by the standard of reason. Thus 1) -3) no longer can be used to generate any contradiction.

To bring the opacity of explanatory contexts to bear on 1) -3) cannot be called *ad hoc*. It is not a device invented for this occasion, but borrowed from Della Rocca's investigation of another important question in Spinoza's thought and, as Della Rocca points out, applicable to many aspects of Spinoza's thought. There is also abundant textual evidence for Spinoza having himself envisaged philosophy and theology as involving separate types of explanation. In addition to the examples I have given the whole of Chapter 15 of the TTP is devoted to arguing for this point.

It is unfortunate that Spinoza offers no theological proof of proposition 1). He is content to deny that there can be a rational demonstration of it and to claim that a theological proof of it could at most achieve moral certainty:

> If we wanted to claim that this fundamental theological assertion [i.e., OA] could be demonstrated by reason, theology would become part of philosophy and there would be no necessity of keeping them separate. But my response to this is to assert absolutely that this fundamental dogma of theology cannot be investigated by the natural light, ... and that revelation was therefore in the highest degree necessary. Nevertheless we can still use our judgement and embrace what has already been revealed with moral certainty.[89]

Spinoza goes on to say that our grounds for accepting OA cannot be better than those available to the prophets who received the original revelations from which OA is derived. These were the ability the prophets received to perform miracles (*signa*) and the conformity of their teaching with sound moral doctrine. The first ground for accepting revealed doctrines, miracles, is therefore largely historical and brings into play the methods of biblical exegesis developed in the TTP.

Spinoza will have no difficulty in persuading contemporary readers that proofs of the kind he envisages for theology fall short of apodictic necessity. The more difficult task will be to assure us that they have any force whatever. It will help to review the grounds that make Spinoza affirm 1). To reconstruct them will also have the advantage of leading into the last of the areas of apparent conflict between the TTP and the *Ethics*, Spinoza's doctrine of love.

Love

The texts in which Spinoza deals with his concept of love are among the most difficult and the least understood in Spinoza's writings and my goal is not to give a definitive account of them. I shall discuss them only to the extent necessary to show how they figure in the differing accounts of salvation given in the TTP and the *Ethics*, and to show that those accounts are logically consistent.

The first step is to establish what kind of love Spinoza intended to identify with salvation. Consider again Dogmas 5 and 6:

Dogma 5:   Worship of God consists in justice and charity or love of neighbour.

Dogma 6:   All who obey God by living in this manner are saved.

The love that is strongly connected, if not identified, with salvation here is charity, and it is said to grow out of obedience. Spinoza uses the term "charity" in the classical Christian sense of love of one's neighbour (*amor erga proximum*).[90]

In other places, however, especially in the later propositions of *Ethics* 5, salvation is identified with a different kind of love, the kind Spinoza calls the intellectual love of God. I shall argue that these two concepts of love belong to different contexts of explanation and are therefore related differently both to obedience and to salvation.

Spinoza recognizes a hierarchy among doers of charity, speaking of those "who exhibit the finest works of charity" as exhibiting the most perfect faith.[91] I shall call the point at which such people aim "perfect charity".

The path that culminates in perfect charity begins in obedience, Spinoza tells us. But what kind of obedience? Earlier in this chapter two kinds were distinguished, deferential and preferential. If the path to salvation was to be open to everyone, as was earlier pointed out, it would have to begin in deferential obedience, since it alone lies "absolutely within the power of all people".[92] But Spinoza also holds that it is the right place to begin our ethical development. If we are ever to gain control of our emotions, the wisest strategy is to begin with dogmas for living (such as the seven dogmas) and simply obey them:

> The best we can do ... until we have perfect knowledge of our emotions is to conceive of a right manner of living or of certain dogmas for living (*dogmata vitae*), to commit them to memory and to apply them continually to the particular situations that often arise in life's way. This should be done until the imagination is completely saturated by them, so that they are always ready for service. For example, we placed among the dogmas (see 4Ep46 and its scholium) that of conquering hate by love or magnanimity (*generositas*), not repaying it with reciprocal hate.[93]

The references to dogma and imagination (the lowest kind of knowledge) accord with the assumption that Spinoza's account of salvation presupposes no more than deferential obedience and thus begins at the bottom end of ethical and spiritual development. In content and tone the above passage would therefore fit well with the discussion of the seven dogmas in Chapter 14 of the TTP. In fact, however, it is taken from the last pages of the *Ethics*, which itself is evidence for the existence of the unified doctrine of obedience and salvation here to be established.

The first step will be to show that deferential obedience can lead to perfect charity. The connection is not obvious because charity is a kind of love and therefore presupposes spontaneity, which is absent from deferential obedience. In the language introduced earlier, charity involves preferential obedience. An intermediate step is therefore necessary to show how one can progress from the lower (loveless) to the higher form of obedience.

What is of interest here is the human capacity for moral development and there is a danger that discussing it in purely abstract, technical terms would lead to taking for granted precisely what needed to be shown. I will therefore particularize my discussion, focusing on an individual to whom no ethical capacity beyond deferential obedience is initially attributed. Spinoza's landlady, Mrs. Van der Spyck, already figures in the secondary literature in that role and can do so again here. Little is known about her beyond the fact that she was a Lutheran and that Spinoza advised her to continue to be one. Nothing else needs to be attributed to her now. In particular, she must not be supposed to have any antecedent will to do good. It can then be investigated whether it would be possible for her to develop an attitude of perfect charity beginning with deferential obedience alone.

By hypothesis she attends the Lutheran church in which Spinoza told her she could find salvation. There she would be likely to encounter examples of the very "dogmas for living" which Spinoza recommended above. They would be presented to her as exhortations to charity in the form of what Spinoza calls "pious dogmas", that is dogmas that are so phrased as to move the heart (*animum*) to obedience.[94] Since only the capacity of deferential obedience has been attributed to her, these dogmas would have to be presented in such a way as either to frighten her into obedience or to lure her into it through hope of reward, for hope and fear are the only emotions that will move her to right action, if she is as we have supposed her to be.[95]

But pious dogmas have the capacity not only to motivate behaviour, but to transform character. Not only will they push her toward charitable activity they will also condition her to feel joy at her actions. Spinoza is fully aware of the extent to which we can be conditioned by education. "Absolutely every act which is habitually called right produces joy", he says. "It depends on our education whether we repent of a deed or glory in it".[96]

The joy she feels at her action will increase her own power of acting,[97] and for the sake of the joy she will do her best to bring about its repeated or, if possible, continuous existence.[98] Thus deferential obedience will tend to give way to what I have called preferential obedience. Moreover, because her acts are charitable, they will tend to awaken the love of those who are affected by her action,[99] and extend their power. The love awakened in them for her will reciprocally awaken more love in her for them. The projectable end of this upward spiral of reciprocal love is the establishment of a society of friends in which "the minds and bodies of all would form, as it were, one mind and one body and all together, as far as possible, strive to maintain their existence".[100] Thus even a single act of charity performed out of deferential obedience tends to bring about first preferential obedience and, ultimately, perfect charity.

What I have just described is admittedly no more than a utopian tendency. No part of that upward journey is inevitable because there are more factors in play than just the actions of Spinoza's landlady and the grateful reactions of those affected by her actions. The main enemy to moral progress is the passive emotions to which all human beings are subject. Spinoza explains that even an agent acting on the basis of adequate ideas can be thrown off course by strong desires arising from the emotions.[101] How much more so an agent like Mrs. Van der Spyck who, by hypothesis, lacks adequate ideas. In real life both she and the beneficiaries of her charity would likely be distracted by their emotions from forming an ideal community linked by love.

All that is necessary for present purposes, however, is to show that it is possible in principle to go from deferential obedience to perfect charity. Real-life realizations of the ideal are always matters of degree, as Spinoza realizes. That is why the Latin expression "*quatenus*" ("insofar as") is so prominent throughout Spinoza's discussion of moral development. Spinoza uses definitions to mark the milestones on the path of salvation, but reminds us over and over, through the use of "*quatenus*", that in the real world these milestones are attained to greater or lesser degrees Bearing that caveat in mind, it is now time to consider how Van der Spyck might move from perfect charity to Spinoza's highest notion of salvation.

The matter appears difficult because even if perfect charity can be achieved, it implies only what above was called "temporal salvation", and that is too little. The sort of salvation Spinoza promised to the obedient involves blessedness, freedom and eternal love toward God.[102] Spinoza's technical term for it is the intellectual love of God.[103] At least three significant properties set it apart from perfect charity. Two of them are suggested by the name itself: the intellectual love of God is directed at God, not at man and is intellectual, rather than emotional in character. In the third place, it is eternal. Van der Spyck's perfect charity, if it can be achieved, will by contrast be man-directed and emotional and will end at the latest with her own life. Though living in perfect charity produces what earlier was called temporal salvation, it is unclear how far it can take anyone like Van der Spyck toward the eternal salvation Spinoza says can be theirs.

Spinoza is of course not committed to the view that everyone must progress from temporal to eternal salvation. He is not a theological universalist. For him, as for orthodox Christianity, many are called, but few are chosen. What must be shown is that there is no barrier preventing even someone like Spinoza's landlady from rising above mere temporal salvation. If the TTP and the *Ethics* are to be consistent, Van der Spyck's present state of perfect charity must open to her the possibility of rising to the intellectual love of God.

It does. The first clue lies in Spinoza's doctrine that, "there is no emotion of which we cannot form clear and distinct conceptions".[104] If Van der Spyck began forming a clear and distinct conception of the emotions that are guiding her, then they would come more and more under her control[105] and other changes would follow. The more her ideas became clear and distinct, the more she could refer them to the idea of God,[106] which, Spinoza says, will cause in turn ever greater love of God.[107]

Once again, all this development hangs on the hypothetical, "if": *if* she forms a clear and distinct conception of her emotions. Just as Mrs. Van der Spyck may only slowly approach perfect charity so her ascent to clear and distinct conceptions of her emotions may be long and steep.

What makes the transition from passive emotions to clear and distinct ideas possible in principle, and even likely in Van der Spyck's case, is that she is, by hypothesis, living out what is prescribed by the seven dogmas. What they prescribe is God's decree and is therefore, Spinoza says, wholly consonant with reason: "Whoever diligently notes these dogmas of life ... and puts them into practice in a short time will assuredly be able to direct most of his actions according to the rule of reason".[108] Thus nothing prevents Van der Spyck from becoming aware of the principles of her actions in the form of eternal truths contained in the nature of God. Spinoza explains this relationship between decrees and eternal truths with a mathematical example early in the TTP:

> For example, if we are only considering that the nature of a triangle is contained in the divine nature from all eternity as an eternal truth, then we say that God has the idea of a triangle or that he understands its nature. But when ... the necessity of the essence of the triangle and of its properties are conceived as depending solely on the necessity of the divine nature and intellect, and not on the nature of the triangle itself, then the very thing that we call God's intellect is called God's will or his decree. For this reason we say one and the same thing about God when we say that God decreed and willed from all eternity that a triangle's three angles should equal two right angles and when we say that he understood it.[109]

The heart of Spinoza's argument in this passage is his explicit identification of God's will with his intellect and his implicit identification of God's individual decrees with eternal truths. Both of these identity-statements are important for understanding salvation in the present context. If Van der Spyck's perfect charitable activity can be understood as a response to God's decrees, then the above passage tells us that she can in turn come to know those decrees as eternal truths.

In response to God's decrees, as expressed in OA+, let us suppose that she has put herself into the relation with other people perfectly exemplifying those decrees insofar as she, a finite individual, is capable of doing so. To the extent that she has perfect charity she will therefore be said to exemplify God's love for mankind as he willed it to be. But in that case, because God's will and understanding are one, she will also exemplify, as far as any finite individual can, God's love for mankind as he *understands* it to be. But that is all that is required to make her capable of the intellectual love of God, since the intellectual love of God and God's love for man are said by Spinoza to be one and the same thing.[110]

Once again it must be emphasized that the path to salvation is gradual and not inevitable. Van der Spyck's supposed condition of perfect charity (which would never be fully attained in fact) contains all the material for salvation but does not in and of itself advance her to that state. It cannot do so, because there is no way to go directly from the first and lowest kind of knowledge, which still characterizes her even in the condition of perfect charity, to the third and highest grade which is associated with salvation.[111] She must first pass through the second grade of knowledge. That means that she would have to become aware of her own behaviour not as merely obeying the decrees of God but as exemplifying one or more eternal truths. Spinoza sees no barrier to anyone's rising to this second kind of knowledge, as has just been shown. But arriving at it is itself only a necessary, not a sufficient, condition for exemplifying the intellectual love of God. Love of that kind can arise only from knowledge of the third kind.[112]

I shall not enter into the difficult scholarly question of what sets the third kind of knowledge apart from knowledge of the second kind,[113] because it is not necessary for resolving the present question. There is sufficient direct textual evidence to show that Van der Spyck would in principle be capable of attaining the intellectual love of God as well. Her mind, "insofar as it involves the essence of the body under the form of eternity is eternal"[114] and "insofar as it is eternal is capable of ... knowing things by the third kind of knowledge".[115] Thus she becomes capable of knowledge of the third kind, and therefore of a salvation that is eternal, God-directed and intellectual, the kind Spinoza identifies with the intellectual love of God.

If the foregoing paragraphs show it to be possible for someone like Van der Spyck to begin with merely deferential obedience and yet arrive at salvation, the argument may be a victim of its own success. How then can Spinoza say that reason cannot account for such a transformation? The answer lies in the fact that all of Van der Spyck's moral progress is only possible, not necessary. Reason deals only with matters that are necessary and therefore cannot demonstrate that any such transformation must occur.[116] The foregoing account of Van der Spyck's moral progress lacks the apodictic certainty that would characterize a demonstration of, for example, the origin of one of the finite modes of extension or of thought.

The attainment of salvation, from a theological point of view, is a miracle, in the strong sense Spinoza gives to that term. It is something that human reason not merely does not explain, but cannot explain. That is not to say that the attainment of salvation constitutes an exception to the determinate operations of nature, any more than miracles do. But it transcends the power of human minds to demonstrate its necessity. That is why Spinoza is entitled to frame his discussion of salvation in religious language, portraying it as finally an act of mercy and grace (Dogma 7). That is also why he is entitled to classify it as a revelation. OA+ is reasonable, but not demonstrable. It does not challenge reason, but complements it. Religion defines a different context of explanation from that defined by philosophy.

The opacity of explanatory contexts accounts for why no inconsistency arises in Spinoza's teachings when proposition 3) is conjoined with 1) and 2). Recognizing it permits us to affirm the consistency of Spinoza's teachings without postulating controversial doctrines after the manner of Alexandre Matheron, and without sliding down the hermeneutical slope into those theories that do not admit Spinoza to be consistent at all. All the major doctrines associated with OA+ are thus transferable to the *Ethics*.

The final chapter will evaluate the Christian dimension of Spinoza's philosophy in that light.

Notes

1   Roothaan [1998], 270 observes this fact. Alexandre Matheron, as discussed in the previous chapter, provides an example.
2   For a discussion of the history and motivation of the doctrine of double truth see Martin Pine [1968] "Pomponazzi and the Problem of 'Double Truth'", in *Journal of the History of Ideas* 29, pp. 163-176. See also his article "Double Truth" in the *Dictionary of the History of Ideas*.

3   Allison [1987], 225.
4   Spinoza [1925] 3, 184 = TTP 15: " quod ...unaquaeque suum regnum obtineat".
5   Spinoza [1925] 2, 239 = 4E37s2 "justum et injustum ... notiones esse extrinsecas".
6   Spinoza [1925] 2, 56 = 1Ep15.
7   The seven dogmas are found at Spinoza [1925] 3, 177f = TTP 14.
8   Spinoza [1925] 2, 270 = 4EA15: "Quae concordiam gignunt, sunt illa, quae ad justitiam, aequitatem, et honestatem referuntur".
9   Spinoza [1925] 2, 172 = 3Ep41s. See also p. 200 = 3EAffd34.
10   E.g., Spinoza [1925] 2, 136 = 2Ep49s; also p. 236 = 4Ep37s1.
11   Spinoza [1925] 2, 250 = 4Ep54.
12   Spinoza [1925] 2 = 4Ed8.
13   Spinoza [1925] 3, 177 = TTP 14.
14   Spinoza [1925] 2, 77f = 1EApp: "sed quia non pauca adhuc restant praejudicia quae ... impedire ... possunt, quominus homines rerum concatenationem eo, quo ipsam explicui, modo amplecti possint, eadem hic ad examen rationis vocare operae pretium duxi".
15   Spinoza [1925] 2, 78 = 1E App.
16   Spinoza [1925] 2, 80 = 1E App.
17   Spinoza [1925] 2, 207 = 4EPref: "Quare ... finalis causa ... nihil est praeter hunc singularem appetitum qui revera causa est efficiens, quae ut prima consideratur".
18   Spinoza [1925] 2, 80 = 1E App.
19   Spinoza [1925] 2, 83 = 1E App: "... nec ideo res magis, qut minus perfectae sunt, propterea quod hominum sensum delectant, vel offendunt; quod humanae naturae conducunt, vel quod eidem repugnant".
20   Spinoza [1925] 2, 78 = 1EApp.
21   Spinoza [1925] 2, 78f = 1EApp.
22   Spinoza [1925] 2, 80 = 1EApp.
23   Spinoza [1925] 2, 73 = 1Ep32c1.
24   Spinoza [1925] 2, 80 = 1E App.
25   Spinoza [1925] 2, 74 = 1Ep33s2.
26   Spinoza [1925] 2, 74f = 1Ep33s2: "... si rem meditari vellent, nostrarumque demonstrationum seriem recte secum perpendere, quin tandem talem libertatemm, qualem jam Deo tribuunt, non tantum, ut nugatoriam; sed, ut magnum scientiae obstaclum, plane rejiciant".
27   Spinoza [1925] 2, 75 = 1Ep33s2.
28   For references in Thomas see Gueroult [1966] *Spinoza*. Vol 1 (*Éthique, 1*) Paris: Aubier, p. 366, note 32; for a discussion of Leibniz's relevance see Hunter [2001], 63, note 6.
29   Spinoza sketches his views of modality in the first scholium to proposition 33. He has both an epistemic and an ontological definition of the fundamental modal terms. Epistemically something is called possible when we are ignorant of whether or not it belongs to the causal order. Ontologically a putative fact is called possible if it is not impossible, i.e., if its non-existence does not follow from the essences of the things involved and if there is some cause of that fact in the causal order. On these definitions ontological possibility turns out to be equivalent to ontological necessity and modal terms turn out to be vacuous.
30   Thomas Aquinas *Quaestiones disputatae de potentia* q. 24, a3: "finis ergo naturalis divinae voluntatis est eius bonitas, quam non velle non potest. sed fini huic non commensurantur creaturae, ita quod sine his divina bonitas manifestari non possit; quod Deus intendit ex creaturis. sicut enim manifestatur divina bonitas per has res quae nunc sunt et per hunc rerum ordinem, ita potest manifestari per alias creaturas et alio modo

ordinatas: et ideo divina voluntas absque praeiudicio bonitatis, iustitiae et sapientiae, potest se extendere in alia quam quae facit".

31 Spinoza [1925] 2, 75 = 1Ep33S2. While discussing this argument no further references will be provided until there is a page-change in the primary text.

32 So Gueroult [1968], *Dieu* (*Éthique, 1*). Vol. 1 of *Spinoza* Paris: Aubier, 372: "si, en effet, on soutient que, au cas où de toute éternité ses décrets eussent été autres, sa perfection eût été la même, on n'a plus aucune raison de prétendre que, s'il les changeait maintenant, sa perfection en serait anéantie".

33 Spinoza [1925] 2, 76 = 1Ep33S2.

34 Spinoza [1925] 2, 76 = 1Ep33S2.

35 Spinoza [1925] 2, 76 = 1Ep33S2: "Fateor, hanc opinionem, quae omnia indifferenti cuidam Dei voluntati subjicit, et ab ipsius beneplacito omnia pendere statuit, minus a vero aberrare, quam illorum, qui statuunt Deum omnia sub ratione boni agere."

36 Spinoza [1925] 2, 76 = 1Ep33S2.

37 Spinoza [1925] 2, 76 = 1Ep33S2: "quod, (ut modo ostendi) magnum est absurdum".

38 Spinoza [1925] 3, 65 = TTP 4.

39 Spinoza [1925] 2, 74 = 1Ep33s2.

40 Spinoza [1925] 3, 111 = TTP 7.

41 Spinoza [1925] 3, 74 = TTP, 5. "Obedientia in eo consistit, quod aliquis mandata ex sola imperantis authoritate exequatur".

42 Spinoza [1925] 2, 303 = (5E36s): "salus seu ... libertas".

43 Spinoza [1925] 2, 46 = 1Ed7.

44 Spinoza [1925] 2, 267 = 4EAppCap4.

45 Spinoza [1925] 2, 308 = 5Ep42s: "ab omnibus fere negligeretur".

46 Cook [1995], 34.

47 Brochard [1954], 341: "... puisqu'il met la foi au dessous de la raison, puisqu'il considère la révélation comme une transposition de la vérité mise à la portée des simples. La foi est une connaissance inadéquate, et, selon l'esprit et la lettre même de sa doctrine, l'idée inadéquate ne diffère guère de l'erreur".

48 Spinoza [1925] 2, 161 = 3Ep28.

49 Matheron [1971], 183.

50 Matheron [1971], 154.

51 Matheron [1971], 155.

52 It was condemned in 543 in the *Canones contra Origenem*. See H. Denzinger [1952] *Enchridion Symbolorum* Freiburg: Herder, p. 97, canon 9.

53 Spinoza [1925] 2, 308 = 5E42s.

54 Matheron [1971], 151.

55 Spinoza [1925] 2, 299 = 5Ep32; Matheron [1971] 151.

56 Matheron [1971], 174.

57 Matheron [1971], 152f.

58 Matheron 152f. Cf. Spinoza [1925] 3, 62 = TTP 4: "ex vera libertate et animo integro et constante".

59 Spinoza [1925] 2, 289 = 5Ep11.

60 Matheron [1971], 173.

61 Matheron [1971], 157f.

62 Spinoza [1925] 2, 235 = 4Ep37 .

63 Matheron [1971], 165.

64 Matheron [1971], 234.

65 Matheron [1971], 242.

66 Matheron [1971], 188.

67 Spinoza [1925] 3, 194 = TTP 15.
68 Spinoza [1925] 3, 44 = TTP 3.
69 Spinoza [1925] 3, 199 = TTP 17: "actio ex mandato". Cf. also op. cit., 74 = TTP 5.
70 Spinoza [1925] 3, 263 = TTP, note 31.
71 Spinoza [1925] 3, 188 = TTP 15.
72 Spinoza [1925], 188 = TTP 15: "... quod simplex obedientia via ad salutem sit".
73 Spinoza [1925], 263 = TTP, note 31: "... satis [est] divina decreta tanquam jura seu mandata amplecti".
74 Spinoza [1925] 3, 264 = TTP, note 34.
75 Spinoza [1925] 2, 303 = 5Ep36s: "...clare intelligimus, qua in re nostra salus ... consistit, nempe in constanti, et aeterno erga Deum amore,...". The adjective "intellectualis" is implicit, the scholium being an explication of proposition 36 in which it is used.
76 Spinoza [1925] 2, 89 = 2Ep7.
77 Spinoza [1925] 2, 90 =2Ep7s.
78 Spinoza [1925] 2, 141 = 3Ep2.
79 Spinoza [1925] 2, 144 = 3Ep2.
80 Or can easily be made to be. It is sufficient to restate i) as "M has an explanation to which M* is essential" and ii) as "M does not have an explanation to which P* is essential".
81 A complete guide up to ca. 1996 is contained in the bibliography of Della Rocca [1996].
82 Della Rocca [1996], 118ff.
83 In fact he explicitly argues that opacity in Spinoza goes beyond the context of explanation (p. 124), but that is not crucial to the present discussion.
84 Spinoza [1925] 3, 184 = TTP 15: "Theologia vero nihil praeter hoc [i.e., homines sola obedientia possint esse beati] dictat nihilque prater obedientiam imperat ...".
85 See chapter 6.
86 Spinoza [1925] 3, 184 = TTP 15.
87 Spinoza [1925] 3, 188 = TTP 15: "[P]hilosophia a theologia separanda [est] ... et ... neutra neutri ancilletur".
88 Spinoza [1925] 3, 184f = TTP 15: "Theologiam enim sic acceptam, si ejus praecepta sive documenta vitae spectes, cum ratione convenire, et si ejus intentum et finem, nulla in re eidem repugnare comperies, et propterea omnibus universalis est" .
89 Spinoza [1925] 3, 185 = TTP 15.
90 Spinoza [1925] 3, 177 = TTP 14.
91 Spinoza [1925] 3, 179 = TTP 14: "qui optima ostendit opera justitiae et charitatis".
92 Spinoza [1925] 3, 188 = TTP 15.
93 Spinoza [1925] 2, 287 =5Ep10s.
94 Spinoza [1925[3, 176 = TTP 14: "dogmata ... quae animum ad obedientiam movent".
95 Spinoza [1925] 2, 307 = 5Ep41s: "nisi haec spes et metus hominibus inessent, at contra si crederent, mentes cum corpore inteire, ne sestare miseris, Pietatis onere confecti, vivere longius, ad ingenium redirent, et ex libidine omnia moderarir, et fortunae potius, quam sibi parere, vellent".
96 Spinoza [1925] 2, 197 = 3EAffd27.
97   Spinoza [1925] 2, 274 = 4EAppCap30.
98 Spinoza [1925] 2, 161 = 3Ep28.
99 Spinoza [1925] 2, 172 = 3Ep41.
100 Spinoza [1925] 2, 223 = 4Ep18s.
101 Spinoza [1925] 2, 220 = 4Ep15: "Cupiditas, quae ex vera boni ... cognitione oritur, multis aliis cupiditatibus, quae ex affectibus, quibus conflicatmur, oriuntur, restingui, vel coerceri potest".
102 Spinoza [1925] 2, 303 = 5Ep36s.

103 Spinoza [1925] 2, 300 = 5Ep32c.
104 Spinoza [1925] 2, 282 = 5Ep4c.
105 Spinoza [1925] 2, 282 = 5Ep3c.
106 Spinoza [1925] 2, 290 = 5Ep14.
107 Spinoza [1925] 2, 239 = 5Ep10s.
108 Spinoza [1925] 2, 282 = 5Ep15.
109 Spinoza [1925] 3, 62f = TTP 4.
110 Spinoza [1925] 2, 303 = 5Ep36c.
111 Spinoza [1925] 2, 297 = 5Ep28.
112 Spinoza [1925] 2, 300 = 5Ep32c, 33.
113 A meticulous discussion of it can be found in Gueroult [1974], *Spinoza* 2 (*L'âme*) Paris: Aubier, pp. 416-487.
114 Spinoza [1925] 2, 296 = 5Ep23s.
115 Spinoza [1925] 2, 299 = 5Ep31dem.
116 Spinoza [1925] 2, 122 = 2Ep41.

Chapter Eight

Spinoza and Christianity

The preceding chapters have emphasized the radical Protestant dimension of Spinoza's religious thought. Collegiants were Spinoza's closest friends and their religious views were clearly congenial to him. In his *Tractatus Theologico-Politicus* Spinoza achieved the simplification of Christian dogma they aimed at. In keeping with broader Reformation ideals Spinoza is dismissive of tradition, viewing Scripture alone as essential to the Catholic Faith and proposing a new hermeneutic for the proper understanding of it.

Spinoza acknowledges the Christian Bible to be a revealed text. It is a collection of prophetic writings whose claim on our attention derives on the one hand from the miracles attesting to the prophets' authority and on the other from the conformity of their message with what reason recognizes as moral truth. However Spinoza does not see the prophets as mere recorders of divinely authored texts. He is like later liberal theologians in treating them as men of their own time, not transcending the particularities of their context and language, still less the limitation of their own abilities. They are always fallible, even to the point of being superstitious and ignorant.

In most cases it is the prophets' vivid imaginations that fit them for their task, according to Spinoza. But that does not imply that their prophecies are merely imaginary. Prophets really articulate the mind of God, Spinoza says, even though they do it subjectively and imperfectly. The difficulty of separating the kernel of their message from the chaff of subjectivity only increases as we recede from them in time and context and progressively lose information about them as individual writers and thinkers. Spinoza's great legacy to theology is the scientific method he develops to cope with these obstacles and uncover Scripture's fundamental message.

When he applies his method he finds that there is only one main teaching to which all Scripture attests and which can therefore be counted by readers of later periods as a revelation. It is that all who obey the commands of God can be saved. That proposition, which I have called the "obedience axiom" (OA), and its logical consequences form the whole subject matter of theology.

To say that there is only one revealed teaching in all of Scripture is to outrage traditional orthodox Christianity. That alone would explain and to some extent justify the inveterate hostility of sectarian commentators toward him. However, to allow for even one revealed teaching also puts in doubt the resolutely horizontal commitment to immanentism and naturalism with which Spinoza is usually credited. OA is after all treated as a moral certainty, though it is neither knowable nor refutable by reason.

Because of OA and all that it entails theology and philosophy must learn to coexist. Neither can absorb the other and if they conduct themselves properly neither contradicts the other. The TTP unfolds a complete blueprint for the harmonious coexistence of the two disciplines, which is said to be both desirable for the sake of increasing piety and crucial for ongoing political stability in the Republic.

As I have represented him, Spinoza shares a concern that animated many of the best seventeenth century thinkers: how to make Christian culture work in the modern age. It puts him in the company of Descartes, Hobbes, Malebranche, Leibniz, Locke and many others, who tried with varying degrees of success to accommodate Christian teachings to their age. None of the philosophers just named escaped being censured for their religious views by sectarian critics, though only Hobbes could rival Spinoza for the degree and sheer quantity of opprobrium heaped upon him.[1]

Spinoza may have been the most radical theologian of his age, but the centuries that separate us from him diminish the shock of his originality and enable us to see more clearly the continuity of his concerns with those of his time. It is possible for us to see, as few of his contemporaries could, that Spinoza's radicalism is still internal to Protestant Christianity. It shares Protestant concern for the future and purity of the Christianity. It does not anticipate the views of Voltaire, or Marx, or Nietzsche who wished for the Faith's abolition.

It would be a weighty objection against this view of the TTP if adopting it made Spinoza inconsistent with himself by making the TTP inconsistent with the *Ethics*. However in the previous chapter I showed this not to be the case. The TTP can be understood as presenting a version of radical Protestantism and still be shown to be consistent with the philosophical positions taken in the *Ethics*. It is far more difficult to reconcile the Protestant Spinoza to the different pictures of him found in the secondary literature, so many of which agree in depicting him as hostile to Christianity in any form.

That is not to say that the present account is everywhere in conflict with others. As stressed in the Introduction, I have not put Spinoza's radical Protestantism forward as a key to his whole philosophy, nor even as the only source of this thought. Nothing I have said precludes recognizing his debt to a wide variety of other influences, which might include Jewish philosophy or Cartesianism or political radicalism.

There is at least one purported source of Spinoza's thinking with which this account of his radical Protestantism cannot easily agree, however. I would like to conclude with a brief critical examination of an important study of Spinoza's thought in which Yirmiyahu Yovel traces what he sees as the influence of Marranism. According to Yovel in the first volume of his *Spinoza and Other Heretics* Marranism led Spinoza to engage in a deliberately equivocal form of writing, to construct an alternative theory of salvation and, finally, to adopt a secular outlook. In the second volume of his study Yovel argues that Spinoza's religious attitude places him closer to nineteenth century philosophers such as Hegel, Marx and Nietzsche than to his own contemporaries.

Did his Marrano ancestry lead Spinoza to be "a philosopher of immanence and secularization" and perhaps "the first secular Jew"?[2] The claim that it did has not met with universal agreement.[3] But Yovel is certainly entitled to object to critics who represent *Spinoza and Other Heretics* as trying to account for all of Spinoza's thought by appeal to Marranism alone. "It presents Marranism as a *dimension* of Spinoza's career and growth", he says, one "which deepens our understanding of the other dimensions as well, but which is not exclusive".[4] The present study recognizes its own limits in the same way. Nevertheless, partial though they are, Yovel's and my accounts of Spinoza cannot coexist as "dimensions" of the same space. The Spinoza presented in these pages was not secular in his outlook. Neither did he reject Christianity nor anticipate the religious concerns of later centuries.

Yovel's preoccupation with heterodoxy leads him to see Spinoza's critique of religious orthodoxy as if it were directed against historical religion as such. We are told, for example, that Spinoza "distanced himself from both Judaism and Christianity" by the pantheism he developed in the *Ethics*.[5] And again, Spinoza's "hidden esoteric truth" is said to be "not Judaism in opposition to Christianity, but the immanent religion of reason in opposition to all historical religions".[6]

While it is correct that on some points Spinoza was as critical of Christians as he was of Jews, to lump these criticisms together conceals vast differences in his attitude to the two religions. One reason for writing the TTP was to show how the minimalistic Christianity developed in Chapter 14 could be the official religion of a progressive modern state, which Judaism, in his view, could not. Spinoza would have to reject Judaism as a religion, except, possibly, in a form liberal enough to accommodate his version of Christianity.

Of Christianity he rejects only sectarianism. Non-sectarian Christianity is his solution to the political, moral and spiritual problems of Holland.

Failing to take account of the radically Protestant element in Spinoza's religious thought leads Yovel to overestimate the novelty of his doctrine of salvation. He writes of a "new alternate way to salvation" supposedly found in Spinoza, one "which lies neither in Christ nor in the Law of Moses, but in the third kind of knowledge".[7] Yovel is ignoring the explicitly Christian framework in which the doctrine of salvation is elaborated, particularly in TTP 14. He is wrongly presupposing that the third kind of knowledge is incompatible with Spinoza's TTP idea of salvation through obedience. And, finally, he is making Spinoza guilty of the very vice in religious thinkers he excoriates: "the blind and rash passion for interpreting the Scripture and excogitating novelties in religion".[8]

Spinoza's style of writing was deeply affected by Marranism, Yovel thinks. He calls Spinoza "a grand master of dual language and equivocation", a technique which he says "is manifest in those of Spinoza's writings published during his lifetime, especially the *Theologico-Political Treatise* ...". For that reason, Yovel argues, we must not try to construe him literally, even though a literal reading is precisely what he seems to teach in the TTP: "While Spinoza advocated a literal hermeneutic method for the Bible, applying this method to Spinoza's own published works would be a mistake".

What is required instead, Yovel says, is "a rather complex and subtle hermeneutics ..., far removed from the literal reading of the text". As we read things with an apparently orthodox meaning we are to watch for a trick by which Spinoza "would pass a covert message to anyone capable of grasping it, while using a phrase whose literal sense was the opposite, thus misleading the innocent reader".[9]

On its own this suggestion is not much help. When Spinoza writes with apparent sincerity that Christ was the way of salvation (*via salutis*[10]) what exactly is the savvy reader supposed to understand? That Christ is *not* the way of salvation? How could we ever understand anyone, unless his words can be assumed to mean what they say? Yovel acknowledges the methodological dangers implicit in assuming what we read to be "literary equivocation". However beyond the counsel of perfection in which he calls for "sensitivity and moderation, an openness toward this phenomenon along with a healthy critical reserve to keep it in check",[11] he offers little guidance on how to avoid its dangers.

It is interesting, but not surprising, that the purest example he can find of equivocal writing in Spinoza lies in the seven dogmas of TTP 14. For each one Yovel is able to find a latent true meaning until he reaches the seventh which he abandons as "impossible to translate into philosophical language".[12] Yovel was apparently unaware that Matheron had managed to translate all seven in his attempt to supply each dogma with what he (Matheron) calls its "true sense".

I have given my reasons for mistrusting such subtle hermeneutics in Chapter 6. With regard to the seven dogmas in particular I have also shown that they do not have to be translated into philosophically respectable terms for Spinoza to be able to affirm them consistently. Yovel's reading yields a Spinoza who, though dishonest with his contemporaries, holds opinions widely appreciated today. The interpretation I have proposed has the opposite strengths. It diminishes Spinoza's attunement to current opinion, but allows him to speak in the idiom of his contemporaries and mean what he says.

Yovel concedes that Spinoza is a child of his time in cherishing the hope of salvation. But he stands above the age, Yovel thinks, in all that concerns the method of getting there:

> Neither the love of Christ, the Law of Moses, or the confused and ineffable mystical experience can lead the soul to where it necessarily aspires by its nature: this can only be done in ways that, while retaining the basic ambitions of the mystic and the religious devotee, are utterly opposed to their practices.[13]

Yovel is right to say that Spinoza rejects the Law of Moses as an avenue to salvation. But once again he treats Spinoza's attitude to Christianity as if it were merely an addendum to his rejection of Judaism. However, as already pointed out in several different contexts, Spinoza is far from denying the importance of love as Christ understood it, assuming this to be what Yovel means by "the love of Christ". On the contrary the obedience required in the Scripture consists precisely in learning to exemplify the love of Christ (i.e., charity) in our lives. According to the apostles John and James, love is all that is required of those whom Yovel calls "religious devotee[s]" and Spinoza, far from opposing this teaching, sees it as one of the central consequences of the Obedience Axiom. As reported in Chapter 6 he plainly says that only those who are obedient to Christ's way of love can be saved.

There is one final difference to be discussed. Like some of Spinoza's bitterest enemies, Yovel calls him a "heretic". The difference is that Yovel says it with a twinkle in his eye and as a friend:

> As for the word *heretic*, it should be taken with a grain of salt. I use it to designate thinkers who, when properly understood, must be deemed heretical in terms of their own orthodox tradition. Again, no derogatory undertones are

intended; if anything, a reader discerning a shade of ironic sympathy in the title will not be totally mistaken.[14]

It is debatable whether or not the term, when used in this ironic and sympathetic way, clarifies Spinoza's stand on any religion. From the point of view of Jewish orthodoxy, he is surely a heretic in the derogatory sense that Yovel does not mean to invoke. Numerous Christian critics, speaking from the orthodoxy of their own denominations have also been perfectly justified in calling him so. But Spinoza, I think, would have rejected the attempt on the part of Christians to label him as a heretic, and rightly so.

What G.K. Chesterton wrote with characteristic wit about the strange modern notion of heresy would apply to Yovel's inappropriate use of the term in connection with Spinoza:

> In former days the heretic was proud of not being a heretic. It was the kingdoms of the world and the police and the judges who were heretics. He was orthodox. He had no pride in having rebelled against them; they had rebelled against him. The armies with their cruel security, the kings with their cold faces, the decorous processes of State, the reasonable processes of law – all these like sheep had gone astray. The man was proud of being orthodox, was proud of being right. If he stood alone in a howling wilderness he was more than a man; he was a church. He was the centre of the universe; it was round him that the stars swung. All the tortures torn out of forgotten hells could not make him admit that he was heretical. But a few modern phrases have made him boast of it. He says, with a conscious laugh, 'I suppose I am very heretical', and looks round for applause. The word 'heresy' not only means no longer being wrong; it practically means being clear-headed and courageous. The word 'orthodoxy' not only no longer means being right; it practically means being wrong. All this can mean one thing, and one thing only. It means that people care less for whether they are philosophically right. For obviously a man ought to confess himself crazy before he confesses himself heretical. The Bohemian, with a red tie, ought to pique himself on his orthodoxy. The dynamiter, laying a bomb, ought to feel that, whatever else he is, at least he is orthodox.[15]

Spinoza cared for nothing more than being philosophically and religiously right. He did not use the term "heretic" as a jocular compliment and resented any attempt to apply it with its normal connotations to himself. An obviously defensive passage in the *Ethics* points this out, complaining that:

whoever seeks the true causes of miracles, or tries to understand natural events as a learned man, rather than gape at them like a fool, is everywhere taken to be impious and a heretic by those who are commonly revered as interpreters of nature and the gods.[16]

Taken at face value, this passage implies that Spinoza does not see himself as a heretic in either the traditional or the modern sense. Not in the former, because he is right; nor in the latter, because he is serious.

Despite all his seriousness and his conviction of being right, however, it must be admitted that the Christianity without dogma Spinoza advocates could not be judged to be anything less than seriously defective by most denominational Christians. Its picture of Christ without the Cross and without the physical Resurrection is enough to put it beyond the pale for most Christians even today. Those within traditional confessional Christianity are bound to view Spinoza as heretical, and not in Yovel's playful sense. But Spinoza's religious thought remains closer to theirs than is usually believed, closer to the Christians who rejected him than to the atheists of the Enlightenment who adopted him as their own. More importantly, it remains closer to traditional Protestant Christianity than is usually recognized by scholars today. If this book goes any way toward establishing Spinoza's real relationship to the Christian tradition, it will have accomplished something worthwhile.

Notes

1 See e.g., Israel [2001], 159ff; S.I. Mintz [1962] *The Hunting of Leviathan*. Cambridge: Cambridge University Press.
2 Yovel [1989] vol. 1, x.
3 See Seymour Feldman [1992] "Spinoza: A Marrano of Reason?" *Inquiry* 35, 37-53. Interestingly, on p. 45 he even asserts that the influence of radical Protestants likely went deeper.
4 Yovel [1992], "Spinoza and Other Heretics: Reply to Critics" *Inquiry* 35, 89.
5 Yovel [1989], vol. 1, 5.
6 Yovel [1989], vol. 1, 143.
7 Yovel [1989], vol. 1, 33.
8 Spinoza [1925] 3, 97 = TTP 7.
9 Yovel [1989], vol. 1, 29.
10 Spinoza [1925] 3, 21 = TTP 1.
11 Yovel [1989], vol. 1, 151.
12 Yovel [1989], vol. 1, 227.
13 Yovel [1989], vol. 1, 37.
14 Yovel [1989], xi.

15   G.K. Chesterton [1960], *Heretics*, London, Bodley Head, 3f.
16   Spinoza [1925] 2, 81 = 1EApp.

Appendix:
Concordance to TTP-Translations

Bold type references are to Spinoza [1925] 3 (here '**G**'). They are followed by the corresponding pages in the most common English translations: R. H. Elwes (Dover Books) "E", and Samuel Shirley (Hackett) "S".

G	E	S	G	E	S	G	E	S
5	3f	1f	**50**	48f	40	**93**	93f	81f
6	4f	2	**51**	49f	40f	**94**	94f	82f
7	5f	2ff	**52**	50f	41f	**95**	95f	83f
8	6f	4	**53**	51f	42f	**96**	96f	84f
9	7f	4f	**54**	52ff	43f	**97**	98f	86
10	8ff	5f	**55**	54f	44f	**98**	99f	86f
11	10f	6f	**56**	55f	45f	**99**	100f	87f
12	11	7f	**57**	56f	46ff	**100**	101f	88f
15	13f	9	**58**	57f	48f	**101**	102f	89f
16	14f	9f	**59**	58f	49f	**102**	103f	90f
17	15f	10f	**60**	59f	50	**103**	104f	91f
18	16f	11f	**61**	60f	50f	**104**	105f	92
19	17f	12f	**62**	61f	51f	**105**	106f	92f
20	18	13f	**63**	62f	52f	**106**	107f	93f
21	18f	21	**64**	63f	53f	**107**	108f	94f
22	19f	22f	**65**	64f	54f	**108**	109f	95f
23	20f	15f	**66**	65f	55f	**109**	110f	96f
24	21f	16f	**67**	66f	56f	**110**	111f	97f
25	22f	17f	**68**	67f	57f	**111**	112f	98f
26	23f	18	**69**	69f	59	**112**	113f	99
27	24	18f	**70**	70	59f	**113**	114f	99f
28	24f	19f	**71**	70f	60f	**114**	115f	100f
29	25ff	20f	**72**	71f	61f	**115**	116f	101f
30	27f	21f	**73**	72ff	62f	**116**	117f	102f
31	28f	22f	**74**	74f	63f	**117**	118ff	103ff
32	29f	23f	**75**	75f	64f	**118**	120f	105f
33	30f	24f	**76**	76f	65f	**119**	121f	106f
34	31f	25	**77**	77f	66f	**120**	122f	107f
35	32f	25f	**78**	78f	67f	**121**	123f	108
36	33f	26f	**79**	79f	68	**122**	124f	108f
37	34f	27f	**80**	80	68ff	**123**	125f	109f
38	35f	28f	**81**	81f	71	**124**	126f	110f
39	36f	29f	**82**	82f	71f	**125**	127ff	111f
40	37f	30f	**83**	83f	72f	**126**	129f	112f
41	38f	31f	**84**	84f	73f	**127**	130f	113f
42	39ff	32f	**85**	85	74f	**128**	131f	114f
43	41f	33f	**86**	86f	75f	**129**	133f	116
44	42f	34f	**87**	87f	76f	**130**	134f	116f
45	43f	35f	**88**	88f	77f	**131**	135f	117f
46	44f	36f	**89**	89f	78f	**132**	136f	118f
47	45f	37f	**90**	90f	79f	**133**	137f	119f

G	E	S	G	E	S	G	E	S
48	46f	38f	91	91f	80f	134	138f	120f
49	47f	39f	92	92f	81	135	139f	121f
136	140f	122f	184	194f	168f	232	249f	215f
137	141f	123f	185	195f	168f	233	250f	216f
138	142f	124f	186	196f	170f	234	251f	217
139	143f	125f	187	197f	171f	235	252f	218
140	144f	126f	188	198f	172	236	253f	218f
141	145f	127f	189	200f	173f	237	254f	219f
142	146f	128f	190	201f	174	238	255f	220f
143	147ff	129f	191	202f	174f	239	257f	222
144	149f	130f	192	203f	175f	240	258f	222f
145	150f	131f	193	204f	176f	241	259f	223f
146	151f	132f	194	205f	177f	242	260f	224f
147	152f	133f	195	206f	178f	243	261f	225f
148	153f	134f	196	207f	179f	244	262f	226f
149	154f	135f	197	208f	180f	245	263f	227f
150	155f	136f	198	209ff	181f	246	264f	228f
151	156f	137ff	199	211f	182f	247	265f	229f
152	157f	139	200	212f	183f	251	269	–
153	158ff	139f	201	214f	185	252	269f	231
154	160 f	140f	202	215f	185f	253	270f	232
155	161	141f	203	216f	186f	254	271	232f
156	161f	142f	204	217f	187f	255	271f	233f
157	162f	143f	205	218f	188f	256	272f	234
158	163ff	144f	206	219f	189f	257	273	234f
159	165f	145f	207	220f	190f	258	273	235
160	166f	146f	208	221ff	191f	259	273f	235f
161	167f	147f	209	223f	192f	260	274	236
162	168ff	148	210	224f	193f	261	274f	236f
163	170f	148f	211	225f	194f	262	275f	237
164	171f	149f	212	226f	195f	263	276	238
165	172f	150f	213	227f	196	264	276f	238f
166	173f	151f	214	228f	196f	265	277	239
167	175f	153	215	229f	197f	266	277f	239
168	176f	153f	216	230f	198f	267	278	239f
169	177f	154f	217	231f	199f			
170	178f	155f	218	232ff	200			
171	179f	156f	219	234f	201f			
172	180f	157	220	235f	202f			
173	182f	158	221	236f	203ff			
174	183f	158f	222	237f	205f			
175	184f	159f	223	238f	206f			
176	185f	160f	224	239ff	207f			
177	186f	161f	225	241f	208f			
178	187f	162f	226	242f	209			
179	188f	163f	227	243f	209f			
180	189ff	164f	228	244f	210ff			
181	191	165f	229	245f	212f			
182	191f	166f	230	246ff	213f			
183	192ff	167f	231	248f	214f			

Bibliography

Akkerman, F. and Hubbeling, H.G [1979], "The Preface to Spinoza's Posthumous Works (1677) and its Author Jarig Jelles (c. 1619/20 – 1683)" *Lias* 6 (1979) pp. 103-173.

Allison, Henry [1987], *Benedict de Spinoza: An Introduction*, New Haven, Yale University Press.

Bedjaï, Marc [1983], *La lumière sur le candelabre de Pieter Balling: Fragment d'un enseignement Spinoziste et Inedita Spinozana (Textes, traduction et commentaire)*, Paris. (Photocopy of author's typescript. Includes the original Dutch text and a seventeenth century English translation.)

Bloch, Olivier ed. [1990], *Spinoza au XVIIIe siècle*, Paris, Méridiens-Klincksieck.

Blom, Hans W. [1988], "Spinoza et les problèmes d'une théorie de la société commerçante", *Studia Spinozana* 4, pp. 281-301.

Brochard, V. [1954], "Le Dieu de Spinoza", in V. Delbos (ed.), *Études de philosophie ancienne et de philosophie moderne* Paris, Vrin.

Brunschwicg, Léon [1951], "Spinoza" in *Écrits philosophiques*, Paris, Presses Universitaires de France.

Brykman, Geneviève [1972], *La judéité de Spinoza* Paris: Vrin.

Calvin, Jean [1960] *Institutes of the Christian Religion*, 2 volumes, Philadelphia, The Westminster Press.

Coley, R.L. [1957], *Light and Enlightenment: A Study of the Cambridge Platonists and the Dutch Arminians*, Cambridge, Cambridge University Press.

Cook, J. Thomas [1995], "Did Spinoza lie to his Landlady?", *Studia Spinozana* 11, pp. 15-37.

Curley, Edwin [1994], "Notes on a Neglected Masterpiece", in Graeme Hunter (ed.), *Spinoza: The Enduring Questions*, Toronto, University of Toronto Press.

De Dijn, Herman [1996], *Spinoza: The Way to Wisdom*, West Lafayette, Indiana, Purdue University Press.

Della Rocca, Michael [1996] *Representation and the Mind-Body Problem in Spinoza*, New York/Oxford, Oxford University Press.

Donagan, Alan [1996], "Spinoza's Theology" in Don Garrett (ed.), *The Cambridge Companion to Spinoza* Cambridge: Cambridge University Press, pp. 343-382.

Feuer, Lewis [1966], *Spinoza and the Rise of Liberalism*, Boston, Beacon Press.

Fix, Andrew [1990], "Mennonites and Collegiants in Holland 1630-1700", *Mennonite Quarterly Review* 64, pp. 160-175.

Fix, Andrew [1991], *Prophecy and Reason: The Dutch Collegiants in the Early Enlightenment*, Princeton N.J., Princeton University Press.

Francès, Madeleine [1937], *Spinoza dans les pays Néerlandais de la seconde moitié du XVIIe siècle*, Paris, Alcan.

Freudenthal, J. [1899], *Die Lebensgeschichte Spinozas in Quellenschriften, Urkunden und Nichtamtlichen Nachrichten*, Leipzig, Von Veit.

Freudenthal, J. [1927], *Spinoza: Sein Leben und seine Lehre*, Heidelberg, Carl Winter.

Gebhardt, Carl [1914], *Spinoza: Lebensbeschreibungen und Gespräche*, Hamburg, Meiner.

Gebhardt, Carl [1932], "Die Religion Spinozas", *Archiv für Geschichte der Philosophie* 41, pp. 339-362.

Geyl, Pierter [1966], *The Netherlands in the Seventeenth Century*, Vol. 1, 1609-1648, 2nd ed., London, Ernest Benn.

Harrisville, Roy and Sundberg, Walter [1995], *The Bible in Modern Culture: Theology and Historical-Critical Method from Spinoza to Käsemann*, Grand Rapids, Eerdmans.

Hubbeling, Hubertus G. [1984], "Zur frühen Spinozarezeption in den Niederlanden", in Karlfried Gründer and Wilhelm Schmidt-Biggemann (eds), *Spinoza in der Frühzeit seiner religiösen Wirkung*, Heidelberg, Lambert Schneider.

Hunter, Graeme [1996] "Arnauld's Defence of Miracles", in Elmar Kremer (ed.), *Interpreting Arnauld*, Toronto: University of Toronto Press, pp. 111-126.

Hunter, Graeme [2001] "Spinoza: A Radical Protestant?", in Elmar Kremer and Michael Latzer (eds), *Evil in Early Modern Philosophy*, Toronto, University of Toronto Press, pp. 49-65.

Israel, Jonathan I. [1984], "The Changing Role of the Dutch Sephardim in International Trade 1595-1715", in *Dutch Jewish History: Proceedings of the Symposium on the History of the Jews in the Netherlands 1982*, Tel-Aviv-Jerusalem, The Institute for Research on Dutch Jewry, pp. 31-51.

Israel, Jonathan I. [1995], *The Dutch Republic: Its Rise Greatness and Fall*, Oxford, Clarendon Press.

Israel, Jonathan I. [1996], "The Banning of Spinoza's Works in the Dutch Republic (1670-1678)", in van Bunge and Klever (eds), pp. 3-14.

Israel, Jonathan I. [2001], *Radical Enlightenment,* Oxford, Oxford University Press

Kaplan, Yosef [1989], *From Christianity to Judaism*, trans. Raphael Loewe, Oxford, Oxford University Press.

Klever, Wim [1991], "A New Source of Spinozism: Franciscus Van den Enden", *Journal of the History of Philosophy* 29, pp. 613-631.

Kolakowski, Leszek [1969], *Chrétiens sans église*, Paris, Gallimard.

Kolakowski, Leszek [1990a], "Dutch Seventeenth-Century Anticonfessional Ideas and Rational Religion: The Mennonite, Collegiant, and Spinozan Connections", in *Mennonite Quarterly Review* 64, 262-297.

Kolakowski, Leszek [1990b], "Dutch Seventeenth-Century Anticonfessional Ideas and Rational Religion: The Mennonite, Collegiant and Spinozan Connections (Concluded)" in *Mennonite Quarterly Review* 64, 385-416.

Lacroix, Jean [1970], *Spinoza et le problème du salut*, Paris, Presses universitaires de France.

Laux, Henri [1993], *Imagination et religion chez Spinoza*, Paris, Vrin.

Leibniz, G.W. [1978], *Die philosophischen Schriften*, 7 volumes, edited by C.I. Gerhardt, Hildesheim, Olms [Reprint of 1875-90].

Lévinas , Emmanuel [1984], *Difficile liberté*, Paris, Michel.

Levy, Ze'ev [1987], "Sur quelques influences juives dans le développement philosopique du jeune Spinoza", in *Revue des sciences philosophiques et théologiques* 71, 67-75.

Malet, André [1966], *Le Traité théologigo-politique de Spinoza et la pensée biblique*, Paris, Société de belles lettres.

Mason, Richard [1997], *The God of Spinoza*, Cambridge, Cambridge University Press.

Matheron, Alexandre [1971], *Le Christ et le salut des ignorants chez Spinoza*, Paris: Aubier-Montaigne.

Méchoulan, Henry [1991], *Être juif à Amsterdam au temps de Spinoza*, Paris, Albin Michel.

Meinsma, K.O. [1983], *Spinoza et son cercle*, trans. S. Roosenberg and J.-P. Osier, Paris: Vrin.

Mignini, Filippo [1987], "Données et problèmes de la chronologie spinozienne entre 1656 et 1665", *Revue des sciences philosophiques et théologiques* 71, pp. 9-21.

Mignini, Filippo [1995], "La dottrina spinoziana della religione", *Studia Spinozana* 11, pp. 53-79.

Misrahi, Robert [1977], "Spinoza and Christian Thought: A Challenge" in *Speculum Spinozanum (1677-1977)*, London, Routledge, pp. 387-417.

Moreau, F.P. [1992], "Les principes de la lecture de l'Écriture Sainte dans le *Tractatus Theologico-Politicus*" in *Groupe de recherches spinozistes: Travaux et documents 4*, Paris, Presses de l'université de Paris Sorbonne, pp.119-131.

Müller, Sabine [1997], *Das Ketzerverständnis bei Sebastian Franck und Matthias Flacius Illyricus am Beispiel der Katharer*, Wissenschaftliche Hausarbeit zur Erlangung des Magister Artium im Fach Mittlere und Neuere Geschichte. Justus-Liebig-Universität.

Nadler, Steven [1999], *Spinoza: A Life*, Cambridge, Cambridge University Press.

Pelikan, Jaroslav [1984], *Reformation of Church and Dogma (1300 – 1700)*, vol. 4 of Jaroslav Pelikan, *The Christian Tradition*, 5 volumes, Chicago and London, University of Chicago Press.

Pelikan, Jaroslav [1989], *Christian Doctrine and Modern Culture (since 1700)*, vol. 5 of Jaroslav Pelikan, *The Christian Tradition*, 5 volumes, Chicago and London, University of Chicago Press.

Popkin, Richard [1979], *The History of Scepticism from Erasmus to Spinoza*, Berkeley and Los Angeles, University of California Press.

Popkin, Richard [1984], "Spinoza and the Conversion of the Jews", in C. de Deugd (ed.), *Spinoza's Political and Theological Thought*, Amsterdam, North Holland Publishing Company.

Popkin, Richard [1985], "Spinoza and Samuel Fisher", *Philosophia* 15, pp. 219-235.

Popkin, Richard [1988], "Spinoza's Earliest Philosophical Years, 1655-1661", *Studia Spinozana* 4, pp. 37-55.

Popkin, Richard [1996], "Spinoza and Bible Scholarship", in Don Garrett (ed.), *The Cambridge Companion to Spinoza*, Cambridge, Cambridge University Press, 1996, pp. 383-407.

Preus, Samuel J. [1998], "The Bible and Religion in the Century of Genius: Part I: Religion on the Margins: *Conversos* and Collegiants" in *Religion* 28, pp. 3-14

Révah, I.S. [1958], "Spinoza et les hérétiques de la communauté judéo-portugaise d'Amsterdam", *Revue de l'histoire des religions* 154, pp. 173-218.

Révah, I.S. [1959], *Spinoza et le Dr Juan de Prado*, Paris, Mouton.

Révah, I.S. [1995a], "Aux origines de la rupture spinozienne", in *Des marranes à Spinoza*, Paris, Vrin, pp. 221/359 - 245/383.

Révah, I.S. [1995b], "La religion d'Uriel da Costa, Marrane de Porto", in *Des marannes à Spinoza,* Paris, Vrin, pp. 45/77 - 76/108.

Révah, I.S. [1995c] "Les Marranes", in *Des Marranes à Spinoza*, Paris, Vrin, pp. 29/13 - 77/61.

Roothaan, Angela [1998], "Spinoza relève-t-il de la théologie naturelle?", *Revue de théologie et de philosophie* 130, pp. 269-283.

Savan, David [1986], "Spinoza: Scientist and Theorist of Scientific Method" in M. Grene and D. Nails (eds), *Spinoza and the Sciences*, Dordrecht, Reidel, pp. 95-123.

Siebrand, H.J. [1988], *Spinoza and the Netherlanders*, Assen/Maastricht, Van Gorcum.

Smith, Steven [1997], *Spinoza, Liberalism and the Question of Jewish Identity*, New Haven and London, Yale University Press.

Spinoza, B. [1925], *Opera*, 4 volumes, edited by C. Gebhardt, Heidelberg, Carl Winter.

Spinoza B. [1954], *Oeuvres complètes*, trans. Roland Caillois, Madeleine Francès, Robert Misrahi Paris: Gallimard/La Pléiade.

Spinoza, B.[1966], *Correspondence*, trans. and ed. A. Wolf London: Cass. Reprint of 1928.

Spinoza B. [1989], *Tractatus Theologico-Politicus*, translated by Samuel Shirley, Leiden: Brill.

Spinoza [1991], *Theological-Political Treatise*, translated by Samuel Shirley, Indianapolis, Hackett.

Spinoza [1999], *Traité théologico-politique*, vol. 2 of *Oeuvres*, Edited by Fokke Akkerman, Translation and notes by Jacqueline Lagrée and Pierre-François Moreau, Paris, Presses Universitaires de France.

Sprigge, T.L.S. [1995], "Is Spinozism a Religion?", *Studia Spinozana* 11, pp. 137-163.

Strauss, Leo [1965], *Spinoza's Critique of Religion*, New York, Schocken Books.

Tosel, André [1984], *Spinoza, ou, le crépuscule de la servitude : essai sur le traité théologico-politique*, Paris, Aubier.

van Bunge, Wiep and Klever, Wim [1996], *Disguised and Overt Spinozism Around 1700*, Leiden/New York, Brill.

van Bunge, Wiep [2001], *From Stevin to Spinoza: An Essay on Philosophy in the Seventeenth-Century Dutch Republic*, Leiden, Brill.

Van Der Wall, Ernestine [1995], "The Tractatus Theologico-Politicus and Dutch Calvinism, 1670-1700", *Studia Spinozana* 11, pp. 201-226.

Walther, Manfred [1994], "Spinoza's Critique of Miracles: A Miracle of Criticism", in Graeme Hunter (ed.) *Spinoza: The Enduring Questions*, Toronto, University of Toronto Press.

Wolfson, H.A. [1962], *The Philosophy of Spinoza*, Cambridge Mass, Harvard University Press.

Yovel, Yirmiyahu [1989], *Spinoza and Other Heretics*, 2 volumes, Princeton, Princeton University Press.

Zac, Sylvain [1985], "Le problème du christianisme de Spinoza", in *Essais spinozistes* Paris: Vrin, pp. 105-117.

Index

DATE DUE
